Donald Davidson

SIMON EVNINE

Stanford University Press
Stanford, California
1991

Stanford University Press
Stanford, California
© 1991 Simon Evnine
Originating publisher: Polity Press, Cambridge
   in association with Basil Blackwell, Oxford
First published in the U.S.A. by
   Stanford University Press, 1991
Printed in Great Britain
Cloth ISBN 0-8047-1852-0
Paper ISBN 0-8047-1853-9
LC 90-70701
This book is printed on acid-free paper

Donald Davidson

Key Contemporary Thinkers

401
D25Ye

92-1058
24043259

In memory of my father

Contents

Preface

In this book, I have attempted to provide an exposition and critical evaluation of the philosophy of Donald Davidson. Wherever I have used technical terms or concepts I have tried to explain them, so that the book should be accessible even to readers with little philosophical background. Some moderately technical work, however, is inevitable in a full account of Davidson's philosophy. I have tried to confine it to a few specific sections which readers can omit if necessary. These sections are 5.3, 5.4, 7.3 and the Appendix. Section 5.2 is also quite technical, but it is really indispensable for understanding Davidson.

I would like to thank the following people: Oliver Black, George Galfalvi, Jerry Valberg, John Watling, Jonathan Wolff and Michael Wrigley who read all or most of the work in progress and made copious suggestions. Their advice has made this book far better than it would otherwise have been. The anonymous readers for Polity Press and Stanford University Press made many useful criticisms both on points of detail and concerning the organization of material. David Charles and Giovanna Pompele successfully offered advice on problems that were posing difficulties for me. I would also like to thank Oxford University Press for permission to quote from Donald Davidson, *Essays on Actions and Events* (1980) and *Inquiries into Truth and Interpretation* (1984).

Simon Evnine, Los Angeles

Introduction

Donald Davidson is one of today's most distinguished and influential philosophers. His first work of general repute was the paper 'Actions, Reasons, and Causes', published in 1963. Since that time he has produced many articles, most of which, upto the early 1980s, have been collected in two volumes, *Essays on Actions and Events* (1980a) and *Inquiries into Truth and Interpretation* (1984a). All of his articles are terse and compact, making it very difficult to understand one of them without a good knowledge of many of the others. Failure to see the papers in their proper contexts can lead to confusion and misunderstanding.

The systematic nature of Davidson's work makes it particularly difficult to give a linear exposition of it. There is no single logical order of its various parts, but rather many connections on many different planes. For this reason, I attempt, in this introduction, to give a general picture of how the various parts of his system fit together. In the absence of an explanation of these parts, this is bound to be somewhat schematic, but it may be useful as a kind of map of the terrain to be covered in the course of the book. Before we come to this map, however, I propose to say something about the philosophical environment out of which Davidson's ideas have emerged, and from which they have, slowly but surely, separated themselves.

Davidson records that he 'got through graduate school [Harvard] by reading Feigl and Sellars' (1976b, p. 261). Feigl and Sellars (1949) is an anthology of empiricist, and especially logical positivist, writings, and its contents give a fairly good picture of the major influences on Davidson and the philosophical orthodoxy at the time of his apprenticeship.

Academic philosophy in mid-century America was greatly influenced by the arrival in America in the 1930s of refugees from the Vienna Circle of logical positivists. Their philosophy merits the epithet 'empiricist' for two reasons. First, it placed a high premium on science, and particularly physics, which was considered as the model and foundation for all other sciences. Secondly, it gave to sensory experience a fundamental role, attempting to show how the meanings of sentences could be accounted for in terms of the experiences whch would verify them.

Although logically separable, these two tendencies often worked to a common end. For instance, theology and 'metaphysics' were prime examples of unscientific realms of discourse and, as such, clearly came under fire from the scientific hard-heads. But in case an advocate of one of these discredited disciplines should suggest that they were themselves 'scientific' enterprises, it could be replied that their assertions, for instance Heidegger's famous 'the Nothing noths' or Bradley's 'the Absolute participates in but does not partake of change,' bore no relation to experience. No experience, i.e. nothing we could experience with our senses, could possibly confirm or refute such sentences; they could therefore be dismissed as meaningless.

Furthermore, both these empiricist tendencies shared a belief in the possibility of reductionism: in the one case, the reduction of all sciences to physics, and in the other, the reduction of all meaningful sentences to reports about sensory experience. Reductionism is the view that all the sentences of one area of discourse can be translated, without any impoverishment, into the sentences of another area of discourse. Thus, anything that can be said in the reduced area of discourse can be said in that to which the reduction is made. Successful reduction can either be seen as legitimating the reduced area of discourse, or as showing how to dispense with it altogether. (This is a bit like being able to see a glass as half-full or half-empty.)

With the growth and success of physics, many philosophers came to identify its theory as the basic, fundamental description of reality. Other exact sciences, such as chemistry, came to be seen as in some way inferior. The truths of chemistry, such as that oxygen has a valency of two, were viewed as a kind of oblique way of getting at the 'real' facts of the matter, which would be expressed in terms of the microphysical atomic structure of oxygen. It was also held that psychology, the study of the mind and human behaviour, could ultimately be reduced to physics (see Carnap 1932).

Descartes had argued that mind and matter were fundamentally and essentially distinct from each other. If physics is the science of matter, Cartesianism would entail a strong denial of the possibility of reducing psychology to physics. So strong was the lure of reductionism in this area, that it came to be assumed that not only did reductionism entail materialism, but that materialism entailed reductionism. It was taken for granted that the only was to repudiate Cartesian dualism was by a reduction of the mind. The question of the relation of mind and body thus came to rest entirely on the question, can the mental be reduced to the physical?

Physics had another role to play in philosophical empiricism. Not only was it offered as the basic language of reality, it was also taken as a model for all other sciences. Its salient feature, in this respect, is the presence of precise laws. Thus, even if one abandoned, or ignored, the attempt to reduce psychology to physics, one could not ignore the requirement to think of psychology itself as an exact science, with psychological laws on the basis of which one could provide explanations and predictions of psychological phenomena.

The other reductionist tendency which we identified was one which took the language of sensory experience as basic and fundamental. The impetus for this view was primarily epistemological. It was felt that one could never know anything other than one's own sensory experiences. Since our language could not possibly express things of which we know nothing, it must be the case that when, for instance, we talk about tables and chairs, ostensibly independently existing material objects, we must really *mean* something about our sensory experiences. Indeed all meaningful sentences must really be reducible to reports about actual or hypothetical sensory experiences.

To this claim about meaningful sentences, one exception was made. Some sentences, such as 'all bachelors are unmarried,' were considered as true by definition, or analytic. Among analytic truths were also counted truths of logic and mathematics. Analytic sentences were not required to be reducible to sensory experience, but this was because they asserted nothing about the world, but only something about our symbols, our concepts or our language. Thus, mid-century positivism divided all true sentences into the analytic, which contain no information about the world, and the empirical, or synthetic, which are reducible to reports of sensory experiences.

In an essay called 'Two Dogmas of Empiricism', published in 1951, Willard Van Orman Quine challenged two of the characteristic features of the kind of empiricism at which we have been looking. Quine was both a part, and a critic, of the empiricist tradition, and his strictures in this paper have been enormously influential. The first dogma which Quine attacks is the distinction between analytic and synthetic truths. Quine argued that attempts to say exactly what analyticity is in terms of meaning or necessity are doomed to failure since all these notions are interdependent. But he offers another way of characterizing analyticity, in terms of revisability or confirmation. An analytic sentence, such as 'all bachelors are unmarried,' is one the assessment of whose truth no experience could lead us to revise, and hence which, trivially, any experience could be said to confirm.

This leads us to the second dogma that Quine disputes, the dogma of reductionism. This holds, as we have seen, that 'every meaningful statement is . . . translatable into a statement (true or false) about immediate experience' (1951, p. 38). Quine presents an alternative, holistic, picture of language in which all sentences are interconnected in the manner of a web. Thus, although many sentences may have very direct links with immediate sensory experience (so-called observation sentences such as 'this is red'), none will be immune from the influence of other sentences held to be true. Even in the face of the most overwhelming sensory experience in favour of its truth, a sentence like 'this is red' could be held to be false, provided the necessary adjustments were made to other sentences held true (see section 1.2 below for an example of how this might work). If this picture is right, then no sentence will be unrevisable in principle, even if many, such as those expressing logical and mathematical truths, are so well-entrenched that we cannot now see how we ever could be led to revise them. Hence, according to Quine in 'Two Dogmas of Empiricism', there are no analytic sentences.

While the influence of members of the Vienna Circle, such as Carnap, Hempel and Reichenbach, can be distinctly felt in Davidson's work, there is no doubt that Quine has been the greatest single influence, both with his own empiricism and, perhaps more importantly, with his criticisms of empiricism. In many places, Davidson represents himself as merely continuing and elaborating Quine's ideas. Furthermore, much of Davidson's philosophical vocabulary, and his apparent reliance on formal logic and formal semantics, emphasize his part in this continuing historical movement. None the less, it is, I believe, fair to say that Davidson has now wholly removed himself, philosophically speaking, from the empiricist tradition. Given the history of this tradition, which began as early as the eighteenth century, and given its current predominance, this makes Davidson a real philosophical innovator. To appreciate the originality of his thought, though, one must not let oneself be seduced by appearances into thinking of his work as just another step in the historical dialectic which we have been tracing. It is a step in this dialectic, but it is a step which provides a startling and radical shift in philosophical focus.

Davidson embraces Quine's holism, and applies it to both language and the mind (section 1.2 and chapter 7). Indeed, Davidson regards linguistic meaning as inextricably bound up with the mental states of the users of language. Reaching over both these areas is action, by means of which we can express our beliefs and fulfil our desires. Thus, his main philosophical concerns are language, the mental and action – all the ingredients of a philosophical anthropology. This should warn us that his technical work in logic and formal semantics, and his metaphysical work on the nature of events and causation, although important and interesting in its own right, is primarily, for Davidson, apparatus necessary for the completion of his anthropological project.

Davidson believes that mind, action and language are all subject to a set of principles, to which he gives the collective name 'the Principle of Charity' (section 1.2 and chapter 6). These principles are the normative principles of rationality; principles such as 'do not believe a contradiction,' which the rational person will accept just in virtue of being rational. The principles are so related to the mental states, actions and linguistic utterances they govern, that, as Davidson argues, no one can be said to have mental states, perform intentional actions or use language, unless he is, to a great extent, rational.

The importance which Davidson gives to holism and rationality in his theories of the mental puts his position directly at odds with the empiricist views on the same subject. Davidson thinks that psychology is neither a science, on the model of physics, nor in itself reducible to physics (sections 1.3 and 1.4). None the less, breaking the traditional connection between materialism and reductionism, he supports a form of non-reductive materialism (chapter 4). Another positivist thesis (particularly supported by Hempel) was that the reasons for which we perform actions are the causes of those actions. This was taken to have implications for the scientific nature of psychology. Here again, Davidson accepts the basic thesis, but denies its implications (chapter 3).

In both these cases, the causation of actions by reasons, and the identity of mind and body, Davidson manages to avoid what he sees as the unwelcome consequences they were typically thought to have, by elaborating a theory of actions and mental states as particulars, analogous to material objects, which are capable of being given many different descriptions (chapter 2).

With regard to language, Davidson's main focus is on the problem of interpretation. However, the theory of interpretation, of what guides and constrains our assignments of meanings to people's utterances, was introduced into Davidson's work through his discussion of a formal theory of meaning for a language (chapter 5). This theory draws heavily on Tarski's work on truth, and is essentially a theory that gives conditions under which the sentences of a language are true. Hence it is often referred to as truth-conditional semantics. The problem of actually seeing how such a theory could apply to a speaker or community of speakers is the problem of what Davidson calls radical interpretation. It is in the course of discussing radical interpretation that Davidson introduces the notion of the Principle of Charity, which functions as a condition which a truth-conditional theory of a language must meet, if it is to be usable as a theory of interpretation for speakers (chapter 6).

That creatures who are to be seen as speaking a language, as having beliefs and as performing actions *must be*, to a large extent, rational is the most controversial and original aspect of Davidson's work. Not only is it a strong metaphysical thesis itself, but it has a number of other metaphysical and epistemological ramifications. Davidson eventually uses it to mount an attack on the possibility of scepticism, the view that our knowledge of the world is somehow insecure (section 8.2), and on relativism, the view that what counts as true or rational may vary, from group to group, from person to person or from time to time (sections 8.3 and 8.4). It is in these areas that Davidson's rationalism is at its most assertive and aggressive, and the reward is a genuine, non-empiricist philosophical vision.

1

The Anomalism of the Mental

It is one of the central pillars of Davidson's philosophy that the mental is, as he says, anomalous. 'Anomalous' means 'odd' or 'irregular', but Davidson uses it more specifically to mean 'not governed by laws'. In calling the mental anomalous, Davidson is claiming that mental states or events, things like beliefs, desires, perceptions and so on, are not subject to scientific laws in the way that physical states and events are.

There are two kinds of laws which one might have thought applied to the mental: laws which connect mental states and events to physical states and events, psychophysical laws, and laws which relate mental states and events to other mental states and events, psychological laws. Davidson's view that the mental is anomalous means that he denies that there are laws of either of these two kinds. The denial of psychophysical and psychological laws will be looked at in sections 1.3 and 1.4 respectively. In the first two sections of this chapter, we shall look at some general features of Davidson's philosophy of mind. Section 1.1 will be concerned with the interpretative, third-person approach to the philosophy of mind that is common to many contemporary philosophers. Section 1.2 will give a preliminary treatment to two features which particularly characterize Davidson's views on the mental: normativity and holism.

1.1 FIRST- AND THIRD-PERSON PERSPECTIVES

Mental states can be divided into two sorts. On the one hand, there are pains, after-images, tickles and the like. These may be collectively referred to as sensations. On the other hand, there are states such as beliefs, desires, doubts and so on. Those in this latter category are sometimes distinguished as propositional attitudes. (They are also called 'intentional' states. This is a difficult word in philosophy. One must distinguish its use in this context from 'intentional' as applied to actions done on purpose, though these are also considered intentional in the sense under discussion. One must also be on guard against confusion with 'intensional' with an 's', though again, this is related, and will be introduced in section 5.2.)

A look at the expression 'propositional attitudes' will be instructive in appreciating what is important about mental states of this kind. If you fear that the soufflé is about to collapse, and I, somewhat maliciously, hope that it is about to collapse then there is something common to both our mental states. This is the proposition *that the soufflé is about to collapse*. But each of us has a different attitude to this proposition. Your attitude is one of fear, while mine is one of hope. There are many different attitudes one can take to propositions, each indicating a different type of mental state. One can (to give a few examples) hope, believe, fear, regret, expect, desire, notice and understand that the soufflé is about to collapse.

Propositional attitudes can be said to have propositional content. The proposition towards which one has an attitude gives the content of that mental state. Thus one can speak of the content of a belief or a desire. Sensations, by contrast, do not have content. Davidson's views on the mental are almost all confined to content-bearing, propositional mental states.[1] Accordingly, when I use the expression 'mental' it will be to stand specifically for content-bearing mental states unless otherwise indicated.

There are two points from which to examine mental states in general. They can be studied from the inside, or first-person point of view, or as they appear from the outside, from the third-person perspective. The first-person approach is at its most prominent with sensations since these have characteristic ways of seeming which are only experienced by their bearers. I feel my pain in a way in which I don't, and cannot ever, feel someone else's pain. But the first-person perspective has also been applied to propositional attitudes and it would hardly be an exaggeration to say that all modern philosophy, from Descartes, through Hume, to Kant and beyond presupposes it. (Indeed, the distinction between the two types of mental states is not always clearly made by these philosophers.)

Despite its obvious advantages, the first-person approach has certain drawbacks. Principally, it raises the possibility that the mental states of others are radically unknowable. If we think of mental states as things best known by their bearers, we soon run up against the possibility that we may never really know what mental states others have. And even if this consequence is not inevitable, we will still have the serious task of justifying our belief that other people have mental states just as we do.

Problems such as these suggest we take an alternative approach to the mental, based on the third-person perspective. This perspective is particularly apposite for propositional attitudes, as opposed to sensations, because, while it is obvious that there is something about a pain which only its bearer can know (i.e. how it feels), there is not obviously anything that it is like to have a belief that Columbus discovered America. Furthermore, explanation and understanding in terms of rationality is a particularly distinctive, human activity. This kind of understanding is essentially a communal activity, relating very much to action, which is in principle public and observable to all. States like belief and desire play a special role in making sense of or understanding people in this distinctive way. The third-person perspective, applied to propositional attitudes, has by now become common in philosophy.

One reason for the prevalence of the third-person perspective today was the replacement of introspectionist psychology by behaviourist psychology towards the middle of this century. Philosophy followed psychology here, and philosophical behaviourism received its most unequivocal expression in Gilbert Ryle's famous book *The Concept of Mind* (1949). Ryle ridiculed, as the dogma of 'the Ghost in the Machine', the view that:

> minds are not in space, nor are their operations subject to mechanical laws. The workings of one mind are not witnessable by other observers; its career is private. Only I can take direct cognisance of the states and processes of my own mind. A person therefore lives through two collateral histories, one consisting of what happens in and to his body, the other consisting of what happens in and to his mind. The first is public, the second private. (Ryle 1949, p. 11)

Instead of this, Ryle wanted to show that 'when we describe people as exercising qualities of mind, we are not referring to occult episodes of which their overt acts and utterances are effects; we are referring to those overt acts and utterances themselves' (1949, p. 25). This is the central tenet of behaviourism.

Wittgentstein was also influential in this respect. Although his relation to behaviourism is problematic, there is no doubt that he was concerned to downplay the role of inner mental stirrings and bring to the fore considerations of public, communal practice. He correctly saw that, although things may or may not go on 'inside' when various mental states occur, it would be a confusion to assume that these inner goings on were essential to those mental states.

> Introspection can never lead to a definition [of mental terms]. It can only lead to a psychological statement about the introspector. If, e.g., someone says: 'I believe that when I hear a word that I understand I always feel something that I don't feel when I don't understand the word' – that is a statement about *his* peculiar experiences.

Someone else perhaps feels something quite different; and if both of them *make correct use of* the word 'understand' the essence of understanding lies in this use, and not in what they may say about what they experience. (Wittgentstein 1983, para. 212)

Davidson is not a behaviourist, but Quine, whose work has had a strong influence on Davidson, is, and we will see in sections 6.1 and 6.2 how Quine's behaviourism is related to certain aspects of Davidson's own thought; and although Davidson definitely believes that mental states *are* the causes of overt acts and utterances, he would none the less agree with Ryle and Quine in rejecting the dogma of the Ghost in the Machine outlined above. Many philosophers now share Davidson's position in this respect. Though not behaviourists, they have been influenced by behaviourism, and this influence is largely detectable in their adherence to the third-person perspective in studying the mind. (See Lewis 1966, pp. 102–5 and Dennett 1987, pp. 1–11. For a reaction against this approach, see Nagel 1986.)

1.2   NORMATIVE PRINCIPLES AND HOLISM

Suppose we came across some previously undiscovered tribe in some remote part of the world. The members of this community appear to use a language though it is totally unrecognizable to us, and they appear to perform various actions. Both of these appearances presuppose that they have a wide range of beliefs, desires and other mental states. If we could understand their language, we could use it to gain some knowledge of their mental states. If we knew what their mental states were, we could perhaps work out what they were saying. But unfortunately we know nothing about any of this. If we are to interpret them, if we are to attribute beliefs, desires and other mental states to them, assign meanings to their utterances and say what they are doing, we will have to find some way of doing this from scratch. This is the problem of radical interpretation.

In our daily lives we never, or almost never, have to interpret someone from scratch. If we don't know the speaker, and hence already have some knowledge of his specific mental states, we at least come with knowledge of a wide range of mental states he will share with members of his community, and with the expectation that he speaks a certain language whose interpretation we take for granted. The point of studying radical interpretation is thus not to understand an actual process that we engage in. It is a theoretical exercise designed to reveal the interrelations betwen the various intentional, or propositional, states and events like beliefs, desires, linguistic utterances and actions, and the relations between these states and events and non-intentional states and events such as brain states, noises, marks on paper and bodily movements.

For Davidson, radical interpretation is characterized by two features. The first is that it must be guided by normative principles, and the second is that it must proceed holistically. Normativity and holism will be examined at length in chapters 6 and 7, but it is important to have some familiarity with them at this stage if we are to understand Davidson's views on the anomalism of the mental.

Normative principles are principles which say how things should or ought to be, and the normative principles which apply to the mental specify things like which kinds of beliefs should or should not be held, on what bases inferences should be made, what kinds of actions should be performed and so on. This does not mean that they say things like 'believe that grass is green,' or 'believe that people are good.' They are general principles like 'if you believe that p and q, then believe that p' and 'don't believe both that p and that not-p.' (The letters p and q stand for arbitrary sentences or propositions). Similarly, saying that they tell one which actions to perform does not mean that they enjoin particular actions, but rather that they direct one, for instance, always to perform that action which one judges it best to perform, all things considered.

What lies behind Davidson's claim that such normative principles should guide radical interpretation is the fact that mental states as such are capable of *justifying* other mental states and actions. Thus, if someone says to me, in an offended tone, 'Excuse me!', I can explain this by attributing to him the belief that I have insulted him. But this belief doesn't just explain his action, in the way that the movement of one billiard ball can explain the movement of another; it justifies it in the sense that his action becomes reasonable in the light of the belief. It is only things which have propositional content, such as mental states and linguistic acts, that are capable of performing this kind of 'rationalization', or justification. And of course, the identification and attribution of mental states in general are almost always intended to play just this rationalizing role. One could say that that is the main point in attending to the mental states of other people.

The kind of normative principles which Davidson takes to govern interpretation are those which we must think of as applying to other people if we are to be able to see their mental states as playing their characteristic justifying role. The principles, in other words, articulate the conception of rationality against which mental states can rationalize and justify other mental states and actions. In holding that radical interpretation must be guided by normative principles, Davidson is claiming that in interpretation, we must assume that the person whom we are interpreting is rational.

Rationality is a concept which is made use of in many different contexts and it is important to see how uncontroversial Davidson is being here. We have noted that the principles do not enjoin any specific beliefs or actions. The rationality in question, therefore, is not of the sort that a secular physicist might wave in the face of a religious believer, or a hard-headed positivist in the face of an artist. Rationality, in this context, is limited to the standards of logical reasoning (deductive and inductive inference), and to the ways in which mental states should relate to the world, through perception and belief on the one hand, and through action and desire on the other.

What is the relation of these principles to the mental states they govern? One picture of how they could be related is this. We identify a range of examples of actions and of states of belief, desire and so on. We then investigate these cases and find that certain principles seem to hold. For instance, we could identify a group of subjects who believed that *p*, look at their beliefs that *p*, and see whether or not it was in the nature of a belief that *p* that it precluded a simultaneous belief that not-*p* in the same person. This would be like our investigation of gold. We determine that some things are gold, look at them in the laboratory and find that gold does not dissolve in acid, melts at such and such a temperature, etc.

Davidson's view on how the normative principles are related to the mental is quite different. On his view, the applicability of these normative principles is constitutively bound up with the states they govern. What this means is that they are not principles that, as it turns out, happen to be true of beliefs, actions and so on. It is part of what it is for something to be a belief that it is subject to these principles. Thus, for instance, we do not discover that beliefs should not be directly under the control of the will. It is part of the very concept of belief that, as one of the normative principles might say, beliefs should be determined (not that they always are determined) just by how the world is. Similarly, it is part of the concept of intentional action that actions should be based on judgements of what, all things considered, it is best to do. It is *a posteriori* (knowable only after investigation) and contingent that if something is gold, it does not dissolve in acid, but it is *a priori* (knowable without investigation), and necessary, that if someone has beliefs then he generally doesn't believe open contradictions or otherwise go against the directives of these normative principles.

It is worth spending a little more time over this contrast between our knowledge of general principles about gold and about mental states like belief. The normative principles embody knowledge that we all have about mental states. They constitute what is often called folk psychology. Many of us also have some knowledge about gold, and what we know on this score could be called folk chemistry. But folk psychology and folk chemistry are very different with regard to the status of the principles embodied in each. When we classify something as gold, on the basis of its appearance and behaviour, we expect that science could say what is really required for something to be gold. We allow for the possibility, and indeed such a possibility actually obtains, that something might be fake gold, fools' gold, so that it was initially classified as gold but on further inspection turned out to be iron pyrites. This is often put by saying that gold is a natural kind, a kind which may sometimes be identified on the basis of things like yellowness, insolubility in acid and so on, but which constitutes a kind by virtue of other more basic properties, namely, a particular microphysical structure. Folk chemistry recognizes this even though it does not itself include knowledge of the essential microphysical structure. We who employ folk chemistry and classify things as gold may have no idea of just what it is the real chemist knows that allows him to distinguish gold from fools' gold. But we do think that he does know, or at least, could in principle know.

In contrast, folk psychology is not something about which we are prepared to defer to experts in this way. Whatever theoretical knowledge there is to be had about mental states, we folk psychologists already have. This is not to deny that there may be disciplines which are the provinces of experts and go by such names as scientific psychology or neurophysiology. What is at issue is the relevance of such information to folk psychology. The point being urged here is that the knowledge of the chemist supplements folk chemistry in a way in which the knowledge of the psychologist or physiologist does not supplement folk psychology. There is no deeper, scientifically discoverable fact which underlies the principle that a belief that p rationally precludes a belief that not-p.

If something is a natural kind, like gold, we can envisage a situation where we confront some of it and say: 'this is the stuff we want to find out about. As yet we know nothing about it but after we have taken some off to the laboratory and subjected it to our tests, we expect to discover something about it.' Indeed, something like this is just what has happened over the ages. We began to sort things into natural kinds such as wood, stone and metal, long before we knew what really made something metal rather than stone. Our general knowledge of these things is *a posteriori*. It is, paradigmatically, knowledge that has been discovered.

By contrast, our knowledge of folk psychology, our knowledge of the normative principles of rationality, is hardly something we have discovered about beliefs and other mental states. There was never a time when we could identify beliefs but didn't realize that if someone believed that p then he ought not to believe that not-p. No one has ever shouted *eureka* over the simple truth that beliefs ought only to be determined by how the world is. This sort of knowledge is *a priori*. So long as we know a belief when we see one, we know that someone who believes that p ought not at the same time to believe that not-p.

This idea of the *a priori* character of these principles of rationality is of the utmost importance. Of the question, 'whether people might not actually *be* approximately rational and consistent in their patterns of belief and desire', Davidson writes that 'in my view this cannot be a factual question: if a creature has propositional attitudes then that creature is approximately rational' (1985a, p. 245). By saying that it is not a factual question, Davidson is emphasizing that we cannot first identify someone as having beliefs and desires, and then go on to wonder whether these beliefs and desires do or don't conform to the normative principles of rationality. There is no gap between something being a believer and agent, and it being a (more or less) rational believer and agent.

The second feature characteristic of interpretation is the holism of the mental. The main source of evidence we have for telling which mental states somebody has is his behaviour. But the attribution of any one mental state is not fixed by any single piece of behaviour. It must be made against the background of attributions of other mental states. Whether or not certain behaviour warrants us in attributing a certain belief to someone will depend on what other propositional attitudes we take him to have. Any action can warrant the attribution of any attitude, given the assumption that the agent has other appropriate attitudes. Conversely, any attitude can be a reason for any action, given other appropriate attitudes. Davidson writes:

> There is no assigning beliefs to a person one by one on the basis of his verbal behaviour, his choices, or other local signs no matter how plain and evident, for we make sense of particular beliefs only as they cohere with other beliefs, with preferences, with intentions, hopes, fears, expectations, and the rest. (1970b, p. 221)

In order to put this claim in context, it will be helpful to say a little about the views on holism of Quine. In his famous paper, 'Two Dogmas of Empiricism' (1951), Quine was concerned to argue against two ideas which had characterized the empiricist philosophical tradition of which he has, to some extent, been a part. It is the second of the two dogmas that concerns us here. The dogma of reductionism, as Quine called it, was that each meaningful empirical sentence is associated with some circumscribed range of sensory experiences the occurrence of which would either conclusively confirm or disconfirm the truth of that sentence. Against this dogma, Quine argued that there is no correlation between single sentences and experiences which confirm or disconfirm them. Instead, 'statements about the external world face the tribunal of sense experience not individually but only as a corporate body' (Quine 1951, p. 41).

Quine's reason for believing this can be given by an example. Suppose you sincerely assert the sentence 'all swans are white.' Subsequently, you seem to have an experience of a black swan. Clearly, there is an inconsistency lurking. It cannot be the case both that all swans are white, and that you have seen a black swan. Seeing a black swan falls into the category of sensory experiences which disconfirm the sentence 'all swans are white.' According to the empiricist reductionist, you should, on having that experience, give up belief in the sentence 'all swans are white.' But Quine correctly points out that, although this is one possible resolution of the conflict, there are others. One could take one's apparent experience of the black swan to be a hallucination; one could argue that although it is not a hallucination, it is not an experience of a swan, but of another kind of bird which looks just like a swan. These are the most obvious ploys for resolution, but more complicated ones might include adopting the belief that white things appear black to me for six seconds every hundred years. Since I will not live to test the hypothesis again in a hundred years time, nothing in my experience could rule out that possibility. Thus, my (apparent) experience of the black swan does not directly and by itself determine that I must give up the belief that all swans are white. Whether I give up that belief when I have the experience will depend on other beliefs of mine.

The relation between this view and Davidson's claim that propositional attitudes can only be attributed against the background of other propositional attitudes should be clear. Just as there is no connection between individual sentences and confirmatory and disconfirmatory experiences which determine the truth or falsity of those sentences, so there is no relation between individual mental states and behaviour which warrants the attribution of those mental states. Just as statements about the external world face the tribunal of sense experience as a corporate body, so attributions of propositional attitudes face the tribunal of behaviour (including linguistic behaviour) as a corporate body. Behaviour which might ordinarily be thought to force us to withdraw the attribution of some belief could occur without our withdrawing the attribution, if we are prepared to change our attributions of other propositional attitudes.

For example, suppose we attribute to someone a desire to steal a painting by Rothko. It might be thought that he could not have this desire if he had an opportunity to steal a Rothko but didn't take it. But holism means that the attribution need not be withdrawn on his failing to steal such a painting when given the opportunity since there may be any number of other beliefs and desires he could have which would make his desire consistent with his failure to act. He may have a stronger desire not to act dishonestly; he may not believe that he does have an opportunity, and so on. There is no one-to-one correlation between beliefs or desires on the one hand, and actions or other behaviour on the other hand.

Accordingly, when we attribute mental states to someone on the basis of behavioural evidence, we had better try to make as wide-ranging an attribution as possible. Looking at as much of the evidence as we can, we should attribute, in one go, as many mental states as we can. Normativity has a role to play here, since when we attribute a large group of mental states, the normative principles constrain which mental states can rationally go together. The block of mental states which we attribute must be largely consistent and coherent.

Before we begin the next section, a caveat should be entered. There are two questions which might be asked about the intentional states and events which are revealed by radical interpretation. First, what kinds of facts constitute their propositional contents? If someone has a belief that p, what is it that makes it a belief that p, rather than that q? This is a metaphysical question about the very nature of propositional attitudes and it must be answered by a general theory of propositional content. The second kind of question is epistemological. How do we obtain knowledge of intentional states and events? How can we tell what other people think, and what their words mean?

At first glance, it looks as if radical interpretation offers itself as an answer to the epistemological question. This is encouraged by the non-technical sense of interpretation according to which it is conceived of as uncovering meaning, or content, which is in some way already present, but obscured. But, and this point is essential for understanding Davidson, to see his theory of interpretation as merely answering this question would be seriously to misconstrue it. Suppose that the theory of interpretation were addressed only to the epistemological question. There will always then be a further question as to how the success of whatever method we have for finding out what people are thinking and saying relates to the facts in virtue of which they are thinking and saying just that. So, if Davidson's views on interpretation as normative and holistic were intended merely to answer the question of how we tell what people think, say and do, then he would also have to say why that method worked, and why it was the only, or best, method that would work. This could not be done without also answering the question, which kinds of facts constitute the contents of mental states and sentences.

In this section, I have stressed the role of normativity and holism in an epistemological context. Normativity meant that we must assume that people whom we interpret are rational, and holism meant that we could only attribute mental states *en bloc*, since the evidence for the attribution did not relate to individual mental states. In fact, Davidson's views on interpretation are meant as an answer to the constitutive question as well. Mental content is constituted normatively and holistically. Owing to the nature of propositional content, there is no possibility that people who have beliefs and the rest, could have beliefs which did not conform to normative principles that operate over whole groups of beliefs. When we interpret according to Davidson's method of radical interpretation, we are not simply applying a method of discovery to mental content which is constituted by quite different facts. We are articulating, or making explicit, the very facts that constitute the content that we are attributing in interpretation. This is not to say that a person cannot have mental states unless there is someone to interpret him. Interpretation does not cause mental content to arise. Nor does Davidson wish to assert that there is no possibility of a gap between how we interpret someone and what that person actually believes and desires. There is still room for the notion of misinterpretation (see sections 6.4 and 6.5). The constitutive nature of normativity and holism will be developed in chapters 6 and 7 when we come to look at radical interpretation in detail.

1.3 PSYCHOPHYSICAL LAWS

We turn now to the question of why there cannot be psychophysical laws, of why 'mental events such as perceivings, rememberings, decisions, and actions resist capture in the nomological net of physical theory' (Davidson 1970b, p. 207). The reasons why psychophysical laws are seen as desirable, and hence why the denial of their possibility is important, are two. First, such laws would enable us to exploit the precise and advanced knowledge we have of physical theory in the context of the mental. This is particularly clear if one considers issues such as the treatment of mental illness. Psychophysical laws, should they exist, might well open up the prospect of precise pharmacological or surgical treatments for depression, schizophrenia and so on. Secondly, the existence of psychophysical laws will have ramifications for the mind–body problem, the problem of saying how mind and matter are related. These ontological ramifications will be considered in chapter 4. In the present section, we will discuss psychophysical laws from the perspective of the interface between physical theory and our knowledge of the mental (see McGinn 1978 and Kim 1985 for very good discussions of psychophysical laws).

There are two kinds of psychophysical laws which are discussed by Davidson, though he does not clearly distinguish them. The first kind is of laws which link mental states or events with distinct physical states or events, for example the attempt to connect mental states with behaviour that manifests them (as in action), or with the circumstances that cause them (as in perception). Where M denotes some mental state and P some physical state, these laws would say:

(L1a)   for any objects x and y, if x is in M then y is in P,

or

(L1b)   for any objects x and y, if x is in P then y is in M.

(In what follows, I will not systematically distinguish between properties and the predicates which are the linguistic expressions of those properties.)

Typically, we would be interested in cases in which x and y were the same object, where one person's mental state was nomologically connected to a different physical state of the same person, but this is not required by the concept of a psychophysical law of this first kind.

Psychophysical laws of the second kind are often referred to as bridging laws. A bridging law identifies properties from different theoretical discourses. An example of a non-psychophysical bridging law is the identification of being water with being H_2O. A property that features in the everyday, macrophysical description of the world is here identified with one dealt with by chemical theory. Psychophysical bridging laws would identify mental properties, such as believing that London is in England, with physical, probably neurological, properties.[2] They would thus say:

(L2)   for any object x, x is in M if and only if x is in P

(just as we can say that something is water if and only if it is H_2O). In (L2), as opposed to (L1), the connective linking the instantiation of M and P is the stronger 'if and only if' rather than the weaker 'if . . . then . . .', and it is required that the subject of the predicate M is the same as the subject of P. These differences arise because (L2) is specifically about the identity of properties, and identity is a much stronger relation than the nomological connectedness of (L1).

Laws like (L1) are most likely to arise from a combination of bridging laws like (L2) and purely physical laws which relate the physical properties which feature in the bridging laws to other physical properties. Thus, if some physical law links physical properties P_1 and P_2, and a bridging law relates P_1 and M, we will be able to derive a law of the form of (L1) which relates M and P_2. Since it is implausible that there should be laws like (L1) without bridging laws, I shall focus the following discussion on the latter.

Davidson writes that 'nomological statements [i.e. laws] bring together predicates that we know a priori are made for each other – know, that is, independently of knowing whether the evidence supports a connection between them' (1970b, p. 218). Conversely, we should know *a priori* when predicates are not made for each other, and Davidson believes that this is the case with mental and physical predicates. So what exactly is meant by saying that mental and physical predicates are not made for each other? We have already seen the importance of the normative principles of rationality for the mental. Laws connecting two sets of predicates (in this case, mental and physical) would serve as conduits through which principles distinctive of one set would be transmitted to the other set. In recognizing that mental and physical predicates are not made for each other, we are thus recognizing that 'conditions of coherence, rationality, and consistency . . . have no echo in physical theory' (1973e, p. 231).

Let us look in detail at a case where the absence of an echo in physical theory of normative principles means that we cannot have a law linking some mental predicate with some physical predicate. If p is the proposition that there are at least ten apples in my bag, and q is the proposition that there are at least five apples in my bag, then, since p entails q, normative principles tell us that if someone believes that p, he should not believe that not-q. Now suppose that there were psychophysical laws which connected the belief that p with neural state m, and the belief that not-q with neural state n. These bridge laws ought to enable us to infer, from the fact that if someone believes that p, then he should not believe that not-q, that if someone is in neural state m, he should not be in neural state n, But how are we to make sense of this 'should' in the context of a physical law relating two distinct neural states?

If we were performing some physical experiment, we might say, given one result, that some further result should or should not occur. But here the 'should' merely reflects our expectation. We might gloss it as 'we expect it to turn out to be the case that . . .'. This is certainly not how it is meant when we say that someone who believes that p should not believe that not-q. We do not merely mean that, on investigation, we expect that that is what we will find. We mean that someone who believes that p is under some rational injunction not to believe that not-q. We can see in this example that the supposition of psychophysical laws opens the way for the introduction into physical theory of a connection (the 'if . . . then should . . .' connection) which has no proper place there.

Let us now look at a case where the contamination runs from the physical into the mental. Let p be the proposition that some point is green and q be the proposition that that point is extended. Again, suppose there were bridge laws which connected the belief that p and the belief that q with neural states m and n. Scientific investigation might reveal that there was a law which said that whenever someone was in neural state m, he was also in neural state n. So, by our bridge laws, we should infer that whenever someone believes that a certain point is green, he believes that that point is extended. Now it is reasonable enough to suppose that if someone does have the first belief he will have the second. But there may be cases where we do not want to say this. Someone may have other, perhaps strange, beliefs about the nature of colour such that our overall requirements of rationality, the normative principles, would direct us to attribute to him the belief that p and the belief that not-q. Unless we think that 'if anything is green, it is extended' is true by definition (and it is, surely, at least doubtful whether it is), this would not be attributing to him a belief in a contradiction. The point is that the question of what someone believes should not be influenced by any law relating neural states. Once we allow the relevance of such laws in determining what people believe, then the normative principles of rationality no longer constrain the concepts of propositional attitude psychology in the way we have suggested they should.

These examples should explain what Davidson means when he says:

> There are no strict psychophysical laws because of the disparate commitments of the mental and the physical schemes. It is a feature of physical reality that physical change can be explained by laws that connect it with other changes and conditions physically described. It is a feature of the mental that the attribution of mental phenomena must be responsible to the background of reasons, beliefs, and intentions of the individual. There cannot be tight connections between the realms if each is to retain allegiance to its proper source of evidence. (1970b, p. 222)

Davidson emphasizes that what he is objecting to are strict psychophysical laws. These are to be distinguished from what he calls psychophysical generalizations. To appreciate the difference between laws and mere generalizations consider the following situation. All of the objects in some fixed domain (perhaps all of the objects in a particular room) are either green or blue. Also, they are all either edible or inedible. Now it might be true that, as a matter of fact, all the green objects are edible. We could, in that case, formulate a true generalization about this fixed domain of objects:

(G)   if x is green then x is edible.

But (G) is obviously not a law. Laws, for instance, are generally taken to support counterfactual claims about what something would be like if it were described by the antecedent of the conditional, but we do not think that (G) should entitle us to infer of some blue inedible object in our domain, the Conservative Party manifesto, say, that if it *were* green, it *would* be edible. For our fixed domain, therefore, (G) is a true generalization relating edibility to colour, but not a chromatogastric law.

Now Davidson is not concerned to deny that there may be true psychophysical generalizations. As has been pointed out, the truth or otherwise of such generalizations is a purely empirical matter, and of no philosophical interest in itself (Kim 1985, p. 373). Davidson's point is that, even if there are such generalizations, our *a priori* conception of the nature of the mental means that they could never be laws.

1.4 PSYCHOLOGICAL LAWS

The second part of the claim that the mental is anomalous is that there are no purely psychological laws, laws which relate mental properties to other mental properties. If the hallmark of science is the presence of laws, then this claim means that psychology cannot be a science in any strict sense. The impossibility of an exact psychology is of the greatest importance to Davidson.

About two things we should be clear at the outset. First, the normative principles which govern the mental may have some claim to be called psychological laws. In whatever sense they are psychological laws, it is not in this sense that Davidson is denying that there are psychological laws. The laws Davidson denies the existence of are tools for explanation and prediction of particular phenomena with precision. Normative principles do not serve these purposes.

Secondly, many actions are undeniably physical. If I tie my shoelace, at one level all we have is the movement of certain physical objects. But actions are none the less counted by Davidson as mental because in saying what actions someone is performing, as opposed merely to saying what movements his body is undergoing, we are contributing to our interpretation of him. Action is intentional in the sense discussed in section 1.1. Laws which link mental states with actions will therefore count as psychological laws, and not as psychophysical laws. Unfortunately, this is not always made as clear as it should be, and sometimes, confusingly, Davidson does talk of such laws as psychophysical.

Let us now turn to the argument against psychological laws. As with psychophysical laws, the argument hinges on the holistic and normative character of the mental. Davidson says that

> it is an error to compare a truism like 'If a man wants to eat an acorn omelette, then he generally will if the opportunity exists and no other desire overrides' with a law that says how fast a body will fall in a vacuum. It is an error, because in the latter case, but not the former, we can tell in advance whether the condition holds, and we know what allowance to make if it doesn't. (1973e, p. 233)

Suppose the truism about the acorn omelette, call it '(T)', were being considered as a putative psychological law. For the antecedent to obtain, someone must want to eat an acorn omelette. (The antecedent and consequent of a conditional are the sentences governed, respectively, by the 'if' and the 'then'.) But knowing whether this condition holds is part of having some more extensive view of the agent as a rational creature. In particular, whether or not he does eat an acorn omelette could be an important factor in whether or not we interpret him as wanting to eat one. It is not that his eating or failing to eat an acorn omelette is conclusive in determining whether or not he wants to eat one. It is just that the two parts of the putative law, the antecedent desire and the consequent action, both feature in the interpretation of an agent and hence are related to each other as parts of a holistic web.

If we could ever specify all of someone's beliefs and desires individually and independently of each other, then we would be on our way to psychological laws of a scientific nature. But the holistic and normative character of the mental makes that impossible. As Davidson says:

> What is needed in the case of action, if we are to predict on the basis of desires and beliefs, is a quantitative calculus that brings all relevant beliefs and desires into the picture. There is no hope of refining the simple pattern of explanation on the basis of reasons into such a calculus. (1973e, p. 233)

This inability leads to the presence, in psychological generalizations like (T), of clauses which exclude at one stroke the influence of other mental states. In (T) this is expressed as 'if no other desire overrides'. Such clauses make any psychological truisms unsuited to the work of prediction and explanation. For instance, failure of the consequent to obtain would not disconfirm (T) because we could never conclusively rule out the influence of other mental states. Such influence may, especially in the absence of an appropriate avowal from the agent, be a more unnatural way of accounting for his failure to act, but it is not impossible. Just how we interpret the failure to act will depend on much more that we believe about the agent's beliefs and desires.

This argument of Davidson's has been criticized by those who do wish to see psychology as a science. Jerry Fodor, for instance, claims that scientific psychology, with laws containing failsafe clauses, such as 'all other things being equal' or 'and there are no overriding desires', would be in no worse a state than any of the special sciences. Special sciences include 'all empirical explanatory schemes . . . other than basic physics' (Fodor 1987, p. 4), for example, biology, chemistry and geology. Like psychological laws, Fodor argues, the laws of the other special sciences would also have failsafe clauses. Consider the geological generalization 'a meandering river erodes its outside bank.' Strictly speaking this is false, since any number of conditions could obtain which would prevent a meandering river from eroding its outside bank. In order to make the generalization true, we would have to add 'all things being equal'. This general, catch-all phrase is necessary because there is no way, given only the apparatus of geology, of specifying which circumstances would make things unequal. The weather's changing and the consequent freezing of the river, someone's building a dam, and so on, cannot be subsumed under any *geological* description. By contrast, basic physics, the bedrock of the sciences, would ideally be able to specify, in its own vocabulary, just those conditions under which events of one sort are followed, invariably, by those of another. Consequently, the laws of physics do not need failsafe clauses.

Fodor thinks that if Davidson rejects psychological laws because of the necessity of failsafe clauses, he will have to reject as laws the generalizations of all the special sciences and conclude that the only real science is basic physics. This is not obviously an argument against Davidson since he is not committed to the scientific status of the so-called special sciences. But in any case, it is not even clear that psychology is in the same boat as the other special sciences. Whether it is or not depends on whether the failsafe clauses have the same function in both geological and psychological generalizations.

Fodor says that the geological generalization 'all things being equal, a meandering river erodes its outside bank' means something like 'a meandering river erodes its outside bank in any nomologically possible world where the operative idealizations of geology are satisfied' (Fodor 1987, p. 5). What is important in this construal of the generalization is the concept of operative idealizations. Idealization, as Fodor uses it here, is essentially an epistemological device, used to remove 'interference' which might obscure the way things really are underneath. Things like weather changes or the buildings of dams are idealized away because they are seen as occasional and unsystematizable interferences in the underlying geological regularities. The presence of the failsafe clause reflects the fact that geological regularities are contingently subject to interferences which are too diverse themselves to be subsumed by any purely geological description.

Fodor thinks there is a also mental reality which underlies any attempt to interpret it. Consequently, any complications introduced by holism and normativity are simply interferences which can be idealized away. Our difficulty in giving a 'quantitative calculus that brings all relevant beliefs and desires into the picture' is merely an epistemological difficulty. This is why one can compare the generalizations of geology with those of psychology.

For Davidson, the necessity of failsafe clauses in psychological generalizations is not due to the failure of any psychological idealizations. The fact that normativity and holism, which are the sources of the necessity of the failsafe clauses, are constitutive of what people really believe and desire means that there is no underlying mental reality whose laws we can study in abstraction from the normative and holistic perspective of interpretation. In other words, the failsafe clauses in psychological generalizations like (T) reflect a deep fact about the mental in a way in which their counterparts in geological generalizations do not reflect any deep fact about geology. Fodor's disagreement with Davidson over the question of psychological laws is thus really a symptom of a more basic disagreement over whether propositional content in general is dependent on considerations of overall rationality in the way in which Davidson thinks it is. This issue will be discussed further in section 9.1.

2

Events, Causation and Causal Explanation

One of the most important and original aspects of Davidson's work is his attempt to combine the thesis of the anomalism of the mental with two other theses with which it has normally been thought to be incompatible. These other theses are (a) that the reasons for which people perform actions are the causes of those actions, and (b) that mental states are identical to physical states. Both identity and causation have been thought to be such that where they hold, there must be laws relating the kinds of things they hold between. Thus, if someone is caused to act by his reasons, it has been argued that there must be some law which relates reasons of that kind to actions of that kind. Such laws would be psychological or psychophysical laws, and hence their existence would be inconsistent with the anomalism of the mental. Similar considerations apply in the case of the identity of mental and physical states. How Davidson shows that (a) and (b) are not incompatible with the anomalism of the mental will become apparent in chapters 3 and 4. But it will be easier to appreciate Davidson's discussion of these issues if we first look at his views about events and causation.

Davidson's main claims in this area are that events do exist, that they should be conceived of as particulars and, consequently, that there is a distinction between events themselves and the descriptions we use to refer to events. These claims will be the subject of section 2.1. The distinction between events and their descriptions also operates as a distinction between causation, a relation between events themselves, and causal explanation, which requires that events be described in certain ways. Causation and causal explanation will be discussed in sections 2.2 and 2.3 respectively.

2.1 EVENTS AS PARTICULARS

What does it mean to say that events as particulars exist? The question belongs to ontology, the study of what kinds of things exist. In ontology, the existence of various types of entities, such as material objects, numbers, sets, propositions, facts and events, is discussed. But discussion of whether there are instances of some kind of entity cannot be conducted independently of consideration of the nature of that kind of entity. Thus, questions such as 'what are material objects?' or 'what are events?' are inextricably involved with the questions, whether material objects or events exist.

How can questions of existence be decided? If two people are having an everyday argument about whether there is a vase of flowers in the room next door, they can simply go and look. But clearly this cannot work for the ontological question of whether material objects in general exist. Any apparent perception of a material object could be discounted as merely a seeming perception of a material object by someone who wanted to deny their existence. We must, therefore, be wary of expecting conclusive answers to ontological questions. But that does not mean that there are no factors which can help us decide what kinds of entities exist.

Some philosophers favour a principle known as Occam's Razor, that entities should not be multiplied. They argue that we should only countenance the existence of entities that we really need to make sense of things. We should refuse to countenance the existence of anything without whose existence we can still get by, philosophically speaking. Ontological economy is their aim, and their usual budget consists only of concrete particular things, paradigmatically material objects. Such philosophers are called nominalists and Davidson's teacher, Quine, is one of their most prominent contemporary spokesmen. There is, therefore, a certain nominalist streak to Davidson's work, which will become apparent in various places.

Davidson, however, denies that ontological economy is his goal, and another ontological principle is clearly operative in his advocacy of the existence of events. By positing the existence of events, Davidson is able to give a unified and systematic treatment to a number of otherwise disparate areas in philosophy. Generally put, the principle is that it may be good reason to suppose that entities of some category exist that their existence would conduce to simplicity and unity in one's theories.

Economy or simplicity will be to no avail, though, if one cannot provide an account of the individuation of the entities one countenances. If we think of ourselves as picking out such an entity on two occasions, we must be able to say whether we have picked out the same thing twice, or two different things. It is part of the nominalist's rejection of entities like propositions or states of affairs that one cannot provide clear conditions of individuation for them. For this reason, as we shall see, much of Davidson's work on events takes the form of discussion of their identity conditions.

A prominent ontological contrast is that between particulars and universals. A universal, such as the property of being red, is something which is capable of having instances. Many different things can be red, or instantiate the property of being red. When we say that *this* rose is red, we do not assert that it is the same thing as red, but that it instantiates the property of being red. Hence, this rose and that rock can both be red while still being distinct from each other. Universals can stand in various logical relations to each other; for instance, the universals red and coloured are such that the first is somehow logically contained in the second. Anything that has the property of being red *ipso facto* has the property of being coloured.

Particulars, of which material objects are the paradigmatic examples, are not instantiated. We cannot say of many, distinct things that they are this rose. If anything *is* this rose, then it is identical with the rose, and hence not a distinct thing. Nor do particulars stand in logical relations to each other though they may stand in other types of relations, such as spatial relations. For instance, this chair can be next to, or underneath, that table.

If an oak tree grows, then there exists at least one particular, namely, the oak tree. Perhaps, depending on one's ontological views, there must also exist the universal of growing, something that is instantiated by any particular that grows. In claiming that events exist, and that they are particulars, Davidson is committed to the existence of something else in addition to these. If we were to give a list of all the particular things in the universe, we would have to include not only the oak tree but also the event which is the oak tree's growing, or the growing of the oak tree. This event is something which we can, if not physically, at the very least notionally, point to and say of *it*, that it is so-and-so or such-and-such. As we shall see, some philosophers think that events are not particulars, but are more like properties in having many instances.

One important feature of particulars is their susceptibility to redescription. Take some particular object, the Mona Lisa, for instance. This one thing can be given many different, and logically independent descriptions: 'Leonardo's best-known picture'; 'one of Freud's favourite paintings'; 'the Louvre's most prestigious possession'; 'an oil painting'. All of these descriptions apply to the particular in question, some of them uniquely (the first and the third), some of them not. If events are particulars, they too will be subject to redescription in this way. One and the same event can be described as: 'the First World War'; 'a terrible waste of human life'; 'the worst effect of the assassination of the Archduke Ferdinand '; 'one of the causes of the Second World War'; 'coming after the nineteenth century'. Again, some of these apply to the event uniquely (the first and third), and some not.

Davidson's original work on events took the form of a defence of a claim about their identity conditions. As we saw, this kind of work has to be done for any sort of entity we want to admit into our ontology. Davidson proposed that 'events are identical if and only if they have exactly the same causes and effects' (1969c, p. 179). I said above that particulars can stand in various non-logical relations to each other. With material objects, the most prominent kinds of relations are spatial. The examples of descriptions of the First World War in the previous paragraph show that with events, the paradigmatic kinds of relations are temporal, and especially causal. Events can happen before, after or at the same time as each other. And events can be the causes or effects of other events. It is this intuition that led Davidson to the view that their conditions of individuation should be framed in terms of causes and effects.

This proposal says very little about what events are. It only ensures that they are particulars if one also holds that causation is a relation between particulars, and there is little reason to hold this except on the grounds that it relates events and they are particulars. Hence it provides no independent reason for thinking that events are particulars. Furthermore, it says nothing about what kind of particulars events might be. It would, in itself, be consistent with events being concrete, material particulars or abstract, non-material particulars, or some kind of *sui generis* third possibility.

But Davidson's proposal faces a more serious problem. If events typically stand in causal relations to each other, there is a sort of circularity in holding that events are identical if and only if they have the same causes and effects. The causes and effects mentioned after the 'if and only if' of Davidson's proposal are further events. Thus, although what Davidson says about events may be true, it will not serve well as a criterion of their individuation. (In the same way, 'events are identical if and only if they are identical' would be true, but not a good criterion of individuation.) In response to Quine's advocacy of this criticism, Davidson has recently written: '[Quine] says my suggested criterion for individuating events is radically unsatisfactory, and I agree. I accepted it only tentatively . . . Quine has made clearer to me what was wrong with my original suggestion, and I hereby abandon it . . . Quine's criterion is neater, and better' (1985d, p. 175). Quine's criterion is that events are identical if and only if they occur in the same space at the same time.

In 'The Individuation of Events' (1969c) Davidson had considered this criterion and tentatively rejected it. One of his qualms was that the criterion does not distinguish events finely enough. 'If a metal ball becomes warmer during a certain minute, and during the same minute rotates through 35 degrees, must we say these are the same event?' (1969c, p. 178). According to Quine's criterion, the answer is yes. Similarly, if someone walks down Regent Street while whistling lillibullero, the event of his whistling is the same event as his walk down Regent Street. This is certainly a counter-intuitive consequence of the criterion, but may just be something we have to live with.

There is, however, another intuition we might have about this case, namely, that the rotation of a ball on a particular occasion *causes* its warming. Since one thing cannot cause itself, if we did want to hold that the warming was caused by the rotation, we would have to distinguish them. One way to get round this problem would be to segment the warming and the rotation into parts. We could then say that segments of the rotation caused segments of the warming which occurred after them. If the warming started after the rotation, then we could hold, in a Quinean spirit, that all but the beginning of the rotation was identical with all but the end of the warming, while still keeping our causal intuition by claiming that each segment of the warming was caused by a segment of the rotation.[1]

A rather deeper problem with Quine's criterion is this. Events are to be individuated by their space–time locations. But, on a very generally held account, occupancy of a space–time region is the individuating feature of material objects. Objects are identical if and only if they occupy the same space at the same time. So it looks as if Quine's criterion for event identity turns events into material objects. Indeed, this is a conclusion that Quine welcomes: 'a physical object, in the broad sense in which I have long used the term, is the material content of any portion of space–time, however small, large, irregular, or discontinuous. I have been wont to view events simply as physical objects in this sense' (Quine 1985 p. 167).

Davidson, however, is not content with this assimilation. He holds that our ordinary ways of speaking, 'our ways of sorting', call for a distinction between events and objects, and says that given his interest 'in the metaphysics implicit in our language, this is a distinction I do not want to give up' (1985d, p. 176). He argues that Quine's criterion for event identity need not entail the assimilation. If events or objects have the same space–time location, then they are identical; but if a material object and an event share a space–time location, they need not be identical, since 'events and objects may be related to locations in space–time in different ways; it may be, for example, that events *occur* at a time in a place while objects *occupy* places at times' (p. 176).

This attempt to resist the assimilation of events to objects will only work if we are able to make a convincing distinction between occurring and occupying which does not itself rely on the distinction between events and objects. It seems at least doubtful whether this can be done. Davidson's acceptance of Quine's criterion is too recent for it to be apparent whether he would accept it even if it does have the consequence that we must give up the distinction between events and objects. One might just say, however, that given his repeated comparison of events and objects, it is not so surprising that he should end up with a theory which may undermine the distinction between them altogether.

One should, however, note that what is really important to Davidson is the particularity of events, and not their materiality. Davidson does indeed believe that all events are physical, in a sense to be elucidated in chapter 4, but he does not need to hold that events, simply by their nature as events, must be material. And there is reason to think that Davidson did, at some point, conceive of events as not essentially material. Indeed, we saw that his proposal to individuate them by their causes and effects left open the possibility that they were not essentially material. This issue will be discussed at greater length in section 4.2.

It is important to mention that, although Davidson in one place puts the question of whether there are events as 'are there such things as changes?' (1970c, p. 181), and contrasts events, as changes, with states and dispositions (1963, p. 12), the category of events has come to include, in the literature on events, and in Davidson's own work, not only changes, but unchanges or states. This is important since Davidson wishes to use events in his discussions of the mental and we are more accustomed to speaking of mental states than mental events. According to the current usage, which I will adopt, mental states are events, even if they are not changes. What is important is that they are particulars – datable, locatable individual entities.

In order to see what is special about Davidson's advocacy of events as particulars, I propose to give a brief account of two further theories, one an alternate view of events as particulars, the other a view of events as universals.

Jaegwon Kim (1976) has developed an account of events as particulars, according to which events are constructed out of three components, an object, a property and a time. An event $<a, F, t>$ occurs if the object a has the property F at time t. Events are identical if their objects, properties and times are all identical. With Quine's view, we saw it was a problem that it might not individuate events as finely as we would wish. A rotation and a warming which we might intuitively think were different events had to be counted as one event if they occupied the same space and the same time. Kim's view, by contrast, individuates events very finely, indeed too finely for Davidson.

Take the event of Brutus' stabbing of Caesar at some time, and the event of his killing Caesar at the same time. For Davidson we have here one event, but under two different descriptions. For Kim, since the property of stabbing is not the same as the property of killing, we must have two separate events. Thus, in killing Caesar by stabbing him, Brutus performs two events. In fact, almost any attempts to redescribe an event will end up describing a new event, since when we redescribe something, we usually do this by mentioning different properties it has. If I can describe one object as 'a tie' and 'a birthday present' it is because this one object has the property of being a tie, and the property of being a birth-day present. On Kim's view, as Davidson says, 'no stabbing can be a killing and no killing can be a murder, no arm-raising a signalling, and no birthday party a celebration. I protest' (1969a, pp. 133–4). The pos-sibility of redescribing events is of the utmost importance for the use to which Davidson puts them in dealing with action and the mind. Kim's view of their identity conditions, therefore, is unacceptable to him.

Some philosophers, such as Roderick Chisholm (1970, 1971) and Neil Wilson (1974), offer views of events on which events are not particulars at all. Chisholm, for instance, has argued that any theory of events must take account of 'the fact of *recurrence* . . . the fact that there are some things that recur, or happen more than once' (1970, p. 15). One might, perhaps, think of the Olympic Games as an event which happens every four years. If there is *one thing* which happens many times then that one thing cannot be a particular thing, but must be like a universal which has distinct instances. The Olympic Games of 1968 are not the Olympic Games of 1972, yet they are both the Olympic Games. This is like two distinct roses both being red.

What would the instantiation of such a universal event be? Chisholm's own vocabulary suggests that the instantiations are occurrences, or hap-penings. But are not the occurrences, or happenings, of a universal event just particular events? (Just as the instantiations of redness are things like particular red roses.) Is not each instance of the Olympic Games a parti-cular event in Davidson's sense, something with a location in space and time, which can happen before or after or at the same time as other particular events? If Chisholm's theory requires that we have particular events as well as universal events it will not have any advantage over Davidson's theory in terms of ontological economy. Furthermore, as Dav-idson notes, his own theory can quite happily deal with the fact of recur-rence. All that is needed is to point out that certain descriptions, such as 'an international sporting competition conducted according to a certain protocol, and being called "the Olympic Games"' applies to a number of distinct particular events, one of which happened in 1968, one in 1972 and so on. We do not have to posit a further, universal entity which *is* the Olympic Games, as opposed to any occurrence of the Olympic Games.

The main reason, I believe, why philosophers have wanted to think of events as universals, rather than as particulars, is not connected with the problem of recurrence, but rather because of a theory about how events relate to language, and how they affect the truth of sentences. These questions will be taken up in greater detail in section 5.4, when we look at Davidson's work on the semantics of adverbial modification, and section 8.1, where the correspondence theory of truth is discussed. But let us take a cursory preview at what is involved.

Particulars are commonly referred to, in language, by means of what are called 'singular terms'. Names, definite descriptions, such as 'the fastest beetle in Africa' or 'the man who broke the bank at Monte Carlo', and demonstratives, such as 'him', 'this' and 'that', are all singular terms; they are expressions which purport to refer to single things. Since events, for Davidson, are particulars, they too will be referred to by means of these devices. In fact, few events have names (hurricanes may be an example of events that are named). Most are referred to by definite descriptions such as 'the first landing on the moon' and 'the marriage of Ferdinand de Medici and Christine of Lorraine in 1589'.

Singular terms can become parts of sentences. In a sentence like 'Vittoria Archilei sang at the marriage of Ferdinand and Christine' there are four singular terms which refer to four particulars. Three refer to the objects, or people, involved; the fourth, a complex term, refers to the event which was a marriage of Ferdinand and Christine. One might say, in a derivative sense, that the sentence as a whole refers to the people and the event, but it is clear that the relation of the sentence to the particulars is quite different from the relation between the singular terms and what they refer to. If we reserve the term 'reference' for this latter relation, the sentence as a whole does not refer to any of the particulars.

The reason why some philosophers have wanted to see events as universals is because they want events to be referred to, in the strict sense, by entire sentences, and not singular terms. This enables them to say that a sentence is true if it refers to some event, or, as these theorists like to call events, to some fact, or state of affairs. (See the Appendix for Davidson's reaction to the claim that sentences as a whole refer to something like facts or states of affairs.)

If particular events, for Davidson, are referred to by singular terms, and not by sentences, then there remains for him the following problem. Consider the singular term 'the marriage of Ferdinand and Christine' and the sentence 'Ferdinand and Christine were married.' If the singular term does indeed refer to an event, then the sentence must be true. Conversely, if the sentence is false, then there can be no event for the singular term to refer to. Davidson has to account for this relation between the singular term and the sentence.[2]

He does this by suggesting, as a paraphrase for the sentence 'Ferdinand and Christine were married' the following: 'some event occurred which was a marriage of Ferdinand and Christine.' We can now see why if the sentence is false the singular term cannot refer. If no event took place which was a marriage of Ferdinand and Christine, then there can be nothing which the description 'the marriage of Ferdinand and Christine' can correctly apply to. Conversely, if there is something for it correctly to apply to, then the sentence must be true, for some such event will have occurred. Further arguments which support Davidson's paraphrase will be examined in section 5.4.

Paraphrasing types of sentences in this way, to show their connections with other linguistic devices, including other sentences, is called by Davidson 'giving the logical form' of such sentences.

2.2 CAUSATION

Discussions of causation traditionally attempt to ascertain the nature of causal connection. When one thing causes another, what exactly is the relation between them? In his paper 'Causal Relations' (1967b), Davidson disavows any intention of analysing the nature of the causal relation itself. All he is interested in, he says, is in uncovering the logical form of causal sentences.

Consider the sentence 'the explosion caused the collapse of the bridge.' Davidson claims that the logical form of this sentence is just what it appears to be. There are two singular terms which refer to two events, the explosion and the collapse of the bridge, and the relational expression '. . . caused . . .' which relates pairs of things such that the first member of the pair caused the second member of the pair. If the events referred to by the two singular terms are indeed such a pair, if the explosion did cause the collapse of the bridge, then the sentence is true.

Other types of causal sentences will have different, but predictable, logical forms. In 'the explosion caused a catastrophe,' we have only one singular term, 'the explosion'. The expression 'a catastrophe' is not a singular term since it can apply to many different particular events. Thus the logical form could be expressed as follows: 'some event occurred which was a catastrophe and which was caused by the explosion.'

These analyses of the logical forms of two types of causal sentences confirm what we have already seen Davidson suggesting by his first proposal about the identity conditions of events, namely, that causation is a relation between events. Apart from this, his analyses tell us nothing, explicitly, about the nature of the causal relation itself. They are silent about whether the relation itself is, as Hume thought, merely one of constant conjunction between types of events, or whether the relation involves some necessary connection between the events so related. We shall see in section 2.3, however, that a position on the more substantive question of the nature of the causal relation is implied by other things Davidson says.

Above, we saw that a sentence such as 'the explosion caused the collapse of the bridge' would be true if the events referred to by the two singular terms did indeed stand in the causal relation to each other. As particular events, of course, they could be described in many different ways. But because the sentence asserting their causal relation depends only on the relation between the events themselves, it could not be changed from true to false, or false to true, by substituting for either of the singular terms other singular terms which referred to the same events. Thus, if the explosion was the loudest thing to happen on Tuesday, we can infer from 'the explosion caused the collapse of the bridge' the sentence 'the loudest thing that happened on Tuesday caused the collapse of the bridge.' This possibility of substituting co-referring singular terms without affecting the truth of the sentences containing them is called extensionality. (Its opposite is intensionality, with an 's'; both these concepts are discussed in greater detail in section 5.2.) The extensionality of causal sentences is a consequence of Davidson's claims that causation is a relation between events and that events are particulars.

Consider the sentences 'John's sneezing caused Mary to wake up' and 'John's sneezing so loudly caused Mary to wake up.' Assuming that the event referred to by 'John's sneezing so loudly' is the same event as that referred to by 'John's sneezing', the two sentence will have the same truth value, since all that is necessary for them to be true is that the events referred to do stand in the causal relation, and they both refer to the same events. But someone might want to object that it was not just John's sneezing that woke Mary, but the fact that he sneezed so loudly. If he had just sneezed normally, she would have kept on sleeping. So although the sentence 'John's sneezing so loudly caused Mary to wake up' is true, the sentence 'John's sneezing caused Mary to wake up' is false.

Philosophers with this intuition would have to argue that the events referred to by 'John's sneezing' and 'John's sneezing so loudly' are distinct. Kim could distinguish the events because the property of sneezing is distinct from the property of sneezing loudly; hence, when John exemplifies these two properties, even at the same time, there would be two separate events.

Another way to account for the intuition that it was specifically John's sneezing *loudly* that caused Mary to wake up would be to give an alternative analysis of the logical form of causal sentences as follows: 'the fact that John sneezed so loudly caused it to be the case that Mary woke up.' Here we have a relation not between things referred to by singular terms, but by things referred to by whole sentences. Since the sentences 'John sneezed' and 'John sneezed so loudly' are clearly different we would have an explanation of why one of our causal sentences was true and the other false.

Davidson deploys an argument, called 'the Frege argument', to show that the logical form of causal sentences cannot be 'the fact that . . . caused it to be the case that . . .'. The argument is given in an Appendix to this book. Whether or not it is a good argument, Davidson has other things to say, at which we shall now look, which help disarm this counter-proposal to his own suggestion about the nature of events and causation.

2.3 CAUSAL EXPLANATION

The impetus for the idea that the logical form of causal sentences is 'the fact that . . . caused it to be the case that . . .' comes from the feeling that it might be not just John's sneezing, but specifically, his sneezing loudly, that caused something to happen. But, says Davidson, we would be 'wrong in thinking we have not specified the whole cause of an event when we have not wholly specified it' (1967b, p. 156). What caused Mary to wake up was some event. No doubt we understand her waking up better when we include in our description of the cause the information that the event was not just a sneezing by John, but a loud sneezing by John; but any description that picks out just the right particular event will yield a true sentence when inserted into the blank in '. . . caused Mary to wake up'. Any description which picks out the right event specifies the whole of the cause, since the cause just is that event, but some descriptions of the event are fuller than others, not in how much of the cause they refer to, but in how much information they give us about that cause. The same is true of material objects. If I go into a shop and buy something, and you want to know what I bought, the answer 'what I bought' correctly picks out the object in which you are interested, even though it fails to tell you what you want to know about it. In other words,

> we must distinguish firmly between causes and the features we hit
> on for describing them, and hence between the question whether a
> statement says truly that one event caused another and the further
> question whether the events are characterized in such a way that we
> can deduce, or otherwise infer, from laws or other causal lore, that
> the relation was causal. (1967b, p. 155)

The distinction between events and the descriptions we use to pick out those events, a distinction which is a consequence of Davidson's view of events as particulars, is, as we have been seeing, absolutely funda-mental to Davidson's philosophy. In the passage just quoted, the distinc-tion appears in the guise of a distinction between causation and what Davidson calls 'the further question' of causal explanation. Causal expla-nations are attempts to explain the occurrence of events, or the presence of characteristics of events, in terms of their causes. Unlike assertions of causal relations between pairs of events, causal explanations are sensitive to how events are described. Although the two descriptions 'John's sneezing' and 'John's sneezing loudly' may refer to the same event, and hence equally refer to the cause of Mary's waking up, one may serve causally to explain why she woke up, while the other does not.

How does causal explanation work? In the passage just quoted, Davidson speaks of an event being characterized in such a way 'that we can deduce, or otherwise infer, from laws or other causal lore, that the relation was causal.' The significance of 'other causal lore' will become apparent in section 3.4, but for the moment let us look at the place of laws here.

Hume held that causation itself was really only a matter of constant conjunction. This means that singular causal claims such as '*a* causes *b*,' causal claims about particular events rather than types of events, are true only if there is some general truth such as 'every *a*-type event is followed by a *b*-type event.' In Hume's words, 'we may define a cause to be *an object, followed by another, and where all objects similar to the first are followed by objects similar to the second*' (Hume 1975, p. 76). Hume can be taken as saying that wherever one event causes another, there is a causal law which relates types of events of which the two particular events are instances. This has led to a theory of causal explanation, called the deductive-nomological theory, according to which one causally explains some event if one shows how the sentence asserting its occurrence is a deductive consequence of a general causal law and a statement of the occurrence of its cause (see Hempel 1966, pp. 49–54).

Opponents of Hume, such as C. J. Ducasse (1926), have argued that Hume is wrong, since we can judge that *a* causes *b* without knowing any laws which *a* and *b* instantiate. It is not the case that every time we make some singular causal claim we are bringing to bear knowledge of general causal laws. When we say that the movement of one billiard ball causes the movement of another, we do not invoke the laws of mechanics to support our claim, and nor, thinks Ducasse, are they what make it true.

Davidson has argued that the opposition between Hume and Ducasse is more apparent than real and his resolution depends crucially on the distinction between events and their descriptions, between causal statements and explanations in terms of causal laws. Singular causal claims are true in virtue of which events they are about, regardless of how those events are described. It does not follow, from the assertion that a singular causal claim '*a* causes *b*' is backed by some law which *a* and *b* instantiate, that *a* and *b* will instantiate that, or any law, under their given descriptions. We can therefore quite easily make various singular causal claims without any reference to laws that they instantiate and to this extent Ducasse is right.

This does not conflict with the Humean thought that true singular causal claims do imply that there is some law that the events which are causally related do instantiate. Events instantiate laws when described in certain ways and not when described in others: 'Causality and identity are relations between individual events no matter how described. But laws are linguistic; and so events can instantiate laws, and hence be explained or predicted in the light of laws, only as those events are described in one or another way' (Davidson 1970b, p. 215).

Take the case of the billiard balls. If the movement of one causes the movement of the other, then, according to Hume and Davidson, there will be some law which relates events similar to the first to events similar to the second. But of course the law is likely to be a law of mechanics, and mechanics as a science makes no mention of billiard balls. Its laws are framed in terms of motion, velocity, mass, friction and so on. So, although there will be some law which the events instantiate, that law will not subsume the events when described simply as 'the movement of the blue ball' and so on. For our particular events to instantiate the law, they would have to be redescribed as 'the motion of a body of mass m, with velocity v . . .'.

One of Davidson's own vivid examples is as follows:

> Suppose a hurricane, which is reported on page 5 of Tuesday's *Times*, causes a catastrophe, which is reported on page 13 of Wednesday's *Tribune*. Then the event reported on page 5 of Tuesday's *Times* caused the event reported on page 13 of Wednesday's *Tribune*. Should we look for a law relating events of these *kinds?* It is only slightly less ridiculous to look for a law relating hurricanes and catastrophes. The laws needed to predict the catastrophe with precision would, of course, have no use for concepts like hurricane and catastrophe. The trouble with predicting the weather is that the descriptions under which events interest us – 'a cool, cloudy day with rain in the afternoon' – have only remote connections with the concepts employed by the more precise known laws. (1963, p. 17)

In the next chapter, we shall look further at causal explanation, in the context of Davidson's discussion of how reasons explain actions. To sum up what we have established in this section, Davidson's view on causal explanation is one of support for a principle, derived from Hume, which he calls the Nomological Character of Causality. The principle, he says, must be read carefully: 'it says that when events are related as cause and effect, they have descriptions that instantiate a law. It does not say that every true singular statement of causality instantiates a law' (1970b, p. 215).

Although such a principle is widely accepted today, it is worth pointing out that Davidson nowhere gives any argument for it. Hume asserted some such principle because he took himself to have analysed tha nature of causation as constant conjunction. It was, remember, part of his very definition of causation that if one particular event causes another then all events similar to the first are conjoined to events similar to the second. Davidson, by contrast, has disavowed any intention of analysing causation as such, and it is therefore a legitimate question to ask why he upholds the Nomological Character of Causality (see McDowell 1985, pp. 397–8). The best answer is, perhaps, that he does after all have a specific view on the nature of causation itself, namely, a more or less Humean one. But this goes beyond anything he argues for. (See section 4.2 for a suggestion that Davidson should abandon the principle.)

3

Action

In any philosophical discussion of the mental, the concept of action must play a large role. It is by performing actions, by doing things, that people can affect the world they live in, and thus in some measure control their environment. But action is much more than an instrument. It is also a means of self-expression. People's characters, their beliefs, desires, hopes and fears, are revealed by what they do. Indeed, since linguistic utterances are also actions, action is ultimately the only means of deliberate self-expression.

It is partly in the hope of using action to infer the presence of mental states that philosophers have attempted to establish the existence of psychological laws. In chapter 1 we saw that Davidson denies the existence of laws which would make the inference from actions to mental states a potentially scientific enterprise. Actions and mental states mesh together in a holistic network or, to use Quine's metaphor, a web in which everything is connected, either directly or indirectly, to everything else. But notwithstanding, any attempt to interpret someone will face a crucial empirical test when it comes to action.

When we interpret someone, there are three tasks we must accomplish. We must ascribe to him mental states; we must assign meanings to his linguistic productions; and we must say which actions he is performing (in chapter 6 we shall see that, ultimately, the second of these is a special instance of the third). It is the last of these which has the most direct link with the empirical data on which our interpretation is based. If actions are psychological events, parts of a person's biography, many of them are also undeniably physical events that can be apprehended and measured by the physical sciences. (Davidson implicitly treats mental actions, like calculating a sum, as mental states or events. 'Action', in what follows, will be restricted to physical action.) Which actions we describe someone as performing will be constrained by the brute physical facts in a way in which, prima facie, our ascriptions of mental states and linguistic meanings need not be. If meaning, mental states and action interlock in a holistic web, it is action which, in some sense, provides the means of entry into the web.

In the first section of this chapter, we shall look at how the individuation of action is a consequence of Davidson's theory of events. In section 3.2, we shall examine Davidson's causal theory of action, a theory which has been enormously influential, and the third section will address an important criticism of the theory. In section 3.4 we take up the question whether explanation by reasons is a form of causal explanation. Finally, the topic of practical reason will be addressed.

3.1   ACTIONS, EVENTS AND AGENCY

Events, we have seen, are taken by Davidson to be particular, dated occurrences. In this sense, it is clear that actions are events. Going to the opera, proposing marriage, turning right at the next traffic light, these are all events which have locations in space and time. But of course, not all events are actions. This raises the question, what conditions must an event meet to be an action? As a particular event, one action can be given many different descriptions. If I perform an action of chasing a bat, this one event can be described as 'chasing a bat', 'moving my arms at certain angles', 'puzzling the neighbours', and so on. Not all descriptions of some particular are equally revealing. If actions are things we do rather than things that merely happen, not all descriptions of the event in question will reveal that it was an action. If I suddenly turn purple I may puzzle the neighbours, so describing the event of my chasing a bat as puzzling the neighbours does not reveal that the event was something I did rather than something that merely happened to me.

This suggests that, for an event to be an action, it must be describable in a particular way. The most obvious way in which this could work would be if there were some class of descriptions such that any events so described were actions. There are some verbs which do carry this implication. If an event is described as someone's telling a joke or getting married, we know that the event was an action. But many verbs which are capable of describing events *as* actions do not entail that the events described are actions. Thus coughing, jumping, killing, laughing and going somewhere all may or may not be actions. We cannot, therefore, hope to say what it is for an event to be an action by specifying a particular class of descriptions.

What is special about actions is that they are events performed by people for reasons. They are done intentionally. What is important about descriptions if they are to reveal an event as an action is that they relate the event to the agent's reason for performing that event. For example, I might fire a gun because I want to draw attention to myself and believe that firing the gun is a good way to do this. The description of the event as 'firing a gun' thus meshes with the belief and desire which constituted the reason why I fired the gun. But if I happen to shoot the archduke, who later dies, then that same action is describable as 'shooting the archduke' and 'killing the archduke', and described in either of these two ways, it would not match the reason for which it was done. If I intentionally fired the gun, but did not intentionally kill the archduke, and if my firing the gun is the same event as my killing the archduke, then one and the same action is intentional under some descriptions and not under others. Being intentional is not something which qualifies events themselves, but events as described in one or another way.

Killing the archduke was something I did, and therefore my action, but I did not do it intentionally. We should not conclude from this that intentional actions form a subset of actions in the same way that actions form a subset of events. For anything to be an action at all, something I do, rather than something that merely happens, it must have some description under which it is intentional. Actions, therefore, are events which are intentional under some description, the descriptions under which they are rationalized by the contents of the mental states which are the reasons for them.

It may seem implausible to say that 'firing the gun' and 'killing the archduke' are different descriptions of the same action. One seems to be an action concerning a gun, and the other an action involving an archduke and his death. They seem to have different spatial locations. Furthermore, it may be that the archduke's death does not occur until hours after I fire the gun at him. In that case, can I be said to perform an action of killing someone hours before he dies? Can the archduke be killed before he dies (see Thomson 1971)?

We must recall Davidson's admonishment not to confuse specifying the whole of an event with wholly specifying it. The description by means of which we pick out some event may involve reference to many things, people and other events which are not themselves parts of or participants in the event we are referring to. When we refer to my action of firing the gun as 'killing the archduke' we are redescribing it in terms of its consequences, or effects. This is why we should accept that I can kill the archduke before he dies. What we cannot do, of course, is describe the action as a killing until he dies. The same phenomenon occurs with objects when we refer to an ancestor as our great-great-grandmother. This description does not usually become true of anyone until long after her death. Similarly, the description 'killing the archduke' may not become true of an event until after the event occurs.

This stretching out and squeezing of descriptions of events is often effected by the use of the preposition 'by'. I kill the archduke by firing the gun, and I fire the gun by moving my finger. Moving my finger, firing the gun, and killing the archduke are all the same action, though in each case more and more of the consequences of what I do are subsumed by the description. This one action, with its three different descriptions, should not be confused with two other events, the gun's firing, and the archduke's dying. These two events are the effects of my action and are distinct from, and subsequent to, it. The event of my killing the archduke by firing the gun is not the same as the events of the gun's firing and the archduke's dying. But if an action of mine causes those events, then I fire the gun, and I kill the archduke, and I do both of these by moving my finger. As Davidson says, 'an agent causes what his actions cause' (1971, p. 53).

Some philosophers (e.g. Goldman 1970), basing themselves on a view of event individuation like that of Kim's, have objected to Davidson's view on the grounds that, when I fire the gun, I am exemplifying a different property from that which I exemplify when I kill the archduke. In other words, since killing an archduke is a different kind of thing from firing a gun, it cannot be that I only perform one action when I fire the gun and kill the archduke. The observation that the property of firing a gun is not the same as the property of killing an archduke is, of course, quite correct. But this does not have to entail that I perform two actions here, instead of one action under two descriptions, unless one already accepts the property-exemplification theory of events.

Others have objected to Davidson's views on different grounds. In typical cases, I do not move my finger by doing anything else. (In an atypical case, for instance, my trigger-finger may become paralysed, and I may use my other hand to move it.) This is not to say that my moving my finger is uncaused, but only that it is not caused by anything that is an action of mine. Noticing that some actions, such as closing the door, can only be done by doing something else, like moving one's arm, whereas other actions, such as moving one's arm, can be done without doing anything else, Arthur Danto has developed the concept of 'basic actions' (Danto 1963, 1965; in the article 'Agency' (1971), Davidson refers to these as 'primitive actions'). Danto writes that:

(1)   *B* is a basic action of *a* if and only if (i) *B* is an action and (ii) whenever *a* performs *B*, there is no other action *A* performed by *a* such that *B* is caused by *A*.

(2)   *B* is a nonbasic action of *a* if there is some action *A*, performed by *a*, such that *B* is caused by *A*. (Danto 1963, pp. 435–6)

Moving my arm, in a typical case, would be an example of a basic action, whereas closing the door would be a non-basic action, since, according to Danto, I perform the action of closing the door by performing the action of moving my hand, and the latter action causes the former.

This, of course, is directly contrary to Davidson's own view of how moving my hand is related to closing the door when I do the latter by doing the former. For Davidson we simply have two different descriptions of the same action. The description 'closing the door' refers to the action in terms of its consequences. And, of course, my moving my hand cannot cause my closing of the door, since an action cannot cause itself. Davidson writes that Danto's view:

> contains several closely related but quite fundamental confusions. It is a mistake to think that when I close the door of my own free will *anyone* normally causes me to do it, even myself, or that any prior or other action of mine causes me to close the door. So the second error is to confuse what my action of moving my hand does cause – the closing of the door – with something utterly different – my action of closing the door. And the third mistake, which is forced by the others, is to suppose that when I close the door by moving my hand, I perform two numerically distinct actions (as I would have to if one were needed to cause the other). (Davidson 1971, p. 56)

What is wrong with saying that when I do one thing by doing another, there are two actions, the latter of which causes the former, is this. If I move my hand on a certain occasion, as a result of which a door closes, then I have closed the door. If my moving my hand caused me to close the door, rather than just causing the door to close, then there would have to be something I did after moving my hand. But it seems quite clear that, once I have moved my hand, there is nothing left for *me* to do before the door closes. As Davidson says, 'our primitive actions, the ones we do not do by doing something else, mere movements of the body – these are all the actions there are. We never do more than move our bodies: the rest is up to nature' (1971, p. 59). All our actions involve movements of our body, so they will all have descriptions like 'moving one's finger'. If we often have occasion to describe our actions as 'killing the archduke' or the like, this is because of such things as the presence of the gun in my hand, the bullet in the gun, the archduke in the trajectory of the bullet, and so on. Of course, the presence of a gun in my hand when I move my finger need not be coincidental. I may move my finger just because I believe there is a gun in my hand and I want to fire it.

None the less, what happens after I move my finger, whether a gun fires, whether an archduke dies, is 'up to nature', in the sense that nothing more is required from me for these things to come to pass.

We can continue to distinguish between basicness and non-basicness, but these must now be seen as qualifying not actions but descriptions of actions. If I kill the archduke, I can answer the question how I did it by saying 'by firing a gun'. And I fired the gun by moving my finger. But, in typical cases, there is nothing I did by doing which I moved my finger. When we reach a description of an action which cannot be qualified with 'by doing something else', we will have reached a basic description of the action.

We must be careful, though, to avoid an error here. From the fact that all our actions have basic descriptions like 'moving one's finger', it does not follow that they are all intentional under those basic descriptions. Davidson's example is tying one's shoe-lace. Although I tie my shoe-lace by moving my fingers in certain ways, and I do not do this by doing anything else, I may find it very difficult intentionally to move my fingers in the necessary ways, despite the fact that I find it easy intentionally to tie my shoe-lace.

3.2   THE CAUSAL THEORY OF ACTION

We turn now to the question how reasons are related to the actions for which they are reasons. For if it is a necessary condition for an event to be an action that there is some description of it under which the agent has a reason for doing it, this is clearly not sufficient. Suppose I kill my rich, childless uncle and that it is also the case that I want to inherit his fortune and believe that killing him is the most expedient way of satisfying this desire. My belief and desire form a reason for killing him, so it is true that I have a reason to kill him. But must it also be true that this reason is *the* reason why I kill him?

One of the chief merits of Davidson's early paper 'Actions, Reasons, and Causes' (1963) was to draw attention to the difference between something's being *a* reason for an action, and something's being *the reason why* one performs an action. For *a* reason to be *the* reason why an agent acts as he does, Davidson argues that, besides the relation between propositional attitudes and the description of an action that must exist for the former to be *a* reason for the latter, a further condition must hold. This condition is that the reason must cause the action.

When we explain an action by citing the reason for which it was performed, we typically do so by means of sentences such as 'I killed my uncle because I wanted to inherit his fortune.' But suppose I also believed him to be an Albanian spy, and that I was fanatically dedicated to eradicating all vestiges of Albanian interference in this country. That also would have been a reason for me to kill him, yet it was not the case that I killed him because I believed him to be an Albanian spy. As Davidson says, 'a person can have a reason for an action, and perform the action, and yet this reason not be the reason why he did it' (1963, p. 9). So what we need is some extra relation that my desiring to inherit his fortune had to my action of killing him, which was not also had by my belief that he was a spy. We need something to account for the 'because' in 'I killed him because I wanted to inherit his fortune and not because I believed he was a spy.' Now, if the propositional attitudes are particular states of, or events in, the agent, and the action is some distinct event, then what relation could there be to explain the 'because' other than the causal relation? If two distinct events interact, how can it be other than causally? Thus, for it to be the case that I killed my uncle *because* I wanted his fortune, it is not sufficient that I merely had that reason, and performed the action. It must also be true that the reason caused my action.

Of course, by asking the rhetorical question 'what other relation could there be than causation?', we do not prove that there could be no other relation. Davidson's point is rather that with causation we have just the kind of relation we need, and that there seems to be no other appropriate relation to do the job. Davidson has clearly put the burden of proof on someone who wants to deny that the reason why I perform an action causes that performance. This is consistent with Davidson's assertion, quoted in the previous section, that when I do something intentionally, no one, not even myself, causes me to do it, and with his view that actions are not, at least directly, caused by other actions. A reason is neither a person nor another action.

We are now in a position to see how the themes of the first two chapters are combined in Davidson's philosophy. In interpreting someone, we describe certain events in ways which connect them with the mental states we attribute to the agent. These events are the intentional actions of that agent. Since causation is a relation which holds between events, it is natural to see these actions as causally related to other, mental, events and this provides the key to explaining why some propositional attitudes are *the* reason why an agent performs an action, rather than merely *a* reason for performing it. This allows us to give the following condition for intentional action:

(C)   For an event *e*, under a description *d*, to be an intentional action, it must have been caused by something which was a reason for *e* under description *d*.

It looks as if this is an attempt to give a causal analysis of the concept of

intentional action. An analysis of a concept is often taken to be a statement of necessary and sufficient conditions for the application of that
concept, stated without the use of either the concept under analysis, or
other concepts essentially related to that concept. In this sense of analysis,
Davidson admits that (C) is a failure as a causal analysis of the concept of
intentional action.

The reason why it is a failure is that, although (C) gives a *necessary*
condition for intentional action, it still does not give a *sufficient* condition.
There could be cases where the conditions stated in (C) do obtain and yet
the event *e* is not an intentional action. Such cases are known as deviant,
or wayward, causal chains. Here is an example:

> A climber might want to rid himself of the weight and danger of
> holding another man on a rope, and he might know that by loos-
> ening his hold on the rope he could rid himself of the weight and
> danger. The belief and want might so unnerve him as to cause him
> to loosen his hold, and yet it might be the case that he never *chose* to
> loosen his hold, nor did he do it intentionally. (1973b, p. 79)

As Davidson says, 'the point is that not just any causal connection between rationalizing attitudes and a wanted effect suffices to guarantee that
producing the wanted effect was intentional. The causal chain must follow the right sort of route' (p. 78). The problem for a causal analysis of
intentional action is thus how to supplement (C) to specify which routes
are of the right sort or, in other words, how to turn (C) into a sufficient as
well as a necessary condition for intentional action.

It is by no means clear, however, that (C) can be supplemented in a
non-question-begging way. There are two ways in which one could try to
supplement it. One way would be to add conditions in mentalistic vocabulary, restrictions on the interrelations between beliefs, desires and other
mental states. For instance, one might say that in the example of the
climber, the belief and desire must cause the wanted effect by causing
some intermediate mental state such as a desire to loosen his hold which,
in turn, must cause the wanted effect. The trouble with this is that however many restrictions one adds, it is surely always possible that the
restrictions should be satisfied, and yet the causal relations between the
various items in the chain still be deviant.

The second approach to making (C) into a sufficient condition would
be to add restrictions in physical vocabulary specifying which neural paths
were necessary for non-deviancy in a causal chain. The trouble with this is
that it would make particular neurophysiological concepts part of the very
concept of intentional action, making it impossible to say of any creatures
that could not have the appropriate physical states that they could perform intentional actions.[1] Since there could clearly be rational alien agents

with completely different 'hardware' from ours, this consequence is unacceptable.

For these reasons, Davidson writes that he 'despair[s] of spelling out . . . the way in which attitudes must cause actions if they are to rationalize the action' (1973b, p. 79). He does not, however, take the view that the insolubility of the problem of deviant causal chains is an objection to the causal theory of action. Whether this sanguine attitude is warranted is perhaps questionable. In sections 3.4 and 9.2, we shall look at some further difficulties for the causal theory of action, and it may be that, taken in conjunction with these other difficulties, the problem of deviant causal chains will carry more weight than Davidson allows it. (For a complicated attempt to solve the problem of deviancy, see Peacocke 1979, chapter 2.)

3.3   CAN REASONS BE CAUSES?

Aside from the rather esoteric objection of deviant causal chains, the idea that the reasons for an action must cause that action has such an intuitive appeal that one may well wonder what was so special about Davidson's advocacy of it in the early 1960s. In fact, until Davidson's paper 'Actions, Reasons, and Causes' appeared, the view that reasons for actions were not the causes of those actions was more or less standard. It was felt that Hume had shown that any two things which are causally related cannot have a logical relation to each other. Since it was also believed that reasons and the actions for which they are reasons do have some logical connection, the conclusion was drawn that they could not be causally related.

The logical connection thesis, as this position is sometimes called, has never been stated as clearly as one would like, and many of its proponents seem to have had their own special concerns (see Melden 1961, pp. 52–3 and chapter 9; Mackie 1974, pp. 270–96; Stoutland 1970). Bearing that in mind, let us try to see what, in general, this objection amounts to.

Consider the following exposition of the objection, given by Melden:

> A causal explanation . . . does not give us a further characterization of the event thereby explained . . . rather, it offers us an account of how it is that an event whose characteristics are already known is brought to pass . . . As the alleged cause of the action, [the motive, or reason] cannot serve further to characterize the action. As motive it must – for it tells us what in fact the person was doing. It informs us, *qua* motive, that the action of raising the arm was in fact the action of giving information to others to the effect that the driver was preparing to make a turn . . . In short, citing the motive was

giving a fuller characterization of the action; it was indeed providing
a better understanding of what the driver was doing. But no Humean cause could possibly do this; any alleged cause, in this sense,
of the action of raising the arm . . . would merely explain how the
action of raising the arm came to be. From the driver's statement
that he raised his arm in order to inform others of what he was
about to do, it follows logically that he was signalling or at least
attempting to signal. If, then, the motive [on the supposition that
the motive is the cause] were some event either concurrent with or
antecedent to the action of raising the arm, there would needs be a
logically necessary connection between two distinct events – the
alleged motive and the action, however it is described. (Melden
1961, pp. 88–9)

The argument, such as it is, rests on the claim that there cannot be logical
relations between things which are related causally. What does this mean?
The logical connection argument could take two forms (see Valberg
1970). It could proceed by arguing that reasons and actions are related in
a way in which only abstract universals can be related, and that therefore
they cannot be causally related since causal relations can only hold between concrete particulars. The kinds of abstract universals which have
logical as opposed to causal relations with each other are things like
meanings, propositions and facts. One proposition can be said to entail, or
imply another, but can hardly be said to cause another.

The trouble with this construal of the logical connection argument is
that, whether or not we think of reasons as abstract entities, we have seen
that there are good grounds for treating events, and hence actions, as
concrete particulars, and just the sort of things to have causal rather than
logical relations. Melden's argument, in any case, seems to rest on a different construal of logical relatedness. His claim is that 'from the driver's
statement that he raised his arm in order to inform others of what he was
about to do, it follows logically that he was signalling.' It may be true
that there is some logical connection between raising one's arm to inform
others of what one is about to do, and signalling. But Melden is wrong to
imply that this shows there is a logical connection between reason and
action. For Melden's logical connection holds between two descriptions of
the same event. It is the same event, the action, which makes both the
sentences 'he raised his arm in order to inform others of what he was
about to do' and 'he was signalling' true. Melden has been confused by
the fact that first sentence uses in its description of that event an allusion
to the agent's reasons. What Melden needs to show is that, from 'he
wanted to raise his arm in order to inform others of what he was about
to do' it follows logically that he was signalling. But this is obviously

not true, since the agent could have the desire and yet not perform any relevant action at all.

In any case, the Humean view about the independence of distinct particulars, a view with which Davidson would undoubtedly agree, is quite compatible with the observation that genuinely distinct particulars can be described in such a way that one can infer the existence of one from that of the other. Once again, the point can be made in terms of objects as well as events. Charlie and his aunt are quite distinct, and the existence of his aunt in no way necessitates the existence of Charlie. But when she is described as 'Charlie's aunt', we can logically infer that Charlie exists (or has existed).

3.4 CAUSAL EXPLANATION AND REASON EXPLANATION

So far, we have been considering the question whether the reason for an action is the cause of that action. However, in 'Actions, Reasons and Causes' Davidson makes another claim about the relation between reasons and actions, and that is that the former causally explain the latter. We saw in the previous chapter what the difference was between the relations of causation, a relation between events however described, and causal explanation, a relation between events under descriptions. The difference between these two relations means that whether or not reasons causally explain actions is partially independent of whether they cause them. If reasons causally explain actions then they must cause them, but the converse is not true.

There is no doubt, of course, that reasons do explain the actions they are reasons for. In many circumstances, they are the best form of explanation we can have. What is at issue is whether the way in which reasons explain actions is a form of causal explanation. Davidson has been less than clear about this question. His 'official', or strict, view of causal explanation, at which we looked in section 2.3, was that one event causally explains another when they are described in ways which instantiate some causal law. According to this view, there is a problem with the idea that reasons causally explain actions. If there were causal laws which reasons and actions instantiated when described as reasons and actions, this would contradict the thesis of the anomalism of the mental. This thesis asserted precisely that there are no laws which events under mental descriptions instantiate.

However, Davidson actually takes a more relaxed position over what constitutes causal explanation. He gives the idea of a spectrum of possible degrees of causal explanation when he says:

the most primitive explanation of an event gives its cause; more elaborate explanations may tell more of the story, or defend the singular causal claim by producing a relevant law or by giving reasons for believing such exists. But it is an error to think no explanation has been given until a law has been produced. (1963, p. 17; see also David Lewis 1986)

And Davidson also says that there is causal explanation when 'events are characterized in such a way that we can deduce, or otherwise infer, from laws or other causal lore, that the relation was causal' (1967b, p. 155). The point of the phrase 'causal lore' is that the knowledge which allows such inferences goes beyond our knowledge of causal laws in the strict sense. In his argument against the existence of psychophysical and psychological laws, Davidson distinguished between genuine laws and mere generalizations. Psychophysical and psychological generalizations, he allowed, might well exist. It is now apparent why he should have been concerned to allow their existence. If there are no genuine laws in virtue of which reason explanations are causally explanatory, might they not be so in virtue of some non-lawlike generalizations?

This seems to be what Davidson means in the following passage:

> If an event of a certain mental sort has usually been accompanied by an event of a certain physical sort, this often is a good reason to expect other cases to follow suit roughly in proportion. The generalizations that embody such practical wisdom are assumed to be only roughly true, or they are explicitly stated in probabilistic terms, or they are insulated from counterexamples by generous escape clauses. Their importance lies mainly in the support they lend singular causal claims and related explanations of particular events. (Davidson 1970b, pp. 218–19)

What, then, are the generalizations in virtue of which reason explanations are causal explanations?

To attribute to someone a desire, say a desire to crush a snail, is to say of him that when he thinks some course of action would lead to the crushing of a snail, he *tends* to perform it. This avoids being a law because it is insulated from counter-examples by the admission of a mere tendency. The failure of someone to crush a snail, given the opportunity, would not entail that he did not desire to do so. Mental states like desires are thus seen as dispositions to act in certain ways. Dispositions, in turn, are essentially causal; they are states which cause certain types of behaviour under certain circumstances.

Dispositions, of course, play a part in physical explanations. Solubility is a disposition to dissolve when placed in water. When we want to explain a particular sugar cube's dissolving when placed in water, we can do so by adverting to its solubility. Many philosophers, however, have thought that explanation by reference to dispositions is no explanation at all. One of Moliere's characters was supposed to have made a fool of himself by saying that a powder succeeded in putting someone to sleep because of its dormitive virtue. Similarly, it is argued that to hold that someone's action of crushing a snail was caused by a state which tends to promote crushings of snails is unexplanatory.

Davidson admits that explanation by reference to dispositions 'is not high science, but it isn't empty either' (1976b, p. 274). This is because crushing a snail by itself need not be caused by an underlying disposition, just as dissolving in water need not be caused by solubility. Whether some action was caused by an underlying disposition is often of interest to us. For instance, knowing that your crushing a snail was a result of a disposition will stop me from letting you near my pet snails; knowing that it was the result of a chance electrical impulse in your brain will not. In addition, if we explain an action by referring to the particular mental states which caused it, we not only learn that it was the result of some general tendency. We also learn which of the many tendencies that could have caused the action was responsible. This allows us to form an idea of other actions an agent might perform in various circumstances.

Davidson has come to accept that the generalizations implicit in causal dispositions such as beliefs and desires may deserve to be called laws, and he also writes that 'laws relating the mental and the physical are not like the laws of physics' (1987b, p. 45), thereby implying the existence of psychophysical laws of some sort. Thus, to a certain extent, holding that reason explanation is a form of causal explanation does conflict with the anomalism of the mental in the strict sense. However, because of their insulation from counter-examples and their often vague nature, the psychological and psychophysical generalizations involved in reason explanations are in no real conflict with the anomalism of the mental, the object of which was to deny that the mental is subject to laws in the precise and potentially deterministic way in which the physical is (but see section 9.2 for further discussion of this).

There is another way in which the dispositions inherent in reason explanations should not be confused with their physical counterparts. A disposition is a causal propensity, a state which tends to cause certain effects in certain situations. When we advert to dispositions in explanations in the physical sciences, as when we explain why something dissolved by reference to its solubility, we assume that, ideally, we could replace the reference to the disposition by a detailed reference to the micro-structure of the object concerned and the physical laws which state unconditionally which micro-structural properties are connected to which other micro-structural properties. The invocation of the causal propensity itself in the explanation is not, ultimately, necessary.

Things are different when we use dispositions in reason explanations.

Since the holistic and normative character of the mental means that there
are no detailed, unconditional psychological or psychophysical laws, the
reference to the disposition is not even in principle eliminable. Consequently, says Davidson, 'reason-explanations . . . are in some sense low-
grade; they explain less than the best explanations in the hard sciences
because of their heavy dependence on causal propensities' (1987b, p. 42).

3.5   PRACTICAL REASON AND INTENTIONS

We must recognize, however, that in another sense reason explanations
are anything but low-grade. In most circumstances, when we inquire
about a person's actions, they are exactly the kind of explanation we
want. There must, therefore, be another way in which reasons explain
actions in addition to the kind of low-grade causal explanation we have
just looked at. This other mode of explanation is provided by the notion
of practical reason.

Let us look more closely at what makes some mental states a reason for
an action. 'A reason,' Davidson says, 'rationalizes an action only if it leads
us to see something the agent saw, or thought he saw, in his action –
some feature, consequence, or aspect of the action the agent wanted, desired, prized, held dear, thought dutiful, beneficial, obligatory, or agree-
able' (1963, p. 3). A reason, then, must include a 'pro attitude' or, as I
shall say quite generally, a desire. But this is not sufficient. A desire that
he impress his friends will not be a reason for someone's strutting unless
he believes that by strutting he will impress his friends. If desire marks
the goal towards which we strive, belief is needed to show us the way
there.

With cases like that in the previous paragraph, the relation of belief
and desire suggests the familiar pattern of means–end reasoning. The
desire represents the end, and the belief is one about the means needed to
achieve that end. Whether a reason must always contain a belief about
means depends on how the action is described. If the action is described as
impressing my friends, my desire to impress my friends will be a reason
without the addition of a belief about means. If the same action is described as strutting, then for my desire to impress my friends to be part of
a reason for it, it is necessary that I have a belief that by strutting, I will
impress my friends.

But there is another way in which belief and desire relate in explaining
action. Desires are for some 'feature, consequence, or aspect' that the
agent sees in his action. They have a certain generality which makes them
unsuited to connect directly with particular actions. If my goal is to turn
on the light, there are many ways I can do this. I could turn it on with my
thumb, with my index finger, with my eyes open or closed, and so on.

Although, when I turn on the light, I do it in just one of these ways, it would be misleading to suppose that my desire was to perform the very action I did perform rather than any of the many other actions which would have done just as well. But if desire is general in this way, I must at least believe that the actual action that I perform is, indeed, a way of turning on the light. To explain my particular action by saying that I wanted to turn on the light presupposes, in other words, that I took myself to be turning on the light.

Davidson's canonical definition of what he calls a 'primary reason' views the role of belief in this second way. 'Whenever someone does something for a reason . . . he can be characterized as (a) having some sort of pro attitude toward actions of a certain kind, and (b) believing (or knowing, perceiving, noticing, remembering) that his action is of that kind' (1963, pp. 3–4). There is, however, both in Davidson's work and in that of others, a tendency to confuse these two different ways in which beliefs and desires can be related in reasons. All reasons must contain a belief which relates the desire to the action in this second way. The belief serves a demonstrative purpose, focusing the agent's desire on particular performances or particular objects. But not all actions must include a belief which represents a means to fulfilling the desire. And when they do include one, it will be different from the other, demonstrative belief which bridges the gap between the generality of the desired end and the particularity of the action.

It is these relations of belief and desire to action which point the way to seeing how reasons explain actions. Aristotle held that an action is like the conclusion of a syllogism of which the belief and desire which are the reason for the action are the premises. A reason explains an action because, given the reason, the action somehow follows from it logically. For instance, the desire, functioning as the major premise, could be expressed as 'any action of mine which results in a state of affairs S is desirable.' The belief, the minor premise, would be 'ϕing would result in S.' The conclusion which can be deductively drawn from these two premises is that ϕing is desirable, but Aristotle simply identified the conclusion with the performance of a ϕ-type action.[2] (Here, and in what follows, there will be some harmless ambiguity about whether the belief concerns a type of action, thus conforming to the means-end pattern of reasoning, or a particular action, thus serving a demonstrative purpose.)

What remains to be done, then, in examining the explanatory relation between reasons and actions, is to examine this idea of a practical syllogism. A good way to do this is to turn to the question of intention. Wittgenstein asked what has to be added to my arm's rising to make it an action of raising my arm. Since raising my arm, as opposed to my arm's rising, is an intentional action, a number of philosophers have felt that what had to be added is something like an intention, or act of will.

By contrast, Davidson's answer to Wittgenstein's question is that nothing has to be added to my arm's rising to make it an action of raising my arm. As we saw in sections 3.1 to 3.3, what is required, if it is to be an action of raising my arm, something that I do rather than something that happens to me, is that it be caused, non-deviantly, by something which is a reason for it under the description 'raising my arm'. Reasons, construed as beliefs and desires, seemed adequate for an account of intentional action. Intentions as such made no appearance.

Unfortunately, as Davidson was to realize, the situation is not so simple. If the concept of intention is analysed by reference to the reason with which an action is performed, what are we to say of cases where someone intends to do something, but never does; cases, as Davidson calls them, of pure intending? We could, of course, simply posit intentions as a new mental category to account for pure intending. But ideally, we should try to give 'an account of intending (and of forming an intention) that would mesh in a satisfactory way with our account of acting with an intention and would not sacrifice the merits of that account' (1978b, p. 101).

Since the account of intentional action made do only with beliefs and desires, it would be natural to hope that pure intending could be analysed with just these same materials. Is intending to ϕ a belief that one will ϕ? There is certainly some connection between intending to ϕ and believing that one will ϕ but Davidson denies that an intention to ϕ even entails that one believe that one will ϕ, let alone is identical to such a belief. He gives the following example:

> In writing heavily on this page I may be intending to produce ten legible carbon copies. I do not know, or believe with any confidence, that I am succeeding. But if I am producing ten legible carbon copies, I am certainly doing it intentionally . . . [I]t is hard to imagine that the point does not carry over to pure intending. (1978b, p. 92)

Some philosophers think that it is odd to credit someone with an intention to do something which he does not also believe that he will do (for example, Grice 1971). But even if we concede this, that is not sufficient to prove that the intention is identical to such a belief. And Davidson gives another reason against such an identification, namely, 'that reasons for intending to do something are in general quite different from reasons for believing one will do it' (1978b, p. 95).

What about the identification of the intention to ϕ with a desire that one ϕ? It is here that we must return to the practical syllogism. Davidson says that, in 'Actions, Reasons, and Causes', he espoused the view 'that the propositional expressions of the reasons for an action are deductively related to the proposition that corresponds to the action as explained by those reasons' (1980a, p. xii). That is, he accepted, roughly, the equation of an agent's reasons with the premises of a practical syllogism, the conclusion of which can be identified with an action. Since the proposition that corresponds to the action would have something like the form 'a ϕ-type action is desirable,' the idea suggests itself of identifying this proposition as the expression of the intention to ϕ. Where the action is performed, there is no need to separate the intention from the action itself, and the practical syllogism could be taken to explain the intention or the action indifferently. When there is an intention, but no action is performed, we will have an explanation for the intention – the same explanation that we would have had for the action, had it been performed.

This is promising, but there is a difficulty with it. Consider the following two practical syllogisms, concerning one piece of poisoned chocolate. First, any action of mine which is an eating of something sweet is desirable; eating this chocolate would be eating something sweet; therefore eating this chocolate is desirable. And, secondly, any action of mine which is an eating of something poisonous is undesirable; eating this chocolate would be eating something poisonous; therefore eating this chocolate is undesirable. We appear to have two valid arguments, both with true premises, but yielding contradictory conclusions, that eating this chocolate is both desirable and undesirable. Something in our account of practical reasoning has gone wrong. Furthermore, if we did take the step of identifying the conclusion with an intention, we would have to suppose that I did both intend to eat and not to eat the chocolate.

Davidson's diagnosis of the problem is this. Practical reasoning is meant to do justice to the idea of weighing up different considerations in deciding how to act. It would, therefore, be wrong to suppose that we cannot go through something like both the arguments about the poisoned chocolate. On the other hand, this is something we cannot countenance as things stand, since we cannot have two valid arguments from true premises which have contradictory conclusions. If the conclusions were somehow relativized, so that they were no longer directly contradictory, that would solve our problem. This can only be done if we reformulate the premises. The formulation of the minor premise, the belief component, seems unexceptionable. But if we look more closely at the major premise, the desire component, we can see what has gone wrong.

We cannot really mean that any action which is an eating of something sweet is desirable, since this would make an action of eating a poisoned chocolate desirable. Furthermore, we don't think of everything sweet, that eating it would be desirable. What we really mean is that being an eating of something sweet counts in favour of an action. It is one mark on the plus side. When we come to deliberate about certain actions, whether they are eatings of things sweet is something we will want to take into account, but there is no reason to suppose that that alone should settle the issue of whether an action is one we want to perform.

To represent this new way of thinking of the desire, Davidson suggests we introduce a 'prima facie' sentential operator.[3] A sentential operator makes a complex sentence out of one or more sentences. The 'prima facie' operator, the meaning of which could be given by the English expression 'in so far as', makes a complex sentence out of two sentences, one stating that some actions are desirable, and the other stating in which respects they are desirable. The major premises of our two arguments above can now be rewritten as: for any action *a*, *a* is desirable in so far as it is an eating of something sweet; and, for any action *a*, *a* is undesirable in so far as it is an eating of something poisonous. Given our two minor premises, these yield the conclusions that eating this chocolate is desirable in so far as it is sweet and undesirable in so far as it is poisonous. These two conclusions, unlike the conclusions that eating this chocolate is desirable and undesirable, do not contradict each other at all.

Now that we have got the form of the practical reasoning right, we can see what is wrong with identifying the action or the intention with the conclusion of the practical syllogism, as Aristotle wanted, and as Davidson seemed happy to admit in 'Actions, Reasons, and Causes'. When we act, we have got beyond the stage of thinking that the action we perform is desirable in so far as it has some feature or other. Our very acting shows that we have formed a judgement that not only is it desirable in this or that way, it is unconditionally desirable. Judging an action unconditionally desirable doesn't mean not having any reservations about it. The point is that in acting intentionally, we have finished our deliberation and made our decision.

So, on the one hand, we have practical syllogisms, the conclusions of which are judgements about prima facie desirability, and on the other we have actions, which could be said to reflect unconditional, or all-out judgements of desirability. We can now say that an intention is an all-out or unconditional judgement in favour of doing something. In cases where we do act, there is no need to separate this judgement from the action. But where, for whatever reason, we do not act, but where we have gone beyond our judgements of prima facie desirability and made a judgement of unconditional desirability, there we have a case of pure intending.

Do we thus have an account of intending which will mesh with the account of acting intentionally that we started with? Can we make sense of the notion of all-out judgements 'without appeal to the notions of intention or the will'? Davidson suggests that:

> we cannot claim that we have made out a case for viewing inten-
> tions as something familiar, a kind of wanting, where we can dis-
> tinguish the kind without having to use the concept of intention or
> will. What we can say, however, is that intending and wanting

belong to the same genus of pro attitudes expressed by value judgements. Wants . . . provide reasons for actions and intentions, and
are expressed by prima facie judgements; intentions and the judgements that go with intentional actions are distinguished by their
all-out or unconditional form. (1978b, pp. 102)

One undesirable consequence of this account is that a new chasm in
practical reasoning is opened up. The practical syllogism itself, which
contains all our weighing of pros and cons, takes us as far as a judgement
of prima facie desirability. An action or intention is reflected by a judgement of unconditional desirability. The problem is to say how we get
from judgements of the first kind to those of the second. In the nature of
the case, it cannot be through any further process of reasoning, since this
all goes into reaching the prima facie judgements. The other obvious
alternative is that judgements of prima facie desirability usually give rise,
through causal processes, to all-out judgements in favour of an action.
When we look at Davidson's views on irrationality, in section 9.4, we
shall see that this process is presupposed by his treatment of irrational
action. But to suppose that it is the norm, and that all cases of rational
action depend on the brute causal relation between judgements of prima
facie and unconditional desirability, risks compromising the notion that
with practical reason, we have a mode of rational explanation of *action*,
rather than just a mode of rational explanation of judgements of prima
facie desirability. The wider implications of this will be further discussed
in chapter 9.

4

Mind and Matter

In this chapter, we turn to the problem of the relation between mind and body. We shall see that the problem has two aspects. One is the purely ontological question of whether one and the same thing has both material and mental characteristics, or whether the mind requires the existence of something other than matter. The other is the question of whether, and how, something's physical states constrain what mental states it has. It is one of the great merits of Davidson's work in this area that it clearly separates these two questions. His answer to the first question is affirmative, and in this respect he is a materialist. But materialism has usually been taken to imply the existence of psychophysical laws. Such laws would mean that the mental is constrained by the physical in a way which conflicts with the anomalism of the mental. Davidson, therefore, attempts to elaborate a form of materialism which is consistent with the anomalism of the mental. Anomalous monism, as his view is called, is the subject of section 4.1. In section 4.2, we shall look at some criticisms of anomalous monism based on difficulties with the theory of events which underwrites it. Davidson supplements anomalous monism with the claim that the mental is supervenient on the physical. We shall examine supervenience in section 4.3 and ask whether it, too, is consistent with the anomalism of the mental.

4.1 ANOMALOUS MONISM

Traditionally, materialist responses to the mind–body problem have been united in seeing Cartesian dualism as the view most opposed to them. Descartes held that mind was one thing and matter another. He conceived of this difference as one between two different kinds of substance. Substance is a seventeenth-century philosophical notion of something self-subsistent and capable of supporting properties. Mind was a substance whose essential nature was to think; matter a substance whose essential nature was to be extended in space. Descartes denied that there could be something which both thought and was extended in space. He therefore viewed people, the most obvious candidates for things which both think and are extended in space, as unions of two different substances. Mind and matter could interact with each other, he thought, but were fundamentally distinct.

Materialism, by contrast, holds that in some sense mind is identical to matter. For this reason, materialism is often referred to as an identity theory of mind. But the denial that mind and matter are different kinds of substance is only interesting so long as we feel some plausibility in the claim that they *are* different kinds of substance. Since modern metaphysics has largely eschewed the notion of substance, the identity theory has come to be formulated in rather different terms and it is its standard formulation in these more modern terms that provides the view against which Davidson argues for his own distinctive version of the identity theory.

What, then, is the standard modern formulation of the identity theory? Identity theorists have been wont to view the mind–body problem against the background of scientific reduction. Physics, dealing with the ultimate constituents of the universe and their properties in the most undiluted form, is seen as the bedrock of all science. In addition to physics, there are other special sciences, chemistry, geology, neurophysiology and so on, which deal with things and properties less fundamental than those that form the subject matter of physics. There is clearly no doubt that the things of which these disciplines treat, for instance chemicals, volcanoes and nervous systems, are made up of the things of which physics treats, namely particles, electrons and the rest. For someone interested in the relation of, say, chemistry to physics, the chief question is, therefore, not the relation between chemical and physical objects, but the relation between chemical properties, such as having a valency of two, and physical properties, such as having a positively charged electron. The question to be asked is, are chemical properties, in some sense or other, connected to (possibly complex) physical properties?

The view that chemical properties are strongly connected to physical properties is reductionism. The strongest form of connection would be identity, but chemical reductionism does not require that chemical properties be identical to physical properties. It would also be satisfied with the claim that the instantiations of chemical and physical properties are linked by laws. In what follows I shall refer to property identity in describing reductionism, but what I say should also apply to reductionism which only requires nomological connections. For the reductionist, chemistry would be seen as reducible to physics in that any truth statable in chemical terms would be translatable into a truth expressed only in the language of physics. This would be accomplished by means of property identities, or bridging laws (see section 1.3), which connect properties from the different theories. Since the physical properties to which chemical properties are identical are likely to be highly complex, the physicalist expressions of chemical truths will be much more cumbersome than their chemical expressions. This explains why we do not actually replace chemistry and the other special sciences with physics. But such replacement would be theoretically possible.

For much of this century, philosophers, particularly those of the logical positivist school, have been committed to the view that all sciences could be reduced to physics. Since these philosophers also held that psychology either was, or could be made into, a science, they believed that psychological properties are, at least theoretically, reducible to physical properties. For any psychological property, such as believing that whales are insects, there is some property, probably highly complex, belonging to basic physics, which is identical to it (see Carnap 1932 for an incisive expression of this view). To make this claim more plausible, it was allowed that psychology might not be directly reducible to physics, but might instead be reducible to neurophysiology, which in turn would be reducible to physics. But such complications are inessential to the traditional, reductionist construal of the identity theory.

Davidson rejects the reductionist identity theory, but his rejection does not stem from its ontological implications. We shall shortly see how his own answer to the mind–body problem also repudiates the existence of non-physical entities. What makes reductionist theories unacceptable to Davidson is that, by linking mental properties with physical properties, they contravene the thesis of the anomalism of the mental. If there are bridging laws between the mental and the physical, then the attribution of mental states to people will no longer be answerable only to the normative and holistic considerations to which, as we saw in section 1.2, Davidson thinks it ought to be. The possibility will arise that the physical states of some creature will pre-empt the attribution of mental states based solely on the evidence appropriate to such attribution. We described, in section 1.3, the consequences of bridging laws for the anomalism of the mental.

This distinction between the question of ontology and the question of property reduction accounts for Davidson's classification of theories of the relation between mind and body:

> On the one hand there are those who assert, and those who deny, the existence of psychophysical laws; on the other hand there are those who say mental events are identical with physical and those who

deny this. Theories are thus divided into four sorts: *nomological monism*, which affirms that there are correlating laws and that the events correlated are one . . . *nomological dualism*, which comprises various forms of parallelism, interactionism, and epiphenomenalism; *anomalous dualism*, which combines ontological dualism with the general failure of laws correlating the mental and the physical (Cartesianism). And finally there is *anomalous monism*, which classifies the position I wish to occupy.[1] (1970b, pp. 213–14)

To facilitate the explanation of anomalous monism, let me introduce the terminology of types and tokens. In giving a particular event or object a certain description, we subsume the particular under a kind, or type. A type is a set of individual, token objects or events which share some property, or satisfy some description. For instance, the type *lion* is the set of particular things which have the property of being a lion. The bridging laws which relate mental and physical properties can also be seen as positing identities between mental state-types and physical state-types. A law which relates the properties F and G says that anything which is an F-type event or object is a G-type event or object.

In many cases, statements of identity are ambiguous between type-identity and token-identity. If I tell someone that my brother and I have the same car this could either mean that each of us has his own car, and that these two cars are of the same type – both Lamborghinis, for instance – or it could mean that we jointly own a single car. The same distinction applies to actions and events, as well as objects. When Oscar Wilde said 'I wish I had said that' and was told by Whistler 'You will, Oscar; you will,' Whistler did not mean that Wilde would actually perform the very action which had just occurred (which, of course, would be impossible), but that he would perform an action of the same type at a later date.

Anomalous monism is a token-identity theory. Davidson uses his theory of events as particulars, and the distinction between events and their descriptions, to combine non-reductionism with ontological monism. He holds that each individual, token mental event is also a physical event. But to say of some particular mental event, such as my present belief that I am thirsty, that it is a physical event, a certain state of my brain, carries no implications about whether other mental events of the same type, i.e. other people's beliefs that they are thirsty, or my belief on a different occasion, will be identical to physical events of *the same physical type*. Your present belief that you are thirsty may be an entirely different kind of physical event from the physical event to which my belief that I am thirsty is identical. That our two beliefs are each identical to some physical event or other does not entail that there is a single kind of physical event such that our two beliefs are identical to a physical event of that kind. There are thus no links between the property of being a belief that one is thirsty and any single, albeit complex, physical property.

The novelty in Davidson's solution lies in his focusing not on types of mental events, as previous identity theorists had tended to do, but on individual token events. As particulars, token events can be described in many different ways. Nobody would think that, just because one and the same object can be a tie and a birthday present, all ties are birthday presents or all birthday presents are ties. Similarly, just because one particular mental event, my present belief that *p*, is a physical event, a certain synaptic connection, why should one think that all beliefs that *p* must be identical to that type of synaptic connection, or that all instances of such a synaptic connection are identical to a belief that *p*?

The token-identity theory is clearly compatible with the anomalism of the mental. But Davidson maintains something stronger, namely, that together with two other premises, the anomalism of the mental entails a token-identity theory. The three premises which entail the theory are as follows:

(1)   There is causal interaction between the mental and the physical.

(2)   Where there is a true singular causal statement, there is some causal law which it instantiates.

(3)   There are no psychophysical or psychological laws.

(1) asserts that the mental and physical interact causally. An example of such interaction would be the causation of actions (which are physical events, even if they are also psychological events) by reasons, which we examined in chapter 3. The second premise is the principle of the Nomological Character of Causality which was discussed in section 2.3. The final premise is the thesis of the anomalism of the mental, the subject of chapter 1.

The argument for anomalous monism is simple. By (1) there are some true singular causal statements relating mental and physical events. By (2), there must be laws which these singular causal statements instantiate, but by (3) these laws cannot be psychophysical or psychological. They must therefore be physical laws, so the events related in the singular causal statements, including the mental events, must have some physical descriptions under which they instantiate these physical laws. The conclusion is that any mental event which causally interacts with physical events itself has a physical description under which it instantiates a physical law. Davidson admits that this argument does not apply to any mental events which are causally isolated from the physical but considers this a trivial price. The argument also does not apply to sensations since these do not have propositional content and hence are not subject to the normativity and holism of the mental.

4.2   MENTAL AND PHYSICAL EVENTS

Davidson effected a kind of liberation when he showed how one could be a materialist without having to posit unlikely identities between kinds of mental events and kinds of physical events, or between mental and physical properties. As he now says, 'in my view the mental is not an ontological but a conceptual category' (1987b, p. 46). In section 9.1 we shall look at a theory which takes much further the idea of the mental as a conceptual rather than ontological category and, without being dualistic, avoids positing even token-identities between mental and physical events. In this section, however, we shall look at what could be called an ontological difficulty with Davidson's theory.

When Davidson first developed anomalous monism, he was still operating with the view that events were individuated by their causes and effects. On that view, a token mental event would be identical to a token physical event if each had the same causes and effects. But we have seen, in section 2.1, that Davidson now subscribes to a spatiotemporal theory of event individuation. Where does this leave anomalous monism? If we agree to the plausible assumption that anything which exists in space and time is physical, then it follows from this new theory of event identity alone that all mental events are physical events. A mental event, being an event, must have a spatiotemporal location, and therefore must be a physical event. There is no need for the argument for anomalous monism to establish non-reductive materialism.

It might be felt that this constitutes too easy an answer to the mind--body problem. If mental events are identical to physical events, this ought to be the outcome of some argument, and not just a consequence of a theory of the nature of events. Davidson, of course, could restrict the theory of spatiotemporal individuation to physical events. The argument for anomalous monism, if it is good, would then establish that all mental events which interact causally with physical events are physical events without relying on a spatiotemporal theory of events. This then leaves Davidson free to apply the spatiotemporal theory to mental events as well without begging any questions. But although this would serve Davidson's purpose in the context of the mind-body problem, it would mean that he ends up without a general theory about the nature of events. Davidson thus has a choice: he can either keep the spatiotemporal theory as a general theory of event identity, and thus risk proving his materialism on the sly; or, he can restrict his theory of event identity to physical events only, and use his argument for anomalous monism to establish that mental events are physical events. In this case, he forgoes a general theory of events.

This dilemma is not, perhaps, very pressing. In either case, Davidson's conclusions about the relation of mental to physical events are not challenged. What is more interesting is that we can discern two fundamentally different conceptions of events at work here. Underlying the argument for anomalous monism is the idea that events, in themselves, are neither physical nor mental. What makes an event a mental, or physical, event, is whether or not it has a mental, or physical, description. Davidson's choice of the term 'monism', rather than, say, 'materialism', to describe his theory, is a good one. What is important is not so much that all events are physical as that events form a single, and ontologically neutral, class of entities.

This approach to events did raise certain problems for Davidson. He recognized that if one simply identified being a physical event with being describable in physical vocabulary then every event would trivially count as physical, since a physical description like 'occurs on Pluto or doesn't occur on Pluto' would be true of every event. Similarly, every event is describable in mental terms, for instance, as being noticed by Columbus or not noticed by him, and hence every event would be trivially counted as mental.

Davidson's attempt to deal with this is rather half-hearted (see 1970b, pp. 210–12). He introduces the idea of descriptions which use mental or physical vocabulary essentially, but whatever exactly this is supposed to mean, Davidson accepts that it will probably allow all events to be counted as mental. He justifies this by saying that 'we can afford Spinozistic extravagance with the mental since accidental inclusions can only strengthen the hypothesis that all mental events are identical with physical events' (p. 212). He seems to forget, however, that the problem is mirrored by the fact that all events are also describable as physical, which might be thought to strengthen the idealist hypothesis that all physical events are identical with mental events. Since, however, events themselves are considered only as bare particulars, nothing very much hangs on whether they all qualify as mental or physical through being trivially subsumed by mental or physical descriptions.

This view of events as bare particulars contrasts with the view of events as individuated by their spatiotemporal locations. On this new conception, events as such are essentially physical. The underlying commitment is not so much to monism as to materialism (though, of course, materialism is a species of monism). Instead of bare events, on the one hand, and descriptions, mental or physical, on the other, each event is now seen as having one description, the physical description of its space–time location, in a privileged way.

This equivocation may help us to understand a criticism of anomalous monism that has been forcefully urged by Hornsby (1980–1, 1985), though her criticism is not formulated in terms of it. Hornsby asks what assurance there is that the way one form of discourse articulates the world into different events will be the same as another. The events of psychology, beliefs, perceptions and the like, may cut across events as discerned by the neurophysiologist. For example, think of a desire to clench my fist causing me to clench it. A neurophysiological process starts in the brain, travels down my arm and terminates in my fist clenching. Neurophysiology describes what happens in terms of many neurophysiological events, psychology discerns a desire and an action. But why assume that we can superimpose these two accounts and find that there are discrete events that each describes in its own way? Where, exactly, does the action begin and the desire end? How far up my arm does the action begin? Must the desire and action be constituted by neurophysiological events which are continuous, or could there be parts of this chain between the desire and the action?

These questions are particularly pressing on the view of events as bare particulars, for this conception of events provides no reason for not seeing the psychological description as being about one set of bare events, and the neurophysiological description as being about another. The very ontological neutrality of events as bare particulars makes it hard to insist that both descriptions must be of the same set of events.

What is being challenged in this criticism is not Davidson's belief that events, as particulars, *can* be given different descriptions. It is simply being suggested that there are no compelling grounds for thinking that the events picked out by, say, neurophysiology and psychology must be the same things under different descriptions. If they are not the same things under different descriptions, then the identity theory, even in Davidson's non-reductive formulation, is false. Mental events are not the same as physical events.

This challenge to the identity theory does not question the validity of the argument for anomalous monism. If, therefore, anomalous monism were false, at least one of the premises which entail it would have to be abandoned. Hornsby suggests that we give up the principle of the Nomological Character of Causality, since it is this which requires that a mental event that causally interacts with some physical event is the very thing which fits some physical description under which it instantiates a physical law. And we did indeed see, in section 2.3, that Davidson's commitment to the Nomological Character of Causality rested on a view of the nature of causation for which he provided no argument (see Hornsby 1985, pp. 456–8; McDowell 1985, pp. 397–8).

Hornsby does identify a view which could support the idea that, at root, physics and psychology are talking about the very same things in different ways but, as we shall see, she thinks this view is untenable. Some events are complex events, composed out of smaller events. For instance, the event of my writing this sentence is composed of the smaller events of my writing each word in the sentence. The première of the *Marriage of Figaro* was composed out of a number of smaller incidents, such as the singing of various arias, which in turn were composed of smaller events and so on. If we were to suppose that, just as all matter is composed of atoms, all events are composed of some basic event units, then we could explain the fact that physics and psychology may appear to identify different events by regarding each as making different collections out of the same basic event units. So even if some mental events did not correspond exactly to an event as discerned by, say, neurophysiology, we could still support a form of monism by showing that each was a collection from the same basic stock of event units. Hornsby calls this the mereological conception of events.

The trouble with this conception is that, if we are to suppose that events are composed out of smaller events, there must be some principle which says something like this: if e and f are events then there is some event which is the composition of e and f. Such a principle might be thought to be unacceptably permissive. The first performance of *Figaro* and my writing this sentence are events. But should we accept that there is also an event which is the fusion of these two events? As Hornsby says, such 'putative events lack any conceivable value to us in giving explanations . . . [I]nasmuch as it is in the nature of events to cause and be caused, we expect individual events to be members of kinds that pull their weight in illuminating accounts of why one thing followed on another' (1985, pp. 453–4). 'Events' such as the fusion of the première of *Figaro* and my writing some sentence are obviously of kinds which can pull no weight in providing such illuminating accounts. In general, there is nothing which would be explained better by that event than by one of its components. Accordingly, Hornsby thinks, we should reject the mereological conception of events and, with it, the idea that there must be some stock of common events which are of interest to physics, neurophysiology, psychology and all other areas of discourse.

The mereological conception of events does not entail Davidson's spatiotemporal theory of their individuation, but it does work well with it. The basic units out of which complex events are composed could be seen as spatiotemporal point-instants. (Quine has specifically suggested thinking of worlds as patterns of such point-instants, see 1969, pp. 147–52.) In section 2.1 we saw Quine saying that 'a physical object, in the broad sense in which I have long used the term, is the material content of *any portion of space-time*, however small, large, *irregular, or discontinuous*. I have been wont to view events simply as physical objects in this sense' (1985, p. 167; italics mine). So Quine, and presumably now Davidson, would allow that there is an event composed of the première of *Figaro* and my writing this sentence. Davidson seems, that is, to accept a mereological conception of events as a consequence of his view that events are individuated by their spatiotemporal locations and this enables him to answer Hornsby's criticisms. Furthermore, in giving up the theory that events are individuated by their causes and effects, Davidson would no doubt disagree with Hornsby that 'it is in the nature of events to cause and be caused'. Events, on Davidson's new conception of them, may be causes and effects, but it is no longer part of their nature that they are.

4.3   SUPERVENIENCE

Anomalous monism combines ontological monism with the anomalism of the mental. Davidson, however, supplements the theory of anomalous monism with the claim that the mental is supervenient on the physical. Let us first look at what supervenience is, and then ask why Davidson endorses it.

The concept of supervenience was first explicitly introduced into philosophy in discussions of ethical and aesthetic properties such as being beautiful or good. G.E. Moore held that a property like being good was not reducible to any non-evaluative, physical or, as he said, 'natural' properties. But despite this, he was not prepared to countenance the possibility that two things could be exactly alike in all physical respects and yet differ in their possession of some evaluative property. If some object were good or beautiful, then any object which was exactly like it in all physical respects would also be good or beautiful. He thus maintained that evaluative properties were supervenient on physical properties.

Davidson introduced supervenience into discussions of the mental. Like Moore and evaluative properties, Davidson, we have seen, has argued that mental properties are not reducible to physical properties. Yet he too has been unwilling to countenance the possibility that two people could be exact physical replicas and yet differ in which psychological properties they possessed. If some person fears that the end of the world is nigh, then any person exactly like him in all physical respects will also fear that the end of the world is nigh.

Originally, Davidson defined supervenience in two ways. It 'might be taken to mean that there cannot be two events alike in all physical respects but differing in some mental respect, or that an object cannot alter in some mental respect without altering in some physical respect' (1970b, p. 214). These two definitions are not equivalent (see Lewis 1985, pp. 169–70), and I will take the first as definitive. It is the first definition which Davidson chose to reiterate when he wrote, retrospectively, that:

the notion of supervenience, as I have used it, is best thought of as a relation between a predicate and a set of predicates in a language: a predicate p is supervenient on a set of predicates S if for every pair of objects such that p is true of one and not of the other there is a predicate of S that is true of one and not the other. (1985a, p. 242)

(In what follows, I shall take supervenience indifferently to be about mental predicates or mental properties.)

Why does Davidson hold that the mental is supervenient on the physical? Following on from the passage just quoted, he writes that:

> supervenience as I have defined it here is clearly all I needed for the argument in 'Mental Events', since what I was arguing for there was only the identity of mental events with physical events. I wanted to emphasize that such ontological reduction does not imply that mental properties are physical properties, nor that there are causal or bridging laws relating events classed by mental properties with events classed by physical properties. (1985a, pp. 243–4)

It is odd to think that such emphasis is provided by supplementing anomalous monism, which on its own would not rule out two physically identical objects differing with respect to mental properties, with a claim about the dependence of mental properties on physical properties. Supervenience may or may not fall far short of causal or bridging laws but it does represent a tightening of the relation between mental and physical properties compared to anomalous monism. It cannot, therefore, be needed to emphasize the looseness of this connection.

Not only does supervenience represent a tightening of the relation between the mental and the physical, but a number of writers have felt that if it does obtain, then it will, after all, yield lawlike connections. Kim writes: 'If M supervenes on N [M and N are classes of properties] , each property in M which is instantiated has a general sufficient condition in N ... I don't see how such generalizations could fail to be lawlike' (Kim 1978, p. 153). In other words, if someone bears a mental property M, and the mental supervenes on the physical, then, if that person's physical state is P, supervenience will entail that anyone who is P has M. Now this is obviously not intended simply as a mere generalization, in the way that the claim that anything which is green is edible was a mere generalization for our fixed domain of objects considered in chapter 1.[2] So it seems as if we will have psychophysical laws such as:

(S)   For any person x, if x has the physical property P, then he has the mental property M.

Laws like (S) would not amount to the reduction of mental to physical properties since the implication only runs from the possession of P to the possession of M. If M were being reduced to P, it would also have to be the case that:

(S')   For any person x, if x has the mental property M, then he has the physical property P.

Supervenience does not license claims like (S'), so it could not be argued that it led to property reduction. None the less, (S) itself seems like a psychophysical law.

But whether or not we should call generalizations like (S) laws, it is still surely true that the very arguments Davidson uses against the possibility of psychophysical laws tell equally against supervenience claims. If the attribution of mental states is to retain allegiance to its proper source of evidence, if it is to be governed by the normative principles of coherence, consistency and rationality, then which physical properties some object instantiates should be irrelevant to which mental properties it has. Imagine two people alike in all relevant physical respects, one of whom has the mental property M. If we now consider whether the other person also has M, why should we let his physical similarity to the first person be a consideration at all? It might well be the case that the principles of rationality which Davidson takes to govern the attribution of mental content, taken in conjunction with the other mental states already attributed to him, require us to deny that the second person has M.

Quite generally, then, the doctrine of supervenience seems incompatible with the thesis of the anomalism of the mental. (This is recognized by Blackburn 1985, pp. 59–60 and Kim 1985, p. 385 n.28). There is some reason to think that particular supervenience claims would be psychophysical laws, but even if they are not, they still would conflict with the autonomy of rationality constraints in governing the attribution of mental states.

There are further difficulties with the doctrine of supervenience. Suppose that the mental predicate 'x hopes that the sun will rise' bears a relation to some set of physical predicates, S. If the mental predicate is true of one person and not of another, then supervenience says that there will be some predicate in S true of one but not of the other. Which predicates might belong to S? The most plausible answer is all physical predicates true of the person who hopes that the sun will rise. But this means that supervenience will countenance the possibility of two people, one of whom hopes that the sun will rise and the other of whom does not, who are exact physical replicas except for the fact that one has a single eyelash which is slightly longer than its counterpart on the other. These two people, who differed in what they hoped, would satisfy the requirement that there was some predicate in the supervenience base which was true of one but not the other. It is surely absurd, none the less, to think that the physical difference between them in this case could in any way underlie the difference in their mental states.

To avoid this, it would be necessary to narrow down the physical predicates on which a mental predicate supervenes. Perhaps one step would be to say that mental predicates were supervenient on the physical predicates true of people's brains. But then it would be possible to repeat the kind of example of the last paragraph by limiting the physical difference between two otherwise identical people to some completely inert part of the brain. The problems which these examples raise is this. They seem to show that what Davidson really wants out of supervenience is the dependence of mental properties on just those physical properties of a person which are causally relevant to the manifestations of the mental property. Differences in length of eyelash, or in some inert part of the brain, don't count because they play no role in the bringing about of other mental states and actions (see section 9.2 for more on this).

If this is what Davidson wants, it is far from clear that he can legitimately have it, given his other views about the relation of mental and physical properties. The causally relevant properties on which a mental property must supervene will be those which are potentially able to cause all those actions and other mental states with which the given mental state might be rationally connected. But given the fact that there are no laws under which mental states fall when described as mental states, there is no way of specifying exactly which other mental states, and which actions, they might cause. There is thus no way of saying which causal powers the underlying physical properties must have, and, consequently, no way of saying which physical predicates should form the supervenience base for some mental predicate.

Davidson seems faced with a dilemma. He can either admit that we can specify the right predicates to form the supervenience base, which amounts to repudiating the anomalism of the mental, or he must allow that the supervenience base might include predicates specifying causally irrelevant properties such as length of eyelash. In this case, it might be that the only difference between two otherwise identical people, one of whom has some mental state and one of whom lacks it, is the length of their eyelashes.

Davidson's views on supervenience have evolved, however, and it is no longer clear that he holds such a thesis. Compare the statement from 'Mental Events', in which supervenience was first discussed by Davidson, 'there cannot be two events alike in all physical respects but differing in some mental respect' (1970b, p. 214), with the following, from a paper published in 1987: 'we are . . . free to hold that people can be in all relevant physical respects identical while differing psychologically: this is in fact the position of "anomalous monism'" (1987a, p. 453). It is indeed the position of anomalous monism, but not as supplemented by supervenience.

The full reasons for Davidson's shift over the question of supervenience (a shift which he has not explicitly recognized) cannot be appreciated until we have seen the latest developments in Davidson's theory of propositional content in chapter 8. We can, however, say a little at this point. In the more recent statement quoted above, Davidson is, in part, reacting to a kind of example which has become common in philosophical discussions of propositional content, so-called twin-earth examples. Putnam (1975) introduced the idea of two worlds which are exact physical replicas of each other, except for the fact that what on earth is H_2O is on twin-earth some macroscopically indiscernible substance XYZ. If I have some belief which I would express as 'water is clear,' my twin-earth counterpart would have a belief which he would express in exactly the same way. However, my belief would be about water, whereas his belief would be about XYZ and not water. Although our brains are, by hypothesis, in type-identical states, we have different beliefs because of the nature of the stuff our beliefs are about.

Putnam is expressing an externalist view of content. On an externalist view, propositional content, what my belief is a belief that, or what my sentence means, is not determined just by what is going on with me but is affected by the nature of things outside me, the things that my beliefs and sentences are about. 'Meanings,' as Putnam puts it, 'just ain't in the head' (1975, p. 227). Davidson, as we shall see in more detail in chapter 8, also accepts an externalist view of content, indeed, a far more radical externalism than Putnam, and for this reason, he no longer holds to supervenience in the way he originally conceived of it.

The pressure put on supervenience by twin-earth examples, however, is not as serious as that posed by the conflict between supervenience and the anomalism of the mental. Even if twin-earth cases force one to give up the position that mental states are supervenient on the physical states of the person whose mental states they are, they may be accommodated by extending the supervenience base to include not only predicates applying to the person, but also to predicates qualifying the relevant physical environment. The conflict between supervenience and the anomalism of the mental would exist even if the supervenience base were enlarged in this way. In section 9.2 I shall return to this problem and suggest why Davidson did advance the claim that the mental is supervenient on the physical.

5

Meaning and Truth

We turn now to Davidson's work on the philosophy of language. In this chapter we shall look at the formal bedrock of Davidson's theory of meaning: the theory of truth and its logic. Section 5.1 identifies two approaches to the problem of giving a theory of meaning. In section 5.2 the logic of a theory of meaning is considered and in section 5.3 an account is given of Tarski's semantic theory of truth since Davidson proposes to utilize this as the basis of a theory of meaning. This proposal raises three questions the first of which, the applicability of Tarski's theory, originally intended for formal logical languages, to natural languages, is the subject of section 5.4. The remaining two questions, whether a Tarski-style theory of truth is empirically testable, and whether it will indeed serve as a theory of meaning, are dealt with in chapters 6 and 7 respectively.

5.1 TWO APPROACHES TO THE THEORY OF MEANING

What is it for sentences to mean anything in general, and how do they mean what they do in particular? These are the kinds of questions that a theory of meaning for a language sets out to answer. The philosopher's interest, of course, is not in the details of this or that language, so we do not actually need to construct a theory for a particular language. Our work will be done when we show *how* to construct such a theory, what it would look like, what kinds of concepts it would need to use and how it could be empirically confirmed.

To this group of problems there are two approaches. One of these approaches is the application of formal semantics to natural languages and is associated with such figures as Frege, Tarski and Carnap. Davidson's work was developed as part of this tradition, though as we shall see, it now has much wider ramifications. The second approach has been called the 'theory of communication-intention' (Strawson 1970, p. 520) and some of its most famous advocates are the later Wittgenstein, Austin and Grice. The two approaches are fuelled by different, but not necessarily conflicting, intuitions; they are therefore not necessarily exclusive (see, for instance, Lewis 1975). None the less, they have tended to be practised separately and Davidson, certainly, gives the impression that they are antagonistic.

Formal semantics is the study of meaning for formal languages. A formal language is a set of symbols which can be assigned to various categories, together with rules defined over these categories for combining expressions. The application of formal semantics to a natural language such as English thus presupposes that English, or at least some fragment of English, is itself a formal language. Such application, therefore, will consist largely of attempts to describe various types of sentences according to logical categories. We have already seen what this is like when we looked at the logical form of causal sentences, or event sentences like 'Ferdinand married Christine' (sections 2.1 and 2.2).

The intuition that motivates the use of formal semantics for natural languages is that the sentences of natural languages are composed out of words in systematic ways and that their meanings depend on the meanings of their parts. This is known as the principle of compositionality. Formal semantics potentially offers a good way of accounting for the application of this principle to natural languages.

The communication-intention approach starts with the intuition that mere sounds and marks cannot mean anything in themselves. Their meaning must come through the uses to which they are put and the intentions of the people who use them. It thus focuses on the nature of the performances, or 'speech-acts', which constitute the use of sentences, it stresses how language is embedded in a social context, and how the meanings of sentences depend on the intentions with which they are used. Grice, for instance, characterizes what it is for a person A to mean something by a sentence x as follows:

> A must intend to induce by x a belief in an audience, and he must also intend his utterance to be recognized as so intended. But these intentions are not independent; the recognition is intended by A to play its part in inducing the belief, and if it does not do so something will have gone wrong with the fulfilment of A's intentions. (Grice 1957, p. 45)

Although followers of Grice would now give a more complex characterization of meaning, the passage serves to indicate the nature of the approach.

The contrast between these two approaches to the problem of meaning is sometimes put in terms of the priority of the philosophy of mind and the philosophy of language. This exploits an ambiguity in the word 'means', which can either say what a sentence does, or can say what a person does (often by using a sentence), as in the passage from Grice. Formal semantics is supposed to put the philosophy of language first, giving priority to sentence-meaning, while communication-intention theory takes sentence-meaning as dependent on speakers-meaning, thus making the philosophy of mind and the theory of speakers' intentions foundational for the philosophy of language.

One half of this picture is right. Communication-intention theory, at least in the form advocated by Grice, does require that, in order to say what sentences mean, we have first to be able to characterize in much detail the mental states of the people who use those sentences. It does, therefore, presuppose that the task of saying in virtue of what people's mental states have the propositional contents they do is independent of, and prior to, the task of giving a theory of meaning for a language. It is precisely this that leads Davidson to reject the communication-intention approach. For Davidson, the questions of how mental states get their contents, and how sentences get their meanings, are interdependent (see chapter 6). We cannot, therefore, hope to use thought to explain linguistic meaning.

Davidson's objection already indicates why we should be suspicious of the second half of the comparison made above. Formal semantics may, in some cases, seek to account for the meanings of the sentences of a language prior to locating it within the context, social and psychological, of its use. But Davidson is not guilty of this. Although he rejects the elucidation of sentence-meaning in terms of the mental states of speakers by making the projects of attributing mental states to someone and assigning meanings to his linguistic productions interdependent, he clearly recognizes the importance of constraining a theory of meaning by facts about propositional-attitude psychology. There is thus no danger that his theory of meaning will become detached from a theory of the mental states of speakers.

This will become evident in the next chapter, when we come to the theory of radical interpretation. But it is already implicit in the way Davidson, like Frege, follows the injunction 'never to ask for the meaning of a word in isolation, but only in the context of a sentence' (Frege 1953, p. x; see also Wallace 1977). The injunction is intended to emphasize that it is the sentence, the actual vehicle of communication, rather than the word that is the primary bearer of linguistic meaning. Words, in isolation, do not communicate anything. They come alive by being used in sentences.

This does not conflict with the commitment to showing how the meanings of sentences depend on the meaning of the words of which they are composed. Even if sentences are primary, we must still discern semantic structure in them in such a way as to be able to account for the dependence of the meanings of sentences on the meanings of their parts for the following reason. A natural language contains an infinite number of sentences. Given that, at any point, the number of sentences we have actually used or understood is finite, there will always be an infinite number of sentences which are new to us, but which we are capable of using and understanding immediately. But although we can understand and use new sentences in a language, we could not do this if the new sentences were not composed in familiar ways from familiar words. This requires, therefore, that we see sentences as composed out of words, the meanings of which determine the meanings of the sentences they make up.

A theory, in the formal sense, is a collection of axioms (or unproved theorems) and rules of inference from which further theorems can be generated. There is no general reason why a theory cannot have an infinite number of axioms (indeed, some theories do), and a theory of meaning for a language *L* could, therefore, take the form of an infinite number of axioms each of which gives the meaning of one of the infinite number of sentences of *L*. But our ability to use and understand an infinite number of sentences on the basis of limited semantic experience suggests a different form for the theory. It suggests that the theory has a finite number of axioms which give the semantic properties of the words of *L* and the semantic effects of their permissible modes of combination, which together entail an infinite number of further theorems which give the semantic properties of all the sentences of *L*. Davidson sums this up:

> When we can regard the meaning of each sentence as a function of a finite number of features of the sentence, we have an insight not only into what there is to be learned; we also understand how an infinite aptitude can be encompassed by finite accomplishments. For suppose that a language lacks this feature; then no matter how many sentences a would-be speaker learns to produce and understand, there will remain others whose meanings are not given by the rules already mastered. It is natural to say such a language is *unlearnable* . . . [A] learnable language has a finite number of semantical primitives. (1965, pp. 8–9)

(A semantical primitive is something which has its own axiom.)

Before we begin looking in more detail at the nature of a theory of meaning, we should alert ourselves to an important disclaimer which characterizes Davidson's work (and the work of many others) in this area. Giving a theory of meaning for a language is giving a theory such that knowledge of it would enable us to understand, and use, that language.

But in answering the question of what w : *could* know that would enable us to interpret the speakers of some langu..ge, Davidson is careful to stress that he is not also answering the question of what we actually *do* know that enables us to do this, 'for there may easily be something we could know and don't, knowledge of which would suffice for interpretation, while on the other hand it is not altogether obvious that there is anything we actually know which plays an essential role in interpretation' (1973c, p. 125). Similarly, when he talks of how we could come to learn a theory which would enable us to understand a language, it is no part of his project to describe the actual process of language acquisition.

In this respect, Davidson's approach differs sharply from that of someone like Chomsky. Despite the fact that both Davidson and Chomsky agree that actual linguistic forms are to be accounted for in terms of underlying, and often apparently quite different, structures, Chomsky, when he explains surface phenomena on the basis of transformation rules and deep structures, takes himself to be describing actual, if implicit, knowledge on the part of speakers of a language. Davidson's explicit theoretical reconstruction of language mastery, on the other hand, is not intended to reflect actual implicit knowledge. This makes problematic the relation of Davidson's theory to actual language use and mastery (see Strawson 1976).

Davidson does not say very much about this problem. He allows that we may say that 'there is a mechanism in the interpreter that corresponds to the theory [of meaning]. If this means only that there is some mechanism or other that performs that task, it is hard to see how the claim can fail to be true' (1974b, p. 141). In other words, something must enable us actually to interpret. But this does not entail that for each axiom, theorem and rule of inference, there is something in the interpreter which counts as implicit knowledge of that. What allows Davidson to take this cavalier stance is, I think, a more general view that even explicit knowledge and belief is not to be explained in terms of particular representational states in people. But to appreciate this fully, we must wait until section 9.1.

5.2 INTENSIONALITY AND EXTENSIONALITY

So far, I have spoken of a theory of meaning as consisting of axioms which give the semantic properties of words and their modes of combination, and theorems, derived from these axioms, that give the semantic properties of sentences. We must now look more closely at just what these semantic properties are. What exactly is it that a theory should tell us about the words and sentences of the language. We should begin with the question of the semantic properties of sentences, since, as we have seen, it is sentences which are the primary vehicles for linguistic communication. If we can get this right, then we can assign as semantic properties to words whatever is needed to generate the appropriate theorems for sentences.

If we call the language *L* for which the theory is being given the object language, and the language in which the theory is given the metalanguage, the theorems of our theory will be sentences of the metalanguage. These metalanguage sentences will refer to the various sentences of the object language, and tell us what their semantic properties are. An initial suggestion might be that the theorems should have the form:

(M)   *s* means that *p*

where *s* is a metalanguage name of an object language sentence, such as a name formed by putting quotation marks around the object language sentence, and *p* is a sentence of the metalanguage which gives the meaning of the object language sentence. So, if the object language is French and the metalanguage English, one such theorem would be ' "La neige est blanche" means that snow is white.'

Davidson rejects (M) as the form for the theorems which give the semantic properties of sentences. To see why, we shall have to introduce some ideas of traditional philosophical logic. (The following picture essentially reflects the ideas of Gottlob Frege 1952.) We can distinguish two different types of semantic properties of expressions, their intensions (senses, meanings) and their extensions (referents). The extension of an expression is the thing in the world to which it applies. Thus, in the sentence 'Joan of Arc was born in Orleans,' the extension of 'Joan of Arc' is Joan of Arc, the extension of 'Orleans' is Orleans, and the extension of 'was born in' is the set of ordered pairs[1] of people and places, such that the first member of the pair was born in the second member.

The extensions of complex expressions are functions of the extensions of their parts. That is, given the extensions of the parts of a complex expression, one can uniquely determine the extension of the complex expression itself. The extension of a sentence, therefore, is something that remains unchanged if we substitute for any of its constituents co-extensive terms. 'The maid of Orleans' is co-extensive with 'Joan of Arc', and we can substitute it, to obtain 'The maid of Orleans was born in Orleans.' What remains constant through such substitution is the truth of the sentence. As long as we restrict substitution to co-extensive terms, we cannot change the sentence from true to false. We can therefore identify the extensions of sentences as their truth values, either the true or the false.

Although sentences with the same truth value are co-extensive, there are clearly important semantic differences between, say, 'Joan of Arc was born in Orleans' and 'grass is green.' We can account for this by assigning to sentences not only extensions, but intensions (or meanings). The intension of a sentence could be conceived of as the thought it expresses, its cognitive value. Two sentences express the same thought if it is rationally impossible for someone who knows the language of which they are sentences to take different cognitive attitudes to them. On this criterion, 'Joan of Arc was born in Orleans' and 'the maid of Orleans was born in Orleans' express different thoughts. If someone failed to know that 'Joan of Arc' and 'the maid of Orleans' refer to the same person, he could take one sentence to be true and the other to be false. Since the intension of an expression is a function of the intensions of its constituents, we must assign different intensions to the expressions 'Joan of Arc' and 'the maid of Orleans', though they have the same extension.

We can now return to Davidson's theory of meaning. In (M), we use '*s* means that . . .', a sentential operator which attaches to a sentence to make a complex sentence. This operator appears not to allow the substitution of co-extensive terms without affecting truth value (substitution *salva veritate*) in the sentence on which it operates. For instance, from

(1)   'Nine is greater than five' means that nine is greater than five

and

(2)   'Nine' and 'the number of planets' have the same extension,

we cannot infer

(3)   'Nine is greater than five' means that the number of planets is greater than five.

It is, of course, true that the number of planets is greater than five; what is not true is that that sentence gives the meaning of the sentence 'nine is greater than five,' since 'nine' and 'the number of planets' do not have the same sense. The operator 'means that' is sensitive not only to the extensions of the terms that follow it, but also to their intensions. It creates what is called an intensional context.

Many philosophers, including Davidson and especially Quine, are committed to working with purely extensional languages. Davidson rejects (M) as the form for the theorems of a theory of meaning because of this commitment. The reasons for such a preference are complicated, and partly ideological. But we shall see, in what follows, a few considerations which might lie behind the advocacy of extensionality.

We should note, however, that this preference for extensional languages is not, by itself, sufficient for rejecting (M), since someone who favoured (M) as the form for the theorems of a theory of meaning could argue as follows. Any language which contains operators that do not permit the substitution of co-extensive terms *salva veritate*, where extensions are taken to be things like people, places and sets, is equivalent to a language in which such substitution is universally permissible, on the understanding that the extensions of the terms are themselves intensions, or meanings (see Lewis 1974b). Thus 'nine' could be taken to have as its extension not nine itself, but a meaning, or intension. 'The number of planets' would have as its extension a different meaning. We thus keep the principle that co-extensive terms are everywhere substitutable *salva veritate*, while at the same time explaining why we cannot always substitute 'the number of planets' for 'nine'.

This proposal involves reifying, or objectifying, intensions or meanings. They become items, like objects or events, which are referred to by words and sentences. (As to what the nature of these objects is, one powerfully worked out proposal is that they are functions. See Lewis 1970.) Davidson has three reasons for not accepting this proposal. One, the most powerful, will be discussed in section 7.3, when we look at the indeterminacy of meaning. Let us look at the two remaining reasons.

The first of them is Davidson's sympathy with the nominalist tradition of Quine. The aim of nominalism is ontological simplicity and it is characterized by a rejection of many types of things which other philosophers have thought it necessary to posit. Material objects are admitted, as are events, construed as parts of space–time. Meanings, propositions, facts and other shadowy entities, however, are thought to be too ill-defined and abstract. One objection to these kinds of entities, persistently urged by Quine, is that they are not clearly individuated. It is notoriously difficult to say when one meaning is the same as, or different from, another (see Quine 1951). Yet none the less, Davidson insists that 'my objection to meanings in the theory of meaning is not that they are abstract or that their identity conditions are obscure, but that they have no demonstrated use' (1967c, p. 21).

Davidson's point is not that semantics cannot find a place for meanings (much work in semantics, of Church (1951), Frege (1952), the later Carnap (1956) and most recently Montague (1974), has given a very definite place to meanings), but rather that we can do just as well without them. He hopes that we can give a theory of meaning using only extensions, and construing these extensions as what one might call extensional objects, people, tables, electrons, sets of ordered pairs, and so on, rather than as intensional objects like meanings. The question of whether semantics can get by without meanings is therefore tantamount to the question whether some purely extensional theory, such as Davidson's, can be successful. We must therefore resume the discussion of Davidson's positive views about the theory of meaning.

Davidson's own solution to difficulties about the form of the theorems in a theory of meaning is, as he says, 'simple, and radical'.

> Anxiety that we are enmeshed in the intensional springs from using the words 'means that' as filling between description of sentence and sentence, but it may be that the success of our venture depends not on the filling but on what it fills. The theory will have done its work if it provides, for every sentence *s* in the language under study, a matching sentence (to replace '*p*') that, in some way yet to be made clear, 'gives the meaning' of *s*. One obvious candidate for matching sentence is just *s* itself, if the object language is contained in the metalanguage; otherwise a translation of *s* in the metalanguage. As a final bold step, let us try treating the position occupied by '*p*' extensionally: to implement this, sweep away the obscure 'means that', provide the sentence that replaces '*p*' with a proper sentential connective, and supply the description that replaces '*s*' with its own predicate. (1967c, pp. 22–3)

The result is a form for the theorems which looks like this:

(T)   *s* is *T* if and only if *p*.

The quoted paragraph introduces one of Davidson's leading ideas in semantics, so let us go over it at a more leisurely pace.

The theorems are supposed, in some sense, to give the meanings, or semantic properties, of the sentences of the object language. For any sentence of the object language, we will surely be no better able to give its meaning than by using that sentence itself or a translation of it. This thought relies on the difference between using and mentioning a sentence, a distinction which, if overlooked, can make almost any attempt to give a theory of meaning seem trivial. Apparent triviality, for instance, affects the sentence ' "Snow is white" means that snow is white.' But we are mistaken if we think that a theory of meaning is going to give us insight into the meaning of any mentioned sentence by any other means than using language in some way or another. To see that the 'snow is white' example is far from trivial, consider it translated into French. It would now read ' "Snow is white" veut dire que la neige est blanche,' which is potentially very useful for a French speaker wanting to learn English, the object language in this case (see Evans and McDowell 1976, pp. vii–xi.)

Since the chief problem with (M) arose from the 'means that', Davidson suggests we simply cut the Gordian knot and replace it with an extensional, or truth-functional, sentential connective. For the purpose he elects the material biconditional, 'if and only if', which, when plugged into two sentences p and q, will yield a true compound sentence if p and q are either both true or both false and a false compound sentence if p and q differ in truth value. By thus employing a sentential connective, we are faced with the problem that we do not have a sentence to go on the left-hand side. s, of course, stands for the *name* in the metalanguage of a sentence of the object language. It is, therefore, a name and not itself a sentence. Given a name we can make a sentence by attaching a predicate to it, so Davidson signals this with the dummy predicate T, thus yielding

(T) s is T if and only if p

as the form for our theorems. p is either the sentence named by s, if the object language is contained in the metalanguage, or its translation.

The problem that remains is to say what the predicate 'is T' must be, so that it will yield all the instances of (T) obtained by replacing s with the name of an object language sentence, and p with either that sentence itself or a translation of it. In other words, what property do we demand that a sentence such as 'snow is white' should have if and only if snow is white?

By putting the question in this way, the answer is obvious – truth. By interpreting 'is T' as 'is true', any instance of (T) gained by replacing s with the name of a sentence and p with that sentence itself will be true. If s names a true sentence, then p will be true, and 's is true' will be true. If s names a false sentence, such as 'snow is green,' then p will be false, and 's is true' will be false. In either case, the biconditional itself will be true since, as we have seen, a material biconditional is true if both of the connected sentences are true, or both are false.

Davidson writes that 'it is worth emphasizing that the concept of truth played no ostensible role in stating our original problem. That problem, upon refinement, led to the view that an adequate theory of meaning must characterize a predicate meeting certain conditions. It was in the nature of a discovery that such a predicate would apply exactly to the true sentences' (1967c, pp. 23–4). Though true, this is a little disingenuous. It has long been accepted, by many different philosophers, that truth will have something to do with meaning. The intuition is often put by saying that to know the meaning of a sentence one must know its truth conditions, to know how the world must be if the sentence is to be true. Davidson's theory is also a kind of truth-conditional semantics and one might say that in a theorem like ' "Snow is white" is true if and only if snow is white' we are giving the truth conditions of the sentence which is mentioned. But Davidson warns that 'truth conditions are not to be equated with meanings; at best we can say that by giving the truth conditions of a sentence we give its meaning. But this claim too needs clarification' (1970a, p. 56, n.3). It will, I hope, become apparent in section 7.1 how seriously this caveat should be taken.

If the form for the theorems is (T), what should be the form of the axioms which give the semantic properties of the components of sentences? Since truth, in an extensional language, is dependent only on the extensions of component expressions, the axioms will assign extensions to terms. For singular terms, like names, and for mass terms such as 'snow', they will give referents, for instance, '"Caesar" denotes Caesar,' and '"Snow" denotes snow.' For common nouns, predicates, and verbs, they will say what things they apply to, as in '"is white" applies to all and only white things,' and '"married" applies to all and only ordered pairs of which the first member married the second.'

It may not be obvious what is so significant at having arrived at (T) as the form for our theorems. The reason why it is such an important advance in dealing with the question of meaning is that Davidson is now able to connect his project of giving a theory of meaning with the work done on truth by the Polish logician Alfred Tarski. What we wanted from a theory of meaning was a theory which assigned semantic properties to words, and showed how to derive theorems which give the semantic properties of sentences. Tarski has shown how to give a compositional theory with theorems of the form of (T). If giving a metalanguage sentence which is true if and only if an object language sentence is true *is* a way of giving the meaning of the object language sentence, then Davidson can take over Tarski's work on truth and use it as the basis for a theory of meaning. Since Davidson proposes to do just that, it is worth pausing to give a brief account of Tarski's truth theory. (The full, and extremely technical, exposition is in Tarski 1956; other less technical accounts of it can be found in Tarski 1944; Quine 1970; Haack 1978.) Readers wishing to avoid discussions which require a certain degree of logical technicality can skip the remainder of this chapter and go straight to chapter 6.

5.3 TARSKI'S THEORY OF TRUTH

Tarski thought that a formal definition of truth should answer to our pre-theoretical intuitions about what it means for a sentence to be true. Most prominent among these intuitions he takes to be that expressed by Aristotle in his *Metaphysics*: 'To say of what is that it is not, or of what is not that it is, is false, while to say of what is that it is, or of what is not that it is not, is true.' What Tarski attempts to do is to characterize a predicate which will apply to sentences in conformity to this intuition.

To this end, Tarski proposed (T) as a test of any putative definition. The employment of (T) as such a touchstone is referred to as Convention

T. Convention T is a condition of *material adequacy* on a definition of truth because it determines what the extension of the truth-predicate should be, i.e. which sentences it should apply to, but not what it means to call a sentence true. A definition of some arbitrary predicate would indeed be a definition of the predicate 'is true' for a language if it entailed all instances of (T), known as T-sentences, for that language. Any predicate which applied to object language sentences if and only if their translations in the metalanguage were true would be the predicate 'is true'. As Davidson says: 'Convention T and T-sentences provide the sole link between intuitively obvious truths about truth and formal semantics. Without Convention T, we should have no reason to believe that truth is what Tarski has shown us how to characterize' (1973a, p. 66). Tarski also placed a number of formal conditions on any proposal for a theory of truth but I shall omit consideration of these.

Given the condition of adequacy on any definition of truth, let us look at Tarski's proposal, as it would apply to the following, extremely austere, object language L. Our language will contain variables x, y and z, the one-place predicate F and the two-place predicate G, the truth-functional operators of negation, ' $-$ ', and conjunction, '&', and the existential quantifier '$\exists$'. In describing a language there are two things that have to be specified for it, its syntax and its semantics. Tarski's work concerns semantics, or the interpretation of a language, but first we must describe the syntax of L. This involves defining the permissible expressions of L (the well-formed formulae) and showing how expressions combine to form other expressions.

The well-formed formulae (wffs) of L are defined by the following five clauses: (a) a one-place predicate followed by a variable is a wff; (b) a two-place predicate followed by two variables is a wff; (c) if A is a wff, then so is $-A$; (d) if A and B are wffs, then so is A&B; and (e) if A is a wff, then so is the result of prefacing A with the existential quantifier binding any of the variables in A. Thus, since Fx is a wff, so is $\exists x(Fx)$. A variable occurs as free in a wff if it is not bound by the quantifier. In the wff $\exists x(Gxy)$, the variable x is bound while the variable y is free. Let us call wffs with unbound variables open, and those with no free variables closed. The sentences of L are all the closed wffs of L. Despite its extreme simplicity, L has an infinite number of sentences. For example, if A is a sentence, then so is $-A$; if $-A$ is, then so is $--A$, and so on *ad infinitum*.

Let us call a wff simple if it contains no wffs as parts, and complex otherwise. Since all closed wffs must be existential quantifications, or made up out of them, all sentences of L are complex. (But of course, not all complex wffs are sentences. $Fx\&Fy$ is not.)

We turn now to Tarski's work concerning the provision of a semantics, or an interpretation, for L. Tarski shows how to derive the truth of sentences from the interpretations of their parts. A complex sentence *A&B* is true, of course, if and only if *A* is true and *B* is true. Here we define the truth of a complex sentence in terms of the truth of its constituents.

We cannot give a theory of truth along the lines just suggested because of one rather large problem. It is only sentences which can be true or false; but the sentences of *L* are built up out of open wffs. A wff like *Fx* is itself neither true nor false. (Remember, *x* is a variable, not a singular term, so it does not refer to anything.) Tarski's solution is to define another semantic notion, satisfaction, which does apply to the open wffs and of which we can give a theory for all expressions of the language, and then to define truth in terms of satisfaction.

The idea behind satisfaction is that open wffs apply to things according to whether those things satisfy some condition. *Fx* is satisfied by an object if and only if that object is *F*. So, if *F* is interpreted as 'is red', then *Fx* will be satisfied by any object if and only if that object is red. If *G* is the two-place predicate 'beheaded', then *Gxy* will be satisfied by any ordered pair of things such that the first beheaded the second. So it will be satisfied by <Elizabeth I, Mary Queen of Scots>, but not by <Mary Queen of Scots, Elizabeth I> or <Batman, Robin>.

We can now give a definition of satisfaction. First, by giving the interpretations of the predicates, we specify which things satisfy the wffs formed by clauses (a) and (b). Let us suppose that they are interpreted as in the previous paragraph. *F* is 'is red' and *G* is 'beheaded'. Then we give the axioms for satisfaction of complex wffs. Something satisfies − *A* if and only if it doesn't satisfy *A*. For example, Ronald Reagan satisfies − *Fx*, since he doesn't satisfy *Fx*. He doesn't satisfy *Fx* because he is not red, and only red things satisfy *Fx*. Similarly, for '&', something satisfies *A&B* if and only if it satisfies *A* and it satisfies *B*.

What are the conditions for satisfaction of an existentially quantified wff? Intuitively, satisfaction is something which applies to open wffs, and not sentences. Existential quantifications, at least those with no free variables, are sentences. But if Tarski is to define truth in terms of satisfaction, he must define satisfaction for all wffs of *L*. Take $\exists x(Fx)$. This says, given our interpretation of *F*, that there is something red. This is true so long as there is something red, i.e. so long as there is something which satisfies the corresponding open wff *Fx*. As long as something satisfies the open wff *Fx*, everything will satisfy the sentence $\exists x(Fx)$, and if nothing satisfies *Fx*, then nothing will satisfy $\exists x(Fx)$. In other words, since *x* is bound by the quantifier, it doesn't matter what value we assign to it. That value will satisfy it, as long as there is something which satisfies *Fx*.

Now take the more complex example $\exists x(Gxy)$. This says there is something which beheaded *y*. The corresponding open wff is *Gxy*, and this is satisfied by any ordered pair of which the first member beheaded the second member. Since *x* is bound by the quantifier, it doesn't matter what gets assigned to it. The wff will therefore be satisfied by an ordered pair, so long as there is some ordered pair which differs from the first pair only in its first member (i.e. the member assigned as a value to x), and which satisfies Gxy. So the pair <Batman, Mary Queen of Scots> satisfies $\exists x(Gxy)$ ('there is something x which beheaded y'), since there exists a pair, <Elizabeth I, Mary Queen of Scots>, which satisfies Gxy, and which differs from the first pair only in what it assigns to the variable bound by the quantifier.

Since all sentences of L are either existential quantifications with no free variables, or made up from them with the truth functions, we can now complete the definition of truth in L by saying that a true sentence is a sentence which is satisfied by everything, and a false sentence one which is satisfied by nothing.

What Tarski shows is how to define truth for a particular language. Strictly speaking, therefore, the T-sentences ought to say 's is true-in-L if and only if p.' This position, however, should not be confused with a relativism which holds that one interpreted sentence can be true-for-me but not true-for-you (see section 8.3). On our present construal, sentences are uninterpreted. We defined sentencehood in L before we gave its semantics. Saying what language we are defining truth in is thus simply fixing the interpretation of the sentences in the object language. Uninterpreted sentences, mere syntactic strings, can have different interpretations, i.e. could be treated as sentences of different languages. Davidson gives an example: 'the sounds [i.e. the uninterpreted sentence] "Empedokles liebt" do fairly well as a German or an English sentence, in one case saying that Empedokles loved and in the other telling us what he did from the top of Etna' (1968, p. 98). In general, however, I will omit the qualification of saying true-in-L and speak simply of truth.

The language for which we have just given a truth definition is, of course, a very minimal language. But as long as the stock of predicates, for each of which we must provide a separate axiom saying what satisfies it, is finite, there are no principled difficulties in making that stock as large as we like. Furthermore, we can give axioms for satisfaction of complex sentences built with the other truth functions, like disjunction, material implication and material equivalence, as well as for the universal quantifier. This means, in effect, that we can give a theory of truth which satisfies Convention T for any language whose logic is first-order predicate calculus, the kind of logic which is taught in first-year logic courses at universities.

Davidson thinks we should use a Tarski-style theory of truth for a language as a theory of meaning. He suggests that there are three questions to be asked about a theory of truth, all of which must be answered in the affirmative if we are to use it as a theory of meaning. These questions are:

(1)   Is it reasonable to think that a theory of truth of the sort described can be given for a natural language?

(2)   Would it be possible to tell that such a theory was correct on the basis of evidence plausibly available to an interpreter with no prior knowledge of the language to be interpreted?

(3)   If the theory were known to be true, would it be possible to interpret utterances of speakers of the language? (1973c, p. 131)

In the remainder of this chapter we will examine the first of these questions; the second and third of them will be addressed in the following two chapters. Something, however, should be said about the third question here. The theorems of a Tarski-style truth theory link sentences of the object language with metalanguage sentences which are materially equivalent to them (i.e. linked by 'is true if and only if'). It is far from obvious that mere material equivalence will enable us to use the metalanguage sentences to interpret the object language sentences. It was, of course, part of Convention T that the sentences on the right of the T-sentences be translations of those named on the left and, if this were fulfilled, then we could use the T-sentences as interpretations. But, as we shall see in section 7.1, this consideration cannot be invoked in deciding whether some theory can serve as a theory of meaning for a language since it requires that we already know what the sentences of the object language mean. Davidson's answer to this problem will be examined in sections 7.2 and 7.3. But until then, I will be assuming that we *can* treat theorems of the form '*s* is true if and only if *p*' as interpreting, or giving the meaning of, *s*.

5.4   THE THEORY OF TRUTH AND NATURAL LANGUAGES

We turn now to the question, can a Tarski-style theory of truth can be given for natural languages? Before we come to the main question, there is a preliminary point concerning what are called indexical expressions, expressions whose referents vary according to the circumstances in which they are used. These include words such as 'I', 'here' and 'now'. Such expressions are clearly major components of natural languages. The T-sentence for a sentence like 'It is cold here now' will have to be something like ' "It is cold here now" is true-in-English if and only if it is cold in the vicinity of the speaker at the time of the utterance.' We are thus actually giving truth conditions for utterances of sentences or alternatively sentences relativized to times, places and speakers (see Weinstein 1974). Whichever of these options we take, we should note that we are no longer using on the right-hand side of the biconditional either the sentence named on the left or a translation of it. The indexicals demand that we use some sentence which has a weaker relation than identity or translation but which still, in some sense, allows the used sentence on the right to give the meaning of the named sentence on the left. I shall ignore this complication in what follows.

Tarski doubted the applicability of his work to natural languages. His chief worry was this. His theory showed how the truth of sentences could be defined on the basis of the relations between expressions and objects in the world (which satisfy the expressions of the language). It is thus extensional and its logic is, essentially, the logic of first-order predicate calculus. Natural languages, on the other hand, contain many linguistic devices and constructions which appear to be totally unlike those for which Tarski's treatment was shown to work. Some, such as adverbs, appear simply to go beyond the resources of first-order logic; others, such as indirect discourse, appear to require intensional treatment. (Both these examples will be discussed in detail.)

In order to make good his commitment to using a theory of truth as a theory of meaning for natural languages, Davidson has to show how these problems can be dealt with. He envisages that a theory of meaning will have two tiers. First, the Tarski-style theory of truth will be given for some fragment of, say, English, a fragment which consists only of syntactic elements for which Tarski has shown how to give a theory. Secondly, a way must be shown of matching each ordinary sentence of English with one, or in cases of ambiguity more than one, sentence of the regimented fragment:

> Much of what is called for is to mechanize as far as possible what we now do by art when we put ordinary English into one or another canonical notation. The point is not that canonical notation is better than the rough original idiom, but rather that if we know what idiom the canonical notation is canonical *for*, we have as good a theory for the idiom as for its kept companion. (1967c, p. 29)

Here we have the origin of and justification for the idea of logical form, which we encountered in more informal circumstances when we looked at events and causation in chapter 2. The logical form, in Davidson's usage, of a sentence or a type of sentence is the canonical form it must be given in order for it to fall within the scope of the theory of truth. By way of illustration, I propose to look briefly at two examples of Davidson's work on the logical forms of apparently recalcitrant idioms of natural languages.

The first example is the phenomenon of adverbial modification. As Davidson points out:

Modifiers are attendants, not first movers. Sentences can get along without them; remove them from a sentence and you get a sentence. Thus 'intentionally', 'gracefully', 'in the water', and 'on Fridays only' usually leave a sentence behind when dropped from a sentence. Equally impressive is the fact that in very many cases the truncated sentence is entailed by the sentence from which the adverbial phrase was pruned. Aside from some adjectives, no other part of speech has the self-effacing character of the adverb. (1985b, p. 230)

These facts are important because they present a goal for an analysis of logical form. 'To give the logical form of a sentence is to give its logical location in the totality of sentences, to describe it in a way that explicitly determines what sentences it entails and what sentences it is entailed by' (1967a, p. 140). So we will want to explain why a sentence like 'Deborah swam in the morning' entails the sentence 'Deborah swam' and is entailed by 'Deborah swam in the morning at Brighton.' Our problem arises because first-order predicate logic does not contain any adverbial analogues. It contains variables and names, which can represent nouns; predicates, which serve as adjectives, relations, and verbs; and logical constants like 'not', 'and', and the quantifiers 'some' and 'every'. But there is nothing with which we can represent adverbs.

One way of approaching the question of the logical form of the sentence 'Deborah swam in the morning' would be to analyse 'swam' as a two-place predicate, 'swam (x,y)', which applies to a person and time, just in case that person swam at that time. In our example, x would be replaced by 'Deborah' and y by 'the morning'. But consider the analogous treatment for its companions. These would be 'swam (Deborah)' and 'swam (Deborah, the morning, Brighton)'. We would now have a one-place predicate, 'swam (x)', which applies to a person, if that person swam; the two-place predicate, 'swam (x,y)'; and a three-place predicate, 'swam (x,y,z)', which applies to a person, a time and a place, if that person swam at that time, at that place. But there is nothing in the rules of logic that tells us we can infer 'swam (a)' from 'swam (a,b)'. There is thus no way logic alone provides for explaining why 'Deborah swam' is entailed by 'Deborah swam in the morning.' Yet it was a desideratum of an analysis of the logical form of these sentences that it reveal the logical connections they obviously have to each other.

If we wanted, we could provide special, extra-logical rules to license the desired inferences. These would say things like 'if the two-place predicate $F(x,y)$ is satisfied by an ordered pair of objects $<a,b>$, then the one-place predicate $F(x)$ is satisfied by the first member of that ordered pair, a.' Such rules as these are unsatisfactory for Davidson. For one thing, there are simple practical difficulties in the way of doing this. How would we capture the fact that, if $F(x,y,z)$ is interpreted as the three-place predicate satisfied by triples of persons, times and places if and only if that person swam at that time and place, then from $F(a,b,c)$ we can infer $F(a,b)$, $F(a,c)$, $F(a)$ but not $F(b,c)$? Of course, *ad hoc* rules can deal with this, but the point is that they will be *ad hoc*.

But perhaps more important than this is the fact that on this approach, it becomes unclear what contribution is being made by $F(. . .)$ to both $F(x)$ and $F(x,y)$. Our special rules might just as well tell us to infer $G(x)$ from $F(x,y)$. The fact that, in 'Deborah swam in the morning at Brighton,' there is a role being played by 'Deborah swam' which is also played in 'Deborah swam in the morning' is lost.

Davidson proposes an alternative analysis of adverbial modification, the main idea of which we have already briefly encountered in section 2.1. His suggestion is that we analyse 'Deborah swam in the morning at Brighton' as containing a hidden variable which ranges over events, and is bound by the existential quantifier. Its logical form would be represented as follows:

$\exists e$ ((Swam (Deborah, e)) and (In (the morning, e)) and (At (Brighton, e))).

This could be read as 'there is some event which was a swimming by Deborah, and was in the morning, and was at Brighton.' It now becomes simply a matter of applying the logical rule that if a conjunction is true, then so are all of its conjuncts, to infer from 'Deborah swam in the morning at Brighton' the following: 'Deborah swam in the morning,' 'Deborah swam at Brighton,' 'Deborah swam,' as well as 'something happened in the morning and at Brighton.' Adverbial modifiers like 'in the morning' or 'at Brighton' turn out to be relations between events and times, or events and places, namely, the relations which hold when an event occurs in some time and at some place.

One of Davidson's arguments for the existence of events as particulars is precisely that they explain the role of adverbs in language. By treating an event sentence like 'Ferdinand married Christine' as quantifications over events, so that its logical form is 'there is an event which was a marriage of Ferdinand and Christine', Davidson can explain the relations of entailment between it and other sentences, such as 'Ferdinand and Christine did something,' and 'Ferdinand married Christine in 1589.'

Davidson's proposal encounters certain probelms (of which he is not unaware). The main problem is that it fails to deal with all cases of adverbial modification in a satisfactory way. Swimmings in the morning, we could say, form a subset of swimmings. They are all those events which not only satisfy the predicate 'e is a swimming', but also satisfy the predicate 'in (the morning, e)'. But when we looked at action, we saw that we should resist the temptation to think of intentional actions as a subset of actions. Intentional actions are not actions which have some additional property, but rather actions described in certain ways. What this means in the present context is that the adverb 'intentionally' as it occurs, say, in 'Oedipus married Jocasta intentionally,' cannot be represented as a predicate modifying events, in the way that 'in the morning' can. For if we represent the sentence as:

$$\exists e \ ((\text{Married (Oedipus, Jocasta, } e)) \text{ and } (\text{Intentional } (e)))$$

we should be able to infer, from the fact that 'Jocasta' has the same extension as 'Oedipus' mother', that Oedipus married his mother intentionally. As we saw in looking at actions, one and the same event may be intentional under the description 'marrying Jocasta', but not intentional under the description 'marrying Oedipus's mother'. But predicates, in first-order logic, apply to objects or events however they are described. That is what it means to say that such logic is extensional. So Davidson's treatment will not work for so-called 'intensional' adverbs like 'intentionally', 'allegedly', 'unexpectedly', and so on.

There are other adverbs for which Davidson's proposal will not work. Suppose Dotty starts to read *Dracula* to send herself to sleep. After an hour she finishes the whole book and falls asleep. Then even though her sending herself to sleep was her reading *Dracula*, she put herself to sleep slowly but read *Dracula* very quickly. A similar problem is faced by the so-called attributive adjectives. Harry may be a short basketball player but a tall man; Dumbo a light elephant but a heavy animal. 'Short', 'tall', 'light' and 'heavy' cannot, therefore, simply apply to objects, but must really be predicated of objects in relation to some specified type. Similar conclusions apply to the corresponding attributive adverbs 'slowly' and 'quickly'. One and the same event may be slow for a sending oneself to sleep but fast for a reading of *Dracula*.

While Davidson offers no solution to this problem, thus leaving his semantic theory incomplete at this point, he takes it as confirmation of his view that there are concrete events that they should have the same problem with attributive adverbs like 'slowly' as objects do with attributive adjectives like 'slow'. Indeed, by quantifying over events, and treating adverbs as predicates of expressions which refer to events, the problem of attributive adverbs simply is the problem of attributive adjectives.

Whether or not we should take this failure to provide a unified account of all adverbial modification as a reason for abandoning Davidson's theory in those cases in which it works is a question of individual judgement. (See Davidson 1985b and Thalberg 1985 for judgements in favour of Davidson, and Horgan 1978 and Bennett 1985 for ones against.) Events, as construed by Davidson, have other uses besides their role in semantic theory, but we have also, in section 4.2, seen some other problems they face. How one measures the pros against the cons depends on what weight one attaches to the various considerations involved.

The second example of an analysis of logical form concerns indirect speech as represented in sentences such as:

(G)   Galileo said that the earth moves.

The difficulty these examples present is just the difficulty that we saw in connection with the intensional 'means that' (section 5.2). If the semantic property of the expression 'the earth' needed for a theory of meaning is that it denotes the earth, then we should be able to substitute any other expressions with the same extension, such as 'the third planet from the sun', without affecting the truth of the containing sentence. We can do this in the sentence 'the earth moves,' but we cannot do it in (G) since the resulting sentence, 'Galileo said that the third planet from the sun moves,' may be false (for instance, if Galileo believed that the earth was not the third planet from the sun). In other words, in (G), and in similar intensional contexts such as 'means that', 'believes that' and so on, the semantic contribution being made by 'the earth' seems not to be determined by its extension alone.

Frege's classic solution to this problem was that, in such intensional contexts, a term takes as its referent (extension) what is normally its sense (intension). Since 'the earth' and 'the third planet from the sun' normally have different senses, they cannot be substituted for each other in contexts where they take as their referents their usual senses. This solution allows Frege to continue to hold that co-extensive expressions are everywhere substitutable *salva veritate*, since we could still substitute for 'the earth', in (G), any expression which refers to the sense that 'the earth' normally expresses, but to which in contexts like (G) it refers.

As we have seen, Davidson does not like the reification of meanings, or senses, involved in such an approach; but his real objection to this as a solution to the problem of indirect discourse is based on a more serious, and less subjective, foundation. On Frege's view, 'the earth' has two referents, depending on its context: the earth itself, and the sense of the expression 'the earth'. But, of course, we can go on embedding sentences in contexts like 'said that . . .' as in 'Davidson said that Galileo said that the earth moves.' Now we will have to suppose that 'the earth' refers not to the earth, nor to the sense of the expression as it features in 'the earth moves,' but rather to the sense it has in 'Galileo said that the earth moves.' Expressions will thus end up having a potentially infinite number of referents.

Frege's solution is thus ruled out by the necessity of explaining the learnability of language. A language in which expressions had an infinite number of possible referents would be unlearnable. It is for this reason that Davidson rejects the Fregean approach. Instead, he offers his own highly ingenious and controversial solution.

Davidson introduces the notion of samesaying, a relation which holds between two people when they make utterances which mean the same thing. In saying 'Galileo said that the earth moves' I am, says Davidson, saying something like this: 'Galileo uttered a sentence that meant in his mouth what "The earth moves" means now in mine . . . I represent Galileo and myself as samesayers' (1968, p. 104). Yet now there is a new problem. In order for Galileo and myself to be samesayers, I have to say that the earth moves. But on the analysis just suggested I do not do this, since the words 'the earth moves' appear in quotation marks; they are mentioned rather than actually used.

Suppose that Galileo makes his utterance, the one I am reporting in indirect discourse. To make us samesayers, I actually utter the sentence 'the earth moves.' Now I want to add that in making that utterance, Galileo and I are samesayers. How can I do this? All I have to add after I have made my utterance is, 'Galileo said that.' Here, of course, the 'that' is a demonstrative which refers to my utterance of 'the earth moves' and not a conjunction, as it is in (G). But we should by now be aware that in analyses of logical form, the surface appearance of the type of expression to be regimented should not constrain the logical form assigned. Davidson offers 'The earth moves. Galileo said that' (with a demonstrative 'that') as the logical form of 'Galileo said that the earth moves.' (A slight awkwardness in Davidson's analysis is this. The 'that' refers to an utterance I make. Yet Galileo did not say that, i.e. that very utterance. He made a different utterance which meant in his mouth what my utterance meant in mine. The analysis had better read, therefore: 'The earth moves. Galileo samesaid that.')

The essence of Davidson's proposal is that 'from a semantic point of view the content-sentence in indirect discourse is not contained in the sentence whose truth counts, i.e. the sentence that ends with "that"' (1968, p. 106). There are two sentences, not one. The first, the sentence that gives the content of what Galileo said, is 'the earth moves.' The second, the one whose truth counts, is 'Galileo said that.' By removing the content sentence from the report of samesaying, we explain why substitution of 'the third planet from the sun' for 'the earth' will not necessarily preserve the truth of 'the sentence that counts', without introducing intensions. The earth moves. Galileo may have said that, without having said this: the third planet from the sun moves.

Davidson's theory appears as a dazzling conjuring trick, a sleight of hand that leaves you unsure of what you have just seen. This is encouraged by the uneasy relation it bears to philology. As an analysis of logical form, it has no requirement to respect the history of any of the lexical items. Yet his proposal undoubtedly gains in plausibility from the fact that the demonstrative 'that' is the same word as the conjunctive 'that.' Indeed, the *Oxford English Dictionary* explains the origins of the conjunctive 'that' in just the way Davidson's analysis suggests.[2] But if Davidson intends this as an analysis of the logical form of a type of expression, he must mean it to apply to all those non-Germanic languages in which the two sorts of 'that' are represented by etymologically unrelated words (as are the French 'que' and 'cela'). It is, as it were, merely good fortune that English bears out his suggestion so neatly.

There is another, apparently more serious, snag to Davidson's proposal. He may avoid explicit invocation of intensions, or meanings, but is this not accomplished by the introduction of 'samesaying', a relation which holds between two people when they both make utterances with the same meaning? It looks as if meanings, having been ushered out through the front door, are creeping in through the back. Davidson meets this criticism by distinguishing between what is required by the particular concepts expressible in a language, and what is required in the apparatus of the theory as such. Some languages, such as English (and indeed probably all natural languages) include words which attribute samesaying to two people. In English, it is the expression 'says that'. The analysis of this particular concept may or may not require that we talk of two utterances meaning the same, or being synonymous. This is a consequence of a particular idiom.

The inclusion of such a lexical item in the object language, however, is to be distinguished from the use of intensions in the structure of the theory of meaning as such, a theory which will apply to languages whether or not they contain expressions like 'says that'. As Davidson says: 'it is hard to exaggerate the advantages to philosophy of language of bearing in mind this distinction between questions of logical form or grammar, and the analysis of individual concepts' (1967c, p. 31). Whatever the analysis of samesaying may be, Davidson's analysis of 'saying that' shows that the theory of meaning need not invoke intensions or intensional idioms to explain the semantic structure of a certain type of natural language locution (but see section 7.2 for further discussion of this point).

6

Radical Interpretation

A theory of meaning, on Davidson's proposal, is a collection of axioms that give the extensions of the words of a language, and the effects of the different ways of combining these words, which together entail further theorems (T-sentences) which give the semantic properties of the sentences of the object language by giving, for each object language sentence, a metalanguage sentence which is true if and only if that object language sentence is true. They thus have the form: 's is true if and only if p.' In the previous chapter we saw that Davidson asks three questions about this proposal. The first, which we addressed in section 5.4, was whether such a theory, originally modelled on a theory intended for formal, logical languages, could be used for natural languages. Davidson believes that it can, and has devoted much labour to showing how particular, apparently recalcitrant, features of natural languages are to be dealt with by his theory of meaning. In this and the next chapter, we shall turn our attention to the remaining two questions: is a theory of truth for natural languages empirically testable, and do T-sentences really give the meanings of the sentences of the object language? (We will assume an affirmative answer to the last question until we come to discuss it in chapter 7.) In section 6.1 the initial problem with the empirical application of truth theories is raised, and Quine's views on radical translation are discussed. Section 6.2 compares radical translation with Davidson's radical interpretation, and 6.3 introduces the Principle of Charity, one of the leading ideas in Davidson's work. Sections 6.4 and 6.5 look at further refinements of the Principle of Charity, and section 6.6 examines the necessity of its application in the light of Davidson's work on decision theory.

6.1 RADICAL TRANSLATION

A theory of meaning is just a collection of axioms and theorems that attribute semantic properties to words and sentences. But if such a theory is meant to be a theory of a particular language, we must have some way of deciding whether, for that language, the theory is correct; whether the theory really applies to that language. In other words, how is the theory empirically testable?

Suppose that we are giving a truth theory for a fragment of English in a metalanguage which is an extended fragment of English. In that case, there will be an unproblematic answer to our question. Since the theory is given in a language we understand for a language we understand, all we have to do is to look at the T-sentences which the theory produces and see if they are correct. Our knowledge of both the object language and metalanguage will ensure that we are in a position to do this. Each T-sentence that we check and find correct confirms the theory of which it is a consequence. Like any other empirical theory, we can consider our truth theory well enough confirmed when we have checked enough (however many that may be) of its consequences. Whatever problems there may be about confirmation of theories in general, our truth theory will be in no worse a position than any other empirical theory.

This unproblematic answer depends, however, on our being able to say, in advance of giving a theory of meaning for some language, whether or not it is contained in the metalanguage. For a language L to be contained in a language M it is necessary that all the sentences of L are sentences of M, and if the sentences are uninterpreted, this condition can easily be seen to obtain or not prior to our giving a theory of meaning for either language. But of course, if the sentences are uninterpreted, the condition is not sufficient for L to be contained in M since it must also be the case that each sentence of L means the same as its homophone in M. This is because it is possible for one (uninterpreted) sentence to belong to two different languages, with different meanings in each. (Remember the Empedokles example from section 5.3, taken from Davidson 1968, p. 98.)

But now we have a problem. That the sentences of the object language mean the same as their homophones in the metalanguage is something which we can only tell when we know what they mean and, of course, giving a theory of truth for the object language was meant to deliver just this information. We cannot assume in advance of finding out what the object language means that it is part of the metalanguage, even if all its (uninterpreted) sentences occur in the metalanguage. So if we want to know whether a particular truth theory applies to a particular language, we cannot, without begging the very question at issue (what do the sentences of the object language mean), give the unproblematic answer we sketched above.

What we must consider, to see whether a particular Tarski-style truth theory can be established as applying to some language, is how the proposal to use such a theory as a theory of meaning will fare when applied to a language which is totally unknown to us. In such a case, even if the sentences of the object language appear identical to sentences of the metalanguage, we cannot assume that they are metalanguage sentences. It is with respect to this kind of situation, which Davidson calls 'radical interpretation', that the question must be answered. Before we see how Davidson answers it, let us look at what Quine has to say about 'radical translation', a project very similar to radical interpretation, since Davidson often acknowledges the influence of Quine's views on his own. (The *locus classicus* for Quine's views, from which all the ensuing quotations are taken, is 1960, chapter 2.)

Quine considers the case in which an explorer wants to assemble a translation manual for some totally unknown language. The aim of the manual is to be able to produce an English sentence to translate any native sentence. Quine is a behaviourist, and this underlies his views on meaning and translation. Regarding the evidence for a translation manual, he writes: 'What we objectively have is just an evolving adjustment to nature, reflected in an evolving set of dispositions to be prompted by stimulations to assent to or dissent from sentences' (1960, pp. 38–9). For Quine, this constitutes the totality of linguistic behaviour. It follows that what we, as field linguists, can do to solicit evidence for our manual is limited to testing the natives for assent to and dissent from sentences in response to various stimulations. Thus, to give Quine's famous example, suppose we hear a native utter the one-word sentence 'gavagai' as a rabbit runs past. It occurs to us that his sentence might be translated as 'there's a rabbit,' or 'Lo!, a rabbit.' We can set up various test situations, some of which include rabbits and some of which do not, and in each case ask the native 'gavagai?' If he agrees in enough cases where there are rabbits present, and disagrees in enough where there is no rabbit, we can tentatively translate 'gavagai' as 'Lo!, a rabbit.'

This requires some qualification. We would not want to count it against translating 'gavagai' as 'Lo!, a rabbit' that the native assented to it in the presence of a cleverly made model of a rabbit, nor that he dissented from it when, although a rabbit was present, his angle of vision made it impossible to see it. To avoid these problems, Quine suggests that we take as the appropriate conditions not such things as rabbits, but rather patterns of sensory stimulation. The more we exclude from the stimulus things which are external to the responder, the more we remove the possibility of unwanted interference, such as that caused by fake rabbits, contaminating the experiments. In the case of sight, the stimulus would be 'the pattern of chromatic irradiation of the eye' (p. 31), but of course we would have also to identify the forms of stimulation for the other sensory modalities. Quine then formulates the concept of a sentence's 'stimulus meaning'. The stimulus meaning of a sentence is comprised of the set of stimulations which would prompt assent to it and the set of stimulations that would prompt dissent from it. Stimulus meaning is clearly a theoretical concept. The question which should interest us is, how close is stimulus meaning as defined to meaning *tout court?*

Quine's notion of stimulus meaning comes close to a doctrine which, in section 1.2, we saw him arguing against, namely, the dogma of reductionism. However, it has crucial differences from this dogma. The dogma of reductionism seeks to identify the meanings of certain sentences with the experiences which confirm or disconfirm them. If there were sentences to which we always gave assent or dissent on the basis of our sensory stimulations, then stimulus meaning could, for those sentences, serve as plain meaning, in just the way the dogmatist of reduction wants.

But Quine also supports holism, and this distinguishes him from the traditional dogmatist of reduction. Quine suggests a web as a model of a language. The nodes of the web represent sentences. The identity of each node depends on its relations with other nodes and with experience. The nodes at the outer edge of the web will connect predominantly with experience – whatever is beyond the web – while the further in a sentence is, the less direct contact it has with experience and the more its identity is determined by its relations with other sentences. The sentences at the edge are Quine's 'observation sentences', sentences like 'this is red.' They obviously have very strong and direct connections with experience. But for Quine, no sentence is free from connections with other sentences. Hence, even for observation sentences it is not right to identify stimulus meaning with meaning *tout court*, though stimulus meaning pulls most weight with observation sentences. For other sentences further in the interior of the web, such as "Lo!, a bachelor," stimulus meaning is less close to plain meaning because, 'as one says in the uncritical jargon of meaning, the trouble with 'Bachelor' is that its meaning transcends the looks of the prompting faces and concerns matters that can be known only through other channels' (p. 42).

Besides observation sentences, there is another class of linguistic expressions where the evidence available to us, in the form of patterns of assent and dissent, does a lot (or in this case, perhaps all) of what we want of plain meaning. This is the class of truth-functional logical constants. Since a conjunction is true if and only if both its conjuncts are true, we can take a native expression 'blip' to be translated as 'and' if and only if, for any two native sentences p and q, the native will assent to 'p blip q' if and only if he will assent to p and assent to q.

What, then, we have been able to build up so far on the basis of the evidence available to us is a concept of stimulus meaning which will do partial duty for meaning *tout court* in the case of observation sentences, enabling us to translate them well enough but still not with any certainty, and a way of translating truth-functional operators. But language consists of much which these methods do not enable us to translate, sentences like 'Lo!, a bachelor' and 'to every action there is an equal and opposite reaction.'

To deal with this, Quine suggests that the radical translator constructs 'analytical hypotheses'. The most obvious kind of analytical hypotheses would be those which matched native words with English words. Until now, we have been dealing with sentences (although these are sometimes one-word sentences) since it is sentences which are assented to and dissented from. Nothing has determined how we should even segment these sentences into words, let alone how the individual words should be translated. Noticing that certain segments of observation sentences, which we can translate, crop up in other sentences that we cannot yet translate, we can form hypotheses about how those segments, which we may as well call words, correspond to English words. If we form enough analytical hypotheses, we should end up with a way of translating any native sentence into an English one.

Analytical hypotheses go beyond the behavioural evidence which Quine thinks is all the evidence there is for translation. He therefore holds that radical translation shows that translation and meaning are indeterminate. They exceed all possible evidence, and thus nothing in our evidence can determine the fact of the matter about how something should be translated. There is, indeed, no fact of the matter. We shall, however, defer a longer discussion of indeterminacy until section 7.3.

6.2 INTERPRETATION VERSUS TRANSLATION

Let us now return to the question, can we empirically establish that some truth theory, which we are at this stage still assuming we can use interpretatively, applies to a particular language? But in attempting to answer it, let us adopt the new perspective of radical interpretation.

A theory will be correct if it yields correct interpretations of people's utterances and inscriptions. What is it to interpret an utterance or inscription?

We interpret a bit of linguistic behaviour when we say what a speaker's words mean on an occasion of use. The task may be seen as one of redescription. We know that the words 'Es schneit' have been uttered on a particular occasion and we want to redescribe this uttering as an act of saying that it is snowing. (1974b, p. 141)

An utterance is an *action*, and hence an event, and to interpret it we want to give that event a certain description. The description, 'saying that p', will be one which 'gives the meaning' of the uttered sentence. This enables us to see how interpretation connects with Davidson's theories of action and anomalous monism. In both of those cases, we were concerned with events and their descriptions. Events, in themselves, are opaque or meaningless. It is only when they are described in certain ways that we see them as intentional actions, mental events like beliefs or linguistic utterances.

For Quine the question was: how can a theory which translates all the sentences of a native language be based on behavioural evidence? The question which Davidson poses for himself in radical interpretation is similar: how can we support a theory which is 'specifically semantical in nature' with evidence which is 'described in non-semantical terms' (1974b, p. 142)? By describing the theory as 'specifically semantical', Davidson means that it is a theory which will tell us what the sentences of the language mean. By requiring that the evidence be 'described in non-semantical terms', he is ensuring that the theory will not be confirmed by evidence which could only be available to us once we had a confirmed theory of the right kind. As we saw when we looked at a theory for a language known to be contained in the metalanguage, without this requirement, Davidson's proposals would be circular.

The kind of evidence we have for testing a theory of meaning will thus concern speakers and uninterpreted sentences, or utterances of sentences. From the point of view of giving a theory of translation, Quine conceived of testing speakers' assent to and dissent from sentences under certain stimulus conditions. In a similar vein, Davidson proposes to take as evidence for a theory of meaning facts about which sentences a speaker holds true under which conditions. But though these two suggestions are closely related answers to closely related problems, there are some significant differences between both the problems and the solutions.

One extremely important difference between Quine and Davidson, discussion of which will be deferred to section 8.3, is that while Quine chose to construe stimulus conditions in terms of sensory states, Davidson makes much of taking the relevant conditions as involving things and events in the world at large. Davidson, in other words, rejects the concept of stimulus meaning.

Secondly, the theory to be supported in Davidson's case is 'specifically semantical in nature'. All that Quine's theory set out to achieve was to map the sentences of one language onto the sentences of another. In Davidson's case, the theory intends to say what the sentences of the object language mean. To see the difference, just consider how Quine's translation manual could tell you, in English, that the German sentence 'Schnee ist weiss' translates the French sentence 'La neige est blanche' without thereby telling you what the French sentence means. In Davidson's case, if you understand the theory, then you understand the object language for which it is a theory.

The third main difference between Quine and Davidson here is that Davidson is no behaviourist, which means that he and Quine will differ in their conceptions of what the evidence for their theories will look like. The important requirement on the evidence, for Davidson, is not that it should be behavioural, but only that it should not be semantical. This means that any non-behavioural, non-semantical evidence, which would include information about the brain and its workings, would be available for Davidson's but not for Quine's use. In fact, though, Davidson makes little or no use of such evidence, and in the case of reference, to be examined in section 7.4, he argues against those who seek to base their theory predominantly on such evidence.

In requiring that all the evidence for a truth theory be non-semantical, Davidson, as he himself came to realize, was overstating his case. 'Non-semantical' here means that we should use no evidence described in terms of intentional concepts such as meaning, belief, desire and intentional action. (In section 5.1 we saw that Davidson rejected the communication-intention theory precisely because it sought to base sentence-meaning on facts about speakers' beliefs and intentions.) But the evidence for the theory is described as people's holding sentences true under certain conditions, and holding a sentence true is having a belief about that sentence. Although, as Davidson stresses, no semantical facts need creep in when specifying the content of the sentence held to be true, although, that is, we can know that somebody holds a sentence to be true without knowing what that sentence means, we are none the less talking about a belief with a specified content, namely, that a certain sentence, described purely syntactically, is true. This is itself a semantical fact in the sense at issue. Describing someone as holding a sentence true is not simply describing a piece of uninterpreted behaviour. It is describing a mental state in mental terms.

This is important because of the perennial philosophical project of reductionism. It is often hoped that concepts which are problematic, as meaning, belief, desire and other intentional concepts are, can be reduced to other more tractable concepts. The dogma of reductionism embodied such a hope, and even though Quine argued against that dogma on the basis of linguistic holism, his own view is also a form of reductionism, seeking to reduce whatever facts there are about the meaning of an entire language to facts about the behaviour of its speakers. By admitting that the evidence for a theory of meaning is not entirely non-semantic,

Davidson is opposing reductionism. Semantic facts cannot after all be extracted from purely non-semantic facts, as behaviourists and other reductionists have hoped. Davidson's hope is the more modest one that the much simpler structure of people's beliefs about which sentences (described as uninterpreted) are true will establish a theory about the interpretations of those sentences.

This stance is just what we would expect from Davidson, given his argument against the reduction of the mental to the physical, an argument which we looked at in chapters 1 and 4. The argument against reductionism in that case hinged on the role of normative principles which governed the mental, and as we are about to see, these play a vital role here too.

6.3   THE PRINCIPLE OF CHARITY

The evidence for the theory of meaning lies in the conditions under which a speaker holds sentences true. It will thus consist of a number of sentences of the form:

(1)   Mary holds true-in-L 'It is raining' if and only if it is raining in her vicinity.

This, and other sentences like it, are ultimately meant to be evidence for the T-sentences of the theory, sentences like:

(2)   'It is raining' is true-in-L if and only if it is raining, in the vicinity of the speaker.

If it were the case that, if (1) were true, (2) would have to be true as well, then it would be easy to see how establishing sentences like (1) would provide evidence for the T-sentences like (2) which comprise the better part of the theory of meaning. But the relation between (1) and (2) is not nearly that simple. A speaker holds a sentence true because of two things: what the speaker believes and what the sentence means. Thus, if I hold true the English sentence 'the earth is round,' it is because the sentence means that (is true if and only if) the earth is round, and I believe that the earth is round.

If the only evidence for sentences like (2) are sentences like (1), then we face a problem. If (1) is true, it is because both Mary believes that it is raining, and the sentence 'It is raining' is true, in Mary's language, if and only if it is raining. (2), however, records only the second of these conditions. Unless we already know that the first condition is satisfied, unless we already know that Mary believes that it is raining, we cannot use (1) as evidence for (2). The truth of (1) would be compatible with the falsity of (2). For example, suppose that we know that, on many occasions on which it is raining in her vicinity, Mary actually believes that it is not raining. She may just be mistaken, or there may be some more complex and bizarre reason, involving mind-controlling aliens who like to implant false beliefs about the weather in Mary's mind. For present purposes, the explanation of her beliefs doesn't matter. On these occasions, we, who do not as yet understand her language, observe that she holds true the sentence 'it is raining.' Although we may now establish that as a general rule, she holds that sentence to be true if and only if it is raining in her vicinity, our knowledge that on many of these occasions, she actually believes that it is not raining will prevent us from taking (1) as evidence for (2). That is, if we have that knowledge about her belief, we will not even consider taking the fact that she holds some sentence to be true if and only if it is raining as evidence for the fact that the sentence means, in her language, that it is raining.

This example is certainly strange and extreme. But it serves to show how, as Davidson stresses over and over again:

> beliefs and meanings conspire to account for utterances. A speaker who holds a sentence to be true on an occasion does so in part because of what he means, or would mean, by an utterance of that sentence, and in part because of what he believes. If all we have to go on is the fact of honest utterance, we cannot infer the belief without knowing the meaning, and have no chance of inferring the meaning without the belief. (1974b, p. 142)

We seem to face an impasse. (2) gives the form that the theorems of our theory must take; (1) gives the form that all our empirical evidence must take. Yet on their own, sentences like (1) cannot provide evidence for sentences like (2). What we need to overcome this impasse is to be able to make assumptions about what people believe. In this particular case, if we could assume that Mary believes that it is raining if and only if it is raining in her vicinity, then we could take the fact that she held a sentence to be true if and only if it is raining in her vicinity as evidence for the fact that, in her language, the sentence is one that is true if and only if it is raining in its speaker's vicinity. We could, in other words, use (1) as evidence for (2).

If the assumptions about what people believe are to play a general role in the theory of meaning, they will have to be about not specific beliefs such as that it is raining, but rather about more general features of belief. In our little example, the assumption that Mary believes it is raining if and only if it is raining in her vicinity could be seen as an instance of a more general assumption that people believe the obvious. Whether or not it is raining is, in many cases at least, obvious and likely to be registered in the beliefs of people.

In making the assumption that people believe the obvious, the question immediately arises: obvious for whom? If we allow that there are different criteria for what is obvious, then even if we suppose that people do believe the obvious, this will not lead to any more specific characterization of what they believe, even given all the facts about where they are and what perceptual capacities they have. It could be that, for instance, it was not obvious to Mary, though it was to us, that it was raining. If there are different standards of obviousness, we still will not be able to use (1) as evidence for (2), even given the assumption that people believe what is obvious.

The assumption that Davidson is requiring us to make, therefore, is that we take others (the interpretees) to find obvious what we (the interpreters) find obvious. In order to use information about which sentences they believe to be true under which conditions as evidence for a theory that says what conditions those sentences are true under, or what those sentences mean, we must assume that the people whom we are interpreting will believe what we think it is right to believe. This means that in radical interpretation we must assume that the objects of interpretation, by and large, believe what we think is true.

One could put this in either of two, equivalent ways. In order to use facts about which conditions speakers hold sentences true under as evidence for a truth theory, we must assume that they believe what we think they should believe. Or, alternatively, in making our assignment of truth conditions to the sentences of the language under interpretation, we must do it in such a way that the sentences the speakers of the language believe to be true turn out to be (according to us) true.

The method of radical interpretation, writes Davidson:

> is intended to solve the problem of the interdependence of belief and meaning by holding belief constant as far as possible while solving for meaning. This is accomplished by assigning truth conditions to alien sentences that make native speakers right when plausibly possible, according, of course, to our own view of what is right. (1973c, p. 137)

The principle being employed in this method was named (by Neil Wilson in 1959) the Principle of Charity. The Principle raises a number of questions. Is it justifiable to employ it, and if so, why? How do we account for the fact that people have false beliefs? Does a principle which ostensibly deals only with sentences believed true, by interpretees and interpreters, have any connection with truth itself? These questions will be addressed in the remainder of this chapter and in chapter 8. But first let us look a little more closely at how the Principle works.

A good example of the use of the Principle of Charity is provided by Quine when discussing radical translation. Quine claimed that we could identify and translate the truth-functional operators solely on the basis of behavioural evidence (see section 6.1). If a native word, for instance 'bloop', is such that for any sentence *p* a native assents to, he will dissent from 'bloop-*p*,' and for any sentence *p* which he dissents from, he will assent to 'bloop-*p*,' then we can translate his 'bloop' by the English 'not'. And if there is another native word 'blip', such that he will assent to '*p* blip q,' if and only if he assents to *p* and assents to *q*, then we can translate his 'blip' by the English 'and'.

Someone might object to this as follows. Suppose we think we have correctly identified the native's 'and' and 'not'. We put to him a query '*p* blip bloop-*p*?' (what we think is the tranlsation of '*p* and not-*p*?'), confidently expecting him to shake his head in violent disagreement. To our surprise he gives a calm 'yes'. The objector holds that this piece of behavioural evidence can be accommodated by different theories. We can either say that we have mistranslated the native words 'blip' and 'bloop', or that we have correctly translated them but that, remarkably, the native has completely different beliefs about the nature of conjunction and negation, and in particular, does not hold the law of non-contradiction, which says that a sentence and its negation cannot both be true.

Each of these options, says the objector, has something to be said for it. On the side of the mistranslation thesis, we can simply point to the fact that it is entirely unreasonable to accept a sentence and its negation, and nobody could do so, openly and knowingly, as the native appears to have done. On the other side, it can be pointed out that our subject may have all sorts of strange beliefs. We accept that he may believe that thunder is an expression of an angry god, so why should we not accept that he differs from us not only in the properties he takes to be true of thunder, but also in those he takes to be true of conjunction and negation?

Quine's answer is to invoke the Principle of Charity. He puts the Principle here as follows: 'one's interlocutor's silliness, beyond a certain point, is less likely than bad translation' (1960, p. 59). In other words, if our proposed translations make the native seem to deny such obvious truths as that a sentence and its negation cannot both be true, then this is more likely to mean some of our translations are wrong than that the native really does deny such obvious truths. The behavioural evidence alone leaves open the possibility of different explanations; by varying our attributions of belief to the native, we can make the behavioural evidence consistent with different translations. The Principle of Charity rules out all those translations which mean attributing to the native too much silliness. It functions as a constraint on possible translations.

Quine's use of the Principle is limited. He applies it only to the translation of the truth-functional operators and he regards it as saying only that a native's adherence to a sentence we consider a logical falsehood is *far less likely* than a mistranslation. This still leaves open the possibility that the native might accept a contradiction. (In Quine 1970, chapter 6, he advances the stronger claim that we could *never* accept that someone knowingly believed an open contradiction and hence that, in the circumstances described, we should always retranslate.)

Davidson, by contrast, applies Charity 'across the board' (1984a, p. xvii). Not only should we assume that someone does not openly believe logical contradictions, we should also assume that people believe that it is raining if they are in the middle of a rainstorm, or more generally, if they are in perceptual reach of rain. Believing the obvious is construed not just as believing logical truths, but as believing a whole range of non-logical truths which make up the framework of our system of beliefs. Even in genuine anthropological cases, where differences in belief come to the fore, Davidson stresses that we should not overlook the massive body of shared beliefs that different people in different cultures hold in common. This will be taken up in more detail in section 8.3.

6.4   ERROR, LANGUAGES AND CONVENTIONS

It might be thought that the Principle of Charity is in danger of making it impossible for anyone ever to be wrong about whether some sentence is true, that is, for someone to be mistaken. Being wrong is simply believing that the conditions which would make some sentence true obtain when in fact they don't. If the interpretation of a sentence depends on our adopting the policy of treating a speaker's holding it true under certain conditions as evidence for its being true under those conditions, how could anyone be mistaken? To give scope to the notion of a mistake, we need something general from which the speaker's misguided adherence to the truth of some sentence can be judged to deviate. The interpretation of a sentence must depend on more than an individual's current beliefs.

If we were seeking a theory of interpretation for an individual at a particular time, then the Principle of Charity would indeed make it difficult to see how someone could be mistaken. We would go directly from facts about which sentences someone held true under which circumstances to conclusions about the interpretations of those sentences in a way which tied the interpretation to the evidence. In such a case, not only would we not have to attribute to the speaker any false beliefs, we would have no need to attribute any beliefs at all to him (other than beliefs about which syntactically described sentences were true). With no possibility of mistaken belief, there is no real need for belief at all. It is precisely because there does exist some public standard which fixes the interpretation of sentences held true by individuals that we have both the concept of belief and the possibility of mistaken belief. 'Belief is built to take up the slack between sentences held true by individuals and sentences true (or false) by public standards' (1974b, p. 153).

In order to interpret not an individual's idiolect at some time, but a language, a public structure about the truth of whose sentences individuals can have false beliefs, we have to change the form of the evidence we use for the theory. If we are after an interpretation of a language as used by some community, the evidence we want is about which sentences are usually held true by the members of that community. Between (1) and (2), therefore, we should assemble more evidence from other speakers, leading to

(3)   Speakers of L hold true-in-L 'It is raining' when and only when it is raining in their vicinity.

(3), rather than (1), is the proper form of evidence for (2), though of course (3) and its like will be reached by many individual observations of the form of (1). This generalization has the consequence that we can now allow both that an individual can hold a sentence true, and that the correct assignment of truth conditions to that sentence will make it false and the individual who holds it true mistaken.

This does not entirely solve the problem of error, however, since the Principle of Charity must still have some application to the interpretation of individuals and their idiolects as well as communities and their languages. Suppose we arrive at an interpretation of the language of some community in a way which makes speakers of that language generally believers of truths (by our standards). If there were some individual member of the society who, judging from the sentences he held true and their public interpretations, generally believed to be true sentences which were false, the Principle of Charity would exert pressure towards the conclusion that that individual was really speaking a different language from that spoken by the rest of the community.

In other words, although by shifting our focus to languages, and hence communal attitudes to the truth of sentences, we make room for individual error, we must not lose sight of the application of the Principle of Charity to individuals. The Principle allows for individual error by introducing the idea of an interpretation of a public language. But where application of the public interpretation to an individual makes that individual too mistaken, the Principle tells us to treat that individual as speaking a different language. It tells us to reinterpret his words.

Having introduced this public standard to give scope to the notion of error, Davidson has since tended to shift his focus back to the individual.

He has expressed the view that 'there is no such thing as a language, not if a language is anything like what many philosophers and linguists have supposed' (1986, p. 446). What is the philosophers' and linguists' conception of a language that Davidson repudiates? What is at issue is the priority between public and individual interpretation. In denying the existence of languages as traditionally conceived, Davidson is concerned to reject the priority of public interpretation over individual interpretation.

This priority is associated with the philosophical use of the notion of convention. Many philosophers have felt that convention plays an important role in linguistic communication. For communication to take place between two (or more) people, there must be conventions which govern what the sentences they use mean. Without such conventions, no one could be understood by anyone else. This view allots a primacy to public standards by requiring individuals to respect conventions (which, of course, are public by their nature). What I communicate by using a certain sentence is dependent on what convention decrees that sentence means. A language, on this view, is a conventional assignment of interpretations to sentences, and communication is supposed, obviously, to require a language in this sense.

Emphasis of the role of convention is particularly prominent in the work of the theorists of communication-intention. Conventions are characterized in terms of the beliefs of those who adhere to them (see Lewis 1969). Consequently, where conventions enter into communication, the meanings of sentences will rely on the beliefs which constitute the relevant conventions. For Davidson, the interdependence of meaning and belief makes the appeal to convention illegitimate, since we could not attribute to people adherence to the relevant conventions without simultaneously interpreting their language.

Davidson argues that communication does not require convention. This can be brought out by imagining two people who speak no common language being stranded together on a desert island. The fact that they speak no common language is no principled (as opposed to practical) objection to their communicating. All that is required for that is that when one of them uses a sentence, the other understands what the speaker means. Radical interpretation shows how this can be done without already understanding his language, without sharing conventions about what sentences mean. Language, therefore, if seen as a conventional assignment of interpretations to sentences (as philosophers and linguists have tended to see it), is not, after all, required for communication.

In a recent paper (1986), Davidson characterizes the situation of interpretation in terms of 'prior theory' and 'passing theory'. The prior theory includes everything one brings to interpretation, in the form of beliefs about the speaker's beliefs and desires, expectations of what words he will in fact use to convey what content, and so on. When the speaker speaks, the interpreter uses his prior theory to form a passing theory, a theory which actually interprets what the speaker is now saying, in accordance with the Principle of Charity. In the most expeditious circumstances, the prior theory and passing theory will be more or less the same. This is what we understand by 'knowing a speaker's language'. But, of course, even with our neighbours, we must always stand ready to adjust our theory in the name of Charity. This is how we are able to understand people even when, according to public standards and conventions, they misuse language. As Davidson is fond of stressing, malapropisms, confusions, 'mistaken' uses of words, none of these need pose any problem at all to understanding (though, of course, they may). In so far as these phenomena are solecisms, it is only relative to our prior theory; what tells us what people mean is our passing theory, which makes no reference to the conventions in terms of which these phenomena are considered 'mistakes'.

Davidson is not denying that, in practice, convention plays a part. The supposition that, for instance, someone is speaking English, where English is a particular, conventional assignment of interpretations to sentences, is a large part of our prior theory when interpreting people in certain parts of the world. Without this assumption, communication and understanding would be vastly more difficult than they are. 'We do not have the time, patience, or opportunity to evolve a new theory of interpretation for each speaker' (1984b, p. 278). But at the end of the day, such conventions are always expendable if we are ready to take up the challenge of radical interpretation; and in any case, we must always give ultimate authority to considerations of rationality, as embodied in the Principle of Charity, when we form our passing theories, when we actually interpret people. Convention has a pragmatic role, but is not essential to interpretation and communication.

6.5 'EPISTEMOLOGY SEEN IN THE MIRROR OF MEANING'

If Davidson now re-emphasizes the individual speaker and his idiolect over the community with its language, does not the problem with which we began the previous section re-arise? How do we allow that people can be mistaken if the interpretations of the sentences they hold true are directly tied to the actual circumstances in which they hold them true? To some extent, we must just accept the anti-sceptical tendency of the Principle of Charity, and, as we shall see in chapter 8, Davidson makes a virtue of this necessity. But surely we must allow the possibility of some error?

The answer to this problem lies in appreciating that the Principle of Charity is far more sophisticated than has so far been indicated. Until now, our formulation of the Principle of Charity has been solely in terms of agreement, or truth by the interpreter's standards. Davidson admits that this was how he:

> tended to put the matter in the early essays, wanting to stress the inevitability of the appeal to charity. But minimizing disagreement, or maximizing agreement, is a confused ideal. *The aim of interpretation is not agreement but understanding.* My point has always been that understanding can be secured only by interpreting in a way that makes for the right sort of agreement. The 'right sort', however, is no easier to specify than to say what constitutes a good reason for holding a particular belief. (1984a, p. xvii; italics mine)

As his work has developed, the real nature of the Principle has emerged more clearly. Here is a good statement of the more developed conception:

> Some disagreements are more destructive of understanding than others, and a sophisticated theory must naturally take this into account. Disagreement about theoretical matters may (in some cases) be more tolerable than disagreement about what is more evident; disagreement about how things look or appear is less tolerable than disagreement about how they are; disagreement about the truth of attributions of certain attitudes to a speaker by that same speaker may not be tolerable at all, or barely. It is impossible to simplify the considerations that are relevant, for everything we know or believe about the way evidence supports beliefs can be put to work in deciding where the theory can best allow error, and what errors are least destructive of understanding. The methodology of interpretation is, in this respect, nothing but epistemology seen in the mirror of meaning. (1975, p. 169)

Error can be attributed in interpretation where it is explicable. If we can recognize how we, in certain circumstances, would have a certain belief which, in our role as interpreter we think is mistaken, we can, according to the new Principle of Charity, attribute to the interpretee this mistaken belief. This rebuts objections to the Principle of Charity which portray the Principle as requiring the attribution of true beliefs even when we better understand someone on the basis of attributing false beliefs (see, for instance, Grandy 1973; McGinn 1977).

In general, the point of the more sophisticated conception of Charity is summed up by the phrase 'epistemology seen in the mirror of meaning'. Constraints which we recognize as applying to our own beliefs, constraints which we could loosely categorize as epistemological, are to be used as constraints on possible interpretations. Everything which constitutes epistemology in this sense counts in interpretation. The passage just quoted at length introduces the canons of inductive and deductive reasoning. Deductive reasoning, of course, was already pulling its weight in Quine's example of the translation of logical constants. We cannot interpret people so that they have (at least conscious and explicit) beliefs in logical inconsistencies.

Inductive reasoning concerns the probabilistic support which some beliefs give to others. Here Davidson draws on work on induction by his logical positivist mentors. What is important are not the details of their approach to induction, but an aspect of their methodology. 'Carnap and Hempel have argued that there is a principle which is no part of the logic of inductive (or statistical) reasoning, but is a directive the rational man will accept. It is the *requirement of total evidence for inductive reasoning:* give your credence to the hypothesis supported by all available relevant evidence' (1969b, p. 41). This principle is a part of epistemology in the broad sense: it is something 'the rational man will accept'. Accordingly, it should be reflected in the mirror of meaning in that interpretation ought not to attribute beliefs to people which, if held, would make those people turn out to be flouting this principle too much.

By analogy to the principle governing inductive inference Davidson introduces another principle, which he calls the Principle of Continence: 'perform the action judged best on the basis of all available relevant reasons' (1969b, p. 41). This again is something the rational man will accept, and again, it features in interpretation. We should not interpret (and remember, interpreting includes describing events as intentional actions) in such a way that people too often turn out to be acting against their better judgement. If some interpretation did this, it would be evidence that the interpretation was wrong, rather than that the people interpreted happened to be very irrational.

The Principle of Charity, it seems, is not a single principle which governs interpretation, namely, interpret so that the objects of interpretation are generally true believers, but rather a collection of all those principles which together regulate the ways in which beliefs, desires and actions rationally connect with each other. The point about interpreting people so that they come out believing truths, by the interpreter's lights (i.e. the Principle of Charity narrowly conceived), is simply one of the many principles which constitute Charity in its more developed sense.

Davidson's metaphor of the mirror brings out how the Principle of Charity has two states, reflected and unreflected as it were. In its reflected state, it is a constraint on which interpretations of people are acceptable. No interpretation can be judged correct that makes the people to whom it is applied too irrational by the standards of its various directives. But in its unreflected state the Principle of Charity also applies plainly and simply to all of us, as rational people. It says: do not act contrary to your best judgement; draw inductive inferences on the basis of all available relevant evidence; believe only things you take to be true, and so on. It is the sum of all those things the rational person will accept just in virtue of being rational.

6.6 THE NECESSITY OF CHARITY

If Charity begins at home in this way, it may still be objected that its wholesale exportation is illegitimate. Why assume that others must be rational, or that their rationality will be the same as our rationality? The age-old question of cultural relativism will be taken up in section 8.3. For the moment, let us try to understand what lies behind Davidson's insistence that interpretation requires Charity. This insistence is manifest in many places, for instance:

> The methodological advice to interpret in a way that optimizes agreement should not be conceived as resting on a charitable assumption about human intelligence that might turn out to be false. If we cannot find a way to interpret the utterances and other behaviour of a creature as revealing a set of beliefs largely consistent and true by our own standards, we have no reason to count that creature as rational, as having beliefs, or as saying anything. (1973c, p. 137)

Davidson's position here has been succinctly defended by another philosopher, David Lewis, though in a slightly different vocabulary from Davidson's. Lewis (1966 and especially 1972) invokes the idea of the definition of theoretical terms. Theoretical terms are at the other end of the spectrum from observation terms. Sentences using them, to revert to Quine's picture of language, lie towards the interior of the web. Accordingly, their meaning is not to be found in any relatively direct relation to experience or the world. What defines a theoretical term is rather what the theory says about it and, in particular, what observational consquences the theory attaches to it.

Lewis gives the analogy of a detective who summons the suspects in a crime to hear the following story, which introduces the theoretical terms 'X' and 'Y': 'Two people, let us call them "X" and "Y", met two weeks ago at a tennis club of which X, but not Y, was a member, to discuss Smith's murder. The next day X bought some strychnine and gave it to Y, who then mixed it into Smith's martini.' To whom 'X' and 'Y' refer will depend on what the detective's 'theory' says about them. In particular, they will only refer to two people if those two people met two weeks ago to discuss Smith's murder at a tennis club of which the first, but not the second, was a member, and so on. We may allow that some of what the detective says of X and Y does not in fact apply to them, some of the detective's theoretical sentences may be false, but if too many are, then the terms 'X' and 'Y' simply lose their meaning.

'Belief', 'desire', 'action' and 'linguistic meaning' are all, according to Lewis, theoretical terms, and the theory of which they are a part is the everyday theory of folk psychology. This theory is itself made up of a whole host of platitudes which are nothing other than the applications of the directives of the Principle of Charity. Indeed, the Principle of Charity could be taken as the skeleton of the theory of folk psychology. In relation to intentional concepts, belief and desire and so on, the Principle of Charity is true by definition, or analytic. As David Lewis puts it, a person 'might have no beliefs, desires, or meanings at all, but it is analytic that if he does have them then they more or less conform to the constraining principles by which the concepts of belief, desire, and meaning are defined' (1974a, p. 112). Davidson suggests something similar when he writes, of the question 'whether people might not actually *be* approximately rational and consistent in their patterns of belief and desire', that 'in my view this cannot be a factual question: if a creature has propositional attitudes then that creature is approximately rational' (1985a, p. 245). That the question is not a factual one, but is, as it were, answered by definition alone, echoes Lewis's claim that it is analytic that people's beliefs etc. conform to the Principle of Charity.

In the 1950s, Davidson was involved in work on formal decision theory and this has clearly influenced his views on the present subject. 'Decision theory is an attempt to describe in an orderly way what variables influence choices' (Edwards and Tversky 1967, p. 7). The variables which it discerns are subjective probability and expected utility. These theoretical notions correspond to belief and desire respectively. An event's subjective probability for you is how likely you think it is to occur; its expected utility is how much you value its occurrence. Theories of decision contain various constraints on these, and related, notions, such as the constraint of the transitivity of preference, which says that if someone prefers A to B, and B to C, then he should prefer A to C.

Since subjective probability and expected utility are quantified forms of belief and desire, and since decision theory uses them to explain choices, often as manifested in actions, decision theory itself looks like scientific psychology of the sort Davidson now argues against (section 1.4). It is, therefore, no surprise to find Davidson writing of decision theory that 'all we had to do was to give a clear behaviouristic interpretation to "S prefers A to B" and decision theory – that is, a certain set of sentences containing the previously uninterpreted word "prefers" – became a powerful empirical theory, eminently testable, and palpably false' (1976b, p. 270). In other words, if preference, for instance, was given 'a clear behaviouristic interpretation', if we took a particular type of behaviour as evincing preference, the constraints which governed it would simply turn out to be false. Experiments would show that people sometimes prefer A to B, B to C, and C to A.

Davidson thus did not interpret decision theory as a scientific psychology. He did not consider it an empirical theory at all. But he did suggest another way of understanding it. 'It is at least as plausible to take [experiments] as testing how good one or another criterion of preference is, on the assumption that decision theory is true' (1976b, p. 272). We assume that what the theory says about its theoretical terms, i.e. that preference is transitive and so on, is true, and then treat any behavioural, or other empirical, test of preference as deferring to the theory. Nothing counts as evincing preference unless it conforms to the constraints which are constitutive of preference.

Understood in this way, decision theory is just a small-scale version of Davidson's whole theory of intentional content. The Principle of Charity governs the application of various concepts, such as belief, desire, action and meaning. If we take the Principle of Charity as resting on 'charitable assumptions about human intelligence', if we took it, that is, as an empirical theory about people, whose beliefs and so on could be ascertained independently of it, then whatever criteria we took as determining beliefs and other intentional concepts, the Principle of Charity could turn out to be false.

Davidson, however, regards the Principle as being constitutive of the concepts it governs.[1] The concepts of belief, desire, meaning and intentional action are defined by what the 'theory', the Principle of Charity, says about them. If they do not apply in accordance with the Principle, there is no reason to take them as applying at all. To apply those concepts, we must assume that the Principle of Charity is true and measure interpretations against it. Good interpretations, like good empirical criteria of preference, will be those which conform to the constraints. The results of empirical testing, the results of radical interpretation, are, so to speak, recessive with respect to it. Davidson likens such a theory to a theory of measurement of, say, length, which says that if A is longer than B, and B is longer than C, then A is longer than C. 'The theory is in each case so powerful and simple, and so constitutive of concepts assumed by further satisfactory theory (physical or linguistic) that we must strain to fit our findings, or our interpretations, to preserve the theory' (1976b, p. 273).

Decision theory also raises another interesting question in this context. Decision theory is a theory which constrains how subjective probability (belief) and expected utility (desire) can explain actions. Radical interpretation is a theory which uses linguistic meanings and beliefs to explain why people hold true certain sentences under certain conditions.

Ultimately, however, the two theories must merge. In decision theory, we talk of subjects being presented with choices which are linguistically described, and hence it must also explain the subjects' understanding of the choices. If meaning and belief are interdepedent, and belief and desire are interdependent, then, at the end of the day, all three notions are interdependent.

In a number of works (1980b, 1984d, 1985c), therefore, Davidson has pursued a goal of what he calls 'a unified theory of meaning and action', a theory in which 'meaning, belief, and desire will be treated as fully coordinate elements in an understanding of action' (1980b, p. 2). The main means used to achieve this integration is to take as evidence for a theory of what people mean, believe and desire, not information about which sentences those people hold true under which conditions, but rather, under which conditions they prefer one sentence to be true rather than another. Simply holding sentences true was the evidential basis for a theory of belief and meaning; by introducing preference into the evidential base, we are able to incorporate desire into the theory. Using only people's choices between pairs of sentences, Davidson has sketched a method for assigning beliefs and desires to the people and meanings to the sentences they choose between. The method, of course, works in the way we have already seen. It invokes constraints on the possible patterns of relations between these items, constraints which further articulate our conception of the Principle of Charity.

We can now state succinctly the answer to the question with which we began the chapter. A particular truth theory for a language will be correct if it makes the people of whose language it is a theory rational in their beliefs, desires and meanings in just the way the Principle of Charity requires. In showing how a theory of meaning for a language is confirmed, however, we see why Davidson's theory is really a theory of propositional content in general. In fixing the theory of meaning we must, at the same time, fix the theory of what people believe and desire. In section 5.1 the question arose, whether Davidson's use of formal semantics would have the consequence that he treated meaning in abstraction from the social and psychological contexts in which language exists and is used. Far from doing this, Davidson connects language with the study of the mental in the strongest possible way, by offering a single answer to the questions, what determines the meaning of people's languages, and what determines the contents of their mental states?

7

Holism and Meaning

We come now to the third of the three questions which, in section 5.3, we saw Davidson thought had to be answered in the affirmative to justify the claim that a Tarski-style theory of truth could serve as a theory of meaning. This is the question, is giving the truth conditions of a sentence a way of giving an interpretation of that sentence? In section 7.1 we consider the main problem for the view that it is. Davidson's answer to the problem comes in several parts. The first part is considered in section 7.2, but the heart of Davidson's justification for using a Tarski-style truth theory as a theory of meaning is considered in section 7.3. The essence of this justification lies in the doctrine of holism. Semantic holism has been subjected to two main types of criticism. These are discussed in sections 7.4 and 7.5 respectively.

7.1 ARE T-SENTENCES INTERPRETATIVE?

Convention T is the requirement that a theory of truth for a language should yield as theorems a T-sentence for every sentence of the object language, where a T-sentence of the form

(T) s is true if and only if p

is defined as one in which p is either the same as s, or a translation of it. Tarski framed Convention T to ensure that the predicate his theory shows how to define is indeed the truth predicate. Convention T assumes that we have an interpretation for s, that we know what s means, since to apply the Convention we must be able to see whether p is the same as, or a translation of, *s*. Tarski thus uses the notion of meaning, or translation, to elucidate the concept of truth.

Davidson wishes to do just the opposite of Tarski. His proposal is to use a theory of truth *as* a theory of meaning or, in other words, to use the concept of truth to elucidate that of meaning. In order, therefore, to avoid begging the very question at issue, what do the sentences of the object language mean, he cannot require that the theory of truth yield T-sentences in Tarski's sense. Davidson must reconstrue T-sentences as sentences which have the form of (T) but for which we do not require that *p* is the same as, or a translation of, *s* (see 1973c, p. 134). His hope is then that we can justify using these weakly construed T-sentences to give the interpretations of the object language sentences; that we can, in other words, effectively re-read 'is true if and only if' as 'means that'. There appears, however, to be a serious obstacle in the way of doing this.

Let us go over why we should want to use a theory of truth as a theory of meaning. Meaning is, in some sense, a richer concept than truth. To say that a sentence is true, or even to say under which conditions it is true, is to say less about it than what it means since two sentences could be true under the same conditions and yet none the less not be synonymous. A theory of truth is consequently more modest than a theory which attempts to account directly for meaning. This modesty is precisely why it is valuable. One of the ways in which the richness of meaning, as compared to truth, manifests itself is in the intensionality of meaning as opposed to the extensionality of truth. In section 5.2, we saw that if the theorems of our theory of meaning took the form ' *s* means that *p*,' we would run into problems over the logic of such a theory. For example, take the theorem '"Snow is white" means that snow is white.' If, for the sentence being used to give the meaning of the named sentence we substitute the sentence 'grass is green,' which has the same truth value (i.e. the same extension) as 'snow is white,' we get the false theorem '"Snow is white" means that grass is green.' The truth of the sentence used to give the meaning is not, in itself, enough to ensure that it does its job properly.

Standard logic, however, only knows how to account for the truth of sentences in terms of the extensions of their parts. The important things about sentences, therefore, are their extensions, or truth values. Anyone committed to using this logic, as Davidson is, in constructing a theory of meaning, must give up the idea that the theorems of the theory will be of the form '*s* means that *p*.' For this intensional form, we saw that Davidson substituted the extensional form '*s* is true if and only if *p*.' For a theory whose theorems are of this form we can use standard, extensional logic and this Davidson considers a great bonus. It means, in effect, that we have an agreed and well-understood logic at hand in working out the details of a theory of meaning.

But, as they say, there's no such thing as a free lunch. We will have to pay a price for being able to use the modest, well-understood resources of truth and extensionality in our theory of meaning. If '"Snow is white" is true if and only if snow is white' is true, then, precisely because we are confining ourselves to extensional resources, we must recognize that '"Snow is white" is true if and only if grass is green' is also true. Material biconditionals, sentences formed out of two other sentences linked by 'if and only if', are true just so long as the constituent sentences are either both true or both false.

It might be thought that the consequence of this for the theory of meaning is that we must find some extra factor, or constraint, to be able legitimately to rule out putative theorems such as '"Snow is white" is true if and only if grass is green.' In fact, this understates the problem while at the same time failing to show up the philosophical issues which lie behind it. In radical interpretation, we do not know in advance of constructing our theory of meaning what the object language means. Hence, even if the sentences of the object language appear to be the same as sentences of the metalanguage, we cannot assume that they have the same meanings. There is thus no principled way of telling which are the maverick theorems. If we assume that we know the meaning of the object language sentence 'snow is white,' we can tell which is the correct theorem for it, and which is the maverick one. But in radical interpretation this assumption is illegitimate.

The problem we face is that, by using a theory of truth instead of a theory whose theorems would say what object language sentences mean, we will end up with theorems which, because they are in the form of material biconditionals, fail to interpret the object language sentences for which they are theorems. Or rather, in radical interpretation, there would be nothing to determine whether the T-sentences were interpretative or not. By using truth instead of meaning, we end up giving, for each sentence of the object language, a sentence of the metalanguage which is true if and only if the object language sentence is, but which is in no way guaranteed to provide an adequate interpretation of it. Not surprisingly, by going for truth rather than meaning to take advantage of the logical simplicity of truth, we risk ending up with less than meaning. How are we to make up the deficit between truth and meaning? How are we to justify the claim that T-sentences, in Davidson's weak sense, do give interpretations of object language sentences?

Davidson's response to this problem comes in three parts. Two of those parts, holism and indeterminacy, are of the utmost importance, and are central theses of his whole system, integral to his semantic project. We shall examine them in section 7.3. The remaining part, at which we shall look first, is more problematic. (The discussion in section 7.2 is somewhat technical, but the material is not essential for understanding what comes after. Readers wishing to avoid technicality can, therefore, skip to section 7.3.)

7.2   THEOREMS AS LAWS

In making a retrospective assessment of some of his work in this field, Davidson has written:

> Something . . . that was slow coming to me was that since I was treating theories of truth as empirical theories, the axioms and theorems had to be viewed as laws . . . How much of a concession this is to intensionality depends, I suppose, on one's analysis of the concept of law. What seems clear is that whatever the concession comes to, it is one that must be made for any empirical science. (1984a, p. xiv)

Although Davidson, in this connection, also speaks explicitly of the need to see the theorems as 'natural laws' (1984a, p. xviii), this locution is, perhaps, misleading. In what sense could a theorem like '"Snow is white" is true if and only if snow is white' be a law of nature? What is important, though, is not whether the theorems are considered as laws of nature, but the realization that what is needed to interpret an utterance of 'snow is white' in the object language is not simply knowledge of a theorem '"snow is white" is true if and only if snow is white.' What is needed is the knowledge that a truth theory meeting the appropriate constraints (the Principle of Charity discussed in chapter 6) entails that 'snow is white' is true if and only if snow is white.

The importance of this shift in characterization of what an interpreter needs to know can be illustrated by an example. Suppose you came across a community of whose language you had absolutely no knowledge. To understand them, you would have to practise radical interpretation. But suppose also that living amongst them for many years was an English anthropologist. He gives you a list of sentences of the form 'native sentence *s* is true if and only if *p*.' If you knew that these sentences were true, could you use them to interpret utterances of the native sentences they were about? The answer is, only if you also knew that if natives were interpreted on their basis, they would not appear less rational than if interpreted on some other basis. You would also have to know that the T-sentences were compositional, that they showed how the truth-conditions of the sentences depended on the extensions of the words. In other words, you must know that the sentences that the anthropologist offers you are entailed by a theory which conforms to the Principle of Charity and the requisite formal constraints.

The concession to intensionality that this shift brings comes with the locution 'a theory entails that . . . ', since this context does not guarantee to preserve truth with the substitution of co-extensive terms. John Foster has argued that because of this concession to intensionality, 'Davidson's grand design is in ruins' (1976, p. 23). Foster takes Davidson's grand design to be the attempt to give a theory of meaning which uses no intensional concepts. If this were so, then the necessity of using 'a theory entails that . . .' to enable a theory of truth to provide interpretations would indeed be ruinous. But Davidson thinks this mistakes the object of his grand design.

Recall the discussion of indirect discourse at the end of section 5.4. There Davidson admitted that he did not require that a language have no intensional idioms. What was required was that the use of these idioms in forming sentences could be handled by an extensional theory of truth. Thus, although the notion of samesaying may be intensional, in some sense, it enabled Davidson to provide an extensional explanation for the idioms of indirect discourse. Davidson proposes to use his theory of indirect discourse in the present case. The semantic structure of a sentence like 'a theory of truth entails that "snow is white" is true if and only if snow is white' will be given as a relation between an utterance of '"snow is white" is true if and only if snow is white' and the sentence 'a theory of truth entails that,' where the 'that' is a demonstrative.

This avoids the problem of the inability to substitute co-extensive sentences after the 'entails that', but still leaves us with the task of analysing the relation of entailing, just as we were left with the notion of samesaying in the case of indirect discourse. Davidson makes the following suggestion: 'If a theory T entails that "Snow is white" is true in English if and only if snow is white, then T has as logical consequence a sentence synonymous with my utterance of '"Snow is white' is true in English if and only if snow is white"' (1976a, p. 178). This still invokes the apparently intensional notion of synonymy. Davidson thinks this is acceptable because this notion will itself be explained by a theory of meaning, construed as a theory of truth meeting certain formal and empirical constraints which are stated without reference to such synonymy. A theory meeting these constraints will yield the notion of synonymy required to make sense of 'a theory entails that . . . '.

What this means, in effect, is that the admission that to interpret the sentences of the object language we must use not just the theorems of a theory of truth, but also the knowledge that they are entailed by such a theory does not itself contribute to explaining how we can get from truth to meaning. Though this seemed to be the object of the concession, it now appears that the justification for using a theory of truth as a theory of meaning must depend entirely on the arguments about holism and indeterminacy. If these are acceptable in justifying the jump from truth to meaning, then we can allow the notion of synonymy to function in the analysis of 'a theory entails that . . .' without circularity. If they are not, then Davidson's grand design does indeed rest on shaky foundations. Let us now turn to these further arguments.

7.3   HOLISM AND INDETERMINACY

Taken individually, T-sentences say that some sentence of the object language is true if and only if some sentence of the metalanguage is. We saw, in section 7.1, how this relation between sentences of the object language and the metalanguage is not strong enough to ensure that T-sentences are interpretative. Taken sentence by sentence, a Tarski-style truth theory fails to add up to a theory of meaning.

The T-sentences, however, are not the only part of the theory. What is special about such a theory is that it shows how the truth conditions of the sentences are accounted for on the basis of the words of which they are composed and the ways in which these words are combined. Each T-sentence, therefore, is located in a network of relationships with other T-sentences by virtue of the fact that they share various component parts. The theorem '"snow is white" is true if and only if snow is white' will be generated by an apparatus which assigns semantic properties to the elements 'snow' and 'is white', and which uses those elements and their semantic properties to generate other T-sentences such as '"snow is cold" is true if and only if snow is cold' and '"clouds are white" is true if and only if clouds are white.' What is important about each T-sentence is not the material equivalence (the relation of being true if and only if) it posits between a single sentence of the object language and a single sentence of the meta-language, but rather, the fact that it asserts this material equivalence in the context of many other interrelated equivalences. Foster puts this point well:

> It is not intended that our understanding of each sentence be based wholly on the truth-conditional for it which the theory entails. Rather, the theory purports to interpret each sentence by locating its position on the lines of truth determination for the language as a whole, by stating its truth conditions in the framework of the general principles by which the truth conditions of *any* sentence are determined by its structure. (1976, p. 10)

Davidson makes the same point. It is an error, he says:

> to think that all we can learn from a theory of truth about the meaning of a particular sentence is contained in the biconditional demanded by Convention T. What we can learn is brought out rather in the *proof* of such a biconditional, for the proof must

demonstrate, step by step, how the truth value of the sentence depends upon a recursively given structure. (1970a, p. 61)

This means that one can only interpret a single sentence of the object language by means of its T-sentence if one is in a position to interpret many sentences in the same language. Being able to interpret a sentence is not simply knowing the appropriate T-sentence; it is knowing that some sentence is true if and only if some condition obtains *and* that that sentence is composed out of parts which feature in other sentences which are true if and only if other specified conditions obtain.

Behind holism construed as the claim that to interpret one sentence you have to be in a position to interpret many related sentences lies a more profound kind of holism. Davidson writes: 'a belief is identified by its location in a pattern of beliefs; it is this pattern that determines the subject matter of the belief, what the belief is about' (1975, p. 168). Having to be able to interpret many sentences to be able to interpret one sentence is not just an epistemological requirement. If beliefs, and interpretations of sentences, are *individuated* largely by their relations to other beliefs and mental states, then something could not be, say, a belief that whales are not insects, unless it were related to other beliefs about what insects and whales are like and, of course, these in turn will have further ramifications. There is not, needless to say, a specific list of further beliefs that must be held by someone if he is to be credited with the belief that whales are not insects. It is just that, without sufficient background, a belief could not be the belief that whales are not insects.

Beliefs and interpreted sentences are individuated by the relations they have to other beliefs and interpreted sentences. These relations will include entailment, probabilistic support, contradiction and so on, all those kinds of relations, in fact, which come under the scope of the Principle of Charity. This means that one cannot first identify some belief, or interpret a single sentence, and then consider the question of its deductive and evidential relations to other beliefs and interpreted sentences. From the very identification of a belief as a belief that whales are not insects it will follow that the believer so credited will share many beliefs with us about whales and insects. Without this shared background his belief just would not have the content we ascribe to it.

Holism, then, goes part of the way to solving the problem we started out with, can a theory of truth be used as a theory of meaning? But Davidson has more to say. Our initial difficulty was that since T-sentences are material bi-conditionals, if '"snow is white" is true if and only if snow is white' is true, then so is '"snow is white" is true if and only if grass is green.' But these two sentences cannot both give interpretations of the object language sentence 'snow is white.' This is dealt with by insisting that interpretations are provided only by T-sentences taken as parts of a whole theory that, if it were used to provide interpretations, would conform to the Principle of Charity. But Davidson also allows that, in some circumstances, there can be different, non-synonymous metalanguage sentences all of which do give interpretations of one object language sentence. This is the doctrine of the indeterminacy of meaning.

Let us look at the roots of this view in Quine's work on radical translation, which we began to examine in section 6.1. In that section, we saw how behavioural evidence enabled us to make translations of logical constants and, through the notion of stimulus meaning, reasonably good translations of observation sentences. In order to translate other sentences, Quine argued that we should form analytical hypotheses which link native words with English words.

These analytical hypotheses are, precisely, hypotheses; they go beyond our evidence. Because they are underdetermined by our evidence, Quine thinks it possible that we could, for some native language, form several, non-equivalent sets of analytical hypotheses. This would have the consequence that, for some native sentence s, one set of analytical hypotheses could give as a translation for s an English sentence e, while another set could give e', where e and e' are different, non-synonymous sentences.

But Quine's thesis is not just that our evidence might leave open different translations. The evidence which will have run out constitutes the totality of linguistic behaviour, for Quine, since he regards knowing a language simply as having a set of dispositions to respond in various ways to various stimulations. If this set of dispositions leaves open the possibility of rival sets of analytical hypotheses, and hence rival translations, there is nothing else to close it. There would be no fact of the matter about which translation was the right one. The thought that, of two incompatible translations, one of them must be right and the other wrong, is fostered, Quine says, 'by an uncritical mentalistic theory of ideas: each sentence and its admissible translations express an identical idea' (1960, p. 74). Quine takes behavioural dispositions to constitute the meanings of the sentences of a language, and not the expression of mental ideas. Hence, not only translation, but meaning itself is indeterminate. Sentences are meaningful, in that they are used for various social purposes, but there is no such thing as 'the meaning' of a sentence.

Quine's argument is really this: any genuine semantic facts are constituted by behaviour; behaviour does not suffice to determine meaning or translation; therefore there is no such thing as determinate meaning or translation. (Clearly, the most contentious point here is the first premise, and it is around this that most discussion of Quine's views revolves.) So the indeterminacy of translation is connected with the denial of meanings which we saw, in section 5.2, was encouraged by Quine's nominalism.

This kind of indeterminacy carries over into a Davidsonian theory of meaning as well, though in a modified form. The basic point is this. There may be different ways of assigning truth conditions to sentences, that is, there may be different, non-equivalent sentences in the metalanguage which are true if and only if various sentences of the object language are true, such that the different truth theories they allow will equally well conform to all the formal and empirical constraints which enable a theory to be used interpretatively. Since all our intuitions about meaning have gone into formulating these constraints, there will be nothing to choose between any two theories which conform to them equally well. (The kinds of examples of indeterminacy which are actually discussed are esoteric, but it is not necessary to understand the details of the examples for present purposes. See Davidson 1977, 1979; Wallace 1977.)

Superficially, this sounds alarming and disconcerting. If the way we are approaching the task of giving a theory of meaning leaves us unable to rule out the possibility of divergent interpretations, surely this can only mean that we are going about our task in the wrong way. But to react in this way is to miss the point. All the facts which are relevant to meaning are taken account of in the way the theory is constructed and empirically applied. Any resulting indeterminacy in which sentences of the metalanguage we use as interpretations for the object language sentences will stem from facts about those metalanguage sentences which are irrelevant. Davidson writes, echoing some of the views expressed in section 6.6:

> We must view meaning itself as a theoretical construction. Like any construct, it is arbitrary except for the formal and empirical constraints we impose on it. In the case of meaning, the constraints cannot uniquely fix the theory of interpretation. The reason, as Quine has convincingly argued, is that the sentences a speaker holds to be true are determined, in ways we can only partly disentangle, by what the speaker means by his words and what he believes about the world. A better way to put this would be to say: belief and meaning cannot be uniquely reconstructed from speech behaviour. The remaining indeterminacy should not be judged as a failure of interpretation, but rather as a logical consequence of the nature of theories of meaning. (1973d, pp. 256-7)

Davidson makes a helpful analogy with theories of measurement:

> A theory of measurement for temperature leads to the assignment to objects of numbers that measure their temperature. Such theories put formal constraints on the assignments, and also must be tied empirically to qualitatively observable phenomena. The numbers assigned are not uniquely determined by the constraints. But the *pattern* of assignments is significant. (Fahrenheit and Centigrade temperature are linear transformations of each other; the assignment

of numbers is unique up to a linear transformation.) In much the same way, I suggest that what is invariant between different acceptable theories of truth is meaning. The meaning (interpretation) of a sentence is given by assigning the sentence a semantic location in the pattern of sentences that comprise the language. Different theories of truth may assign different truth conditions to the same sentence . . . while the theories are (nearly enough) in agreement on the roles of the sentences in the language. (1977, pp. 224-5)

Just as we can measure temperature in either Fahrenheit or Centigrade, so we can 'measure' meaning with different sets of truth conditions. So long as the pattern between the roles of the sentences is preserved, a pattern which is determined by the formal and empirical constraints placed on the theory, the resulting indeterminacy in not significant.

As a matter of fact, this analogy fails to point up a number of ways in which Davidson's form of indeterminacy may be more acceptable than Quine's. As Davidson notes, by insisting on a Tarski-style truth theory, he is requiring that the object language be seen as, more or less, comprised of the standard devices of first-order quantificational logic. In other words, its sentences will have to be seen as constructed out of singular terms, predicates, quantifiers and truth-functional operators. For Quine, some of this apparatus may show up in the analytical hypotheses, but this is quite fortuitous. Any way of getting from native to familiar sentences will be acceptable, so long as it preserves, or maximizes, sameness of stimulus meaning where this is appropriate and translates the logical constants in accordance with the Principle of Charity. There will thus be no theoretical constraint on how the sentences are segmented. Davidson's added restriction would undoubtedly narrow the possibilities for indeterminacy.

But there is another important factor which will diminish indeterminacy, and which Davidson has come to insist on more and more. In assigning truth conditions, and hence interpretations, to the utterances of some speaker, the Principle of Charity and the doctrine of holism emphasize the relations between sentences as well as the truth of those sentences. But the Principle of Charity is now taken by Davidson to include requirements on how the assignments of truth conditions to sentences accord with the location of a speaker in the network of causal relations with which he is embedded in the world. This was already alluded to in the previous chapter when I said that Davidson's radical interpretation was distinguished from Quine's radical translation in that the former abandoned the notion of stimulus meaning and construed the conditions under which sentences were held true directly in terms of the external world.

Thus, suppose that whenever it rained, there was an increase in the presence of a chemical X in the atmosphere on the other side of the world. When speakers uttered the sentence 'it is raining,' one could, consistently with the requirement that one interpret speakers so that they utter truths wherever possible, assign to that sentence the T-sentence '"it is raining" is true if and only if there is an increase in the presence of X on the other side of the world to that in which the speaker is located.' If the link between rain and the increase of X was a result of some natural law, and not merely a cosmic coincidence, such a T-sentence would even be as lawlike as its more obvious rival which says that the sentence is true if and only if it is raining near the speaker. The extra requirement in the Principle of Charity which we are now considering would none the less rule out, or at least make very improbable, such a T-sentence on the grounds that there was no suitable connection between the increase of X on the other side of the world, and the utterance of the sentence by a speaker. In other words, our evidence for accepting a particular truth theory must include our knowledge of the causal interaction between speakers and the things they talk about. This question of the relation between causation and interpretation will be taken up at greater length in section 8.2.

Before we go on, I can now redeem a promissory note left in section 5.2. Davidson had three reasons for rejecting the existence of meanings. One was his nominalism, which he denied was a significant consideration. The second was the claim that meanings had no demonstrated use in a theory of meaning. We are now in a position to appreciate his third, and I think most forceful, reason. Quine's belief that there is nothing more to language than certain dispositions to behaviour, a belief encouraged by his nominalism, led him to the view that meaning is indeterminate. Beyond a certain point, a point which can be reached just in terms of dispositions to behaviour, there are no facts of the matter about what sentences and words mean.

Davidson, in one place, gives the impression that his own reasoning is the reverse of this. He begins with the intuition that meaning is indeterminate, an intuition fuelled by his holism, and for this reason he rejects meanings. 'Indeterminacy shows . . . that if there is one way of getting it right there are other ways that differ substantially in that non-synonymous sentences are used . . . And this is enough to justify our feeling that there is something bogus about the sharpness questions of meaning must in principle have if meanings are entities' (1968, p. 101; see Burge 1986, pp. 197-200, for a suggestion that Davidson is confused about this).

7.4 ATOMISM: THE CAUSAL THEORY OF REFERENCE

Linguistic holism of the sort we have been examining is one of the most controversial of Davidson's views. It comes under fire principally from two directions, which we will look at in this and the following sections. Both Davidson and his critics can agree on the general shape of the theory. We have axioms which characterize the semantic properties of the basic components of the language, words and their modes of combination. From these axioms, and the rules of logic, we can derive the remaining theorems of the theory, which are the T-sentences.

Which facts will make a purported theory *the* theory (or, given indeterminacy, *a* theory) of meaning for some language? Davidson's answer is that a theory would correctly be taken as a theory of meaning for some language if the totality of the T-sentences conformed to the constraints included in the Principle of Charity. If this condition is met, and is known to be met, then the theory as a whole can correctly be taken as a theory of meaning for the language as a whole though, as we have seen, one cannot remove individual T-sentences and say that they alone give the meanings of the object language sentences which they are about. On this view, the contact between the theory and the world, the empirical clout of the theory, comes at the level of the totality of the T-sentences.

The two positions from which linguistic holism comes under fire differ from Davidson's theory over this issue of where the contact between the theory and the world comes. Let us take first what we may call linguistic atomism (see Field 1972 for a defence of this position). By using the notion of a translation in stating Convention T, the requirement that any theory must meet if it is to be a theory of truth, Tarski hoped to illuminate the concept of truth. For Davidson, this gets things back to front. Truth, he argues, is far more easily understood than meaning or translation. Rather than use these problematic semantic concepts to throw light on truth, Davidson uses the intuitively understood notion of truth to get whatever can be got out of the semantic concept of meaning.

Meaning, however, is not the only semantic concept that features in a theory of meaning. The axioms from which the T-sentences are derived employ the obviously semantic notions of reference and satisfaction. They include axioms such as ' "snow" refers to snow' and ' "is white" is satisfied by all and only white things.' The question therefore arises of how these notions themselves are to be understood. Can we use truth, which enters the theory at the level of sentences by linking object language sentences to metalanguage sentences, to enable us to understand the subsentential concept of reference? Or will we have to give some independent account of what reference is, thereby making semantic concepts co-eval with, or even prior to, truth in the order of explanation? Davidson maintains the former, atomists the latter.

Here is how Davidson puts the conflict:

There are two approaches to the theory of meaning, the building-block method, which starts with the simple and builds up, and the holistic method, which starts with the complex (sentences, at any rate) and abstracts out the parts. The first method would be fine if we could give a non-linguistic characterization of reference, but of this there seems no chance. The second begins at the point (sentences) where we can hope to connect language with behaviour described in non-linguistic terms. But it seems incapable of giving a complete account of the semantic features of the parts of sentences, and without such an account we are apparently unable to explain truth. (1977, p. 221)

(We have seen that it is over-optimistic for Davidson to say that we can give an account of how sentences connect with behaviour in totally non-linguistic terms: we need the notion of people holding certain sentences to be true, which is itself a propositional, or semantic, fact. So the real challenge to the atomist, the building-block theorist, would be to give an account of reference which used no greater linguistic or semantic apparatus than that needed by Davidson to explain truth simply in terms of sentences.)

One of the chief ways in which the atomist seeks to explicate the notion of reference is in causal terms.[1] The inspiration for this approach comes from the apparent success of causal theories of perception. In such theories, it is hoped that one could say what it is for an object to be perceived by someone by stating what kind of causal connection must obtain between that object and the person's experience of it. In the present case, the hope is to say what causal connection must obtain between an object and an utterance of a certain word for the word to refer to that object. It is information like this which will, on the atomistic conception, ultimately confirm the axioms of a truth theory. Then, using these empirically confirmed axioms, one could derive from them the truth conditions of sentences of the language. The theory itself would look just like the kind of theory Davidson advocates. But what would ensure that the theorems gave semantic properties of sentences would be that they were derived from empirically confirmed axioms which treated of reference and satisfaction. Reference and satisfaction, in turn, would be given non-semantic, probably causal, analyses.

As a result of this difference in conception, the atomist would have no need of the Principle of Charity. The Principle was designed as a way of testing theories as a whole, by judging their total assignments of truth conditions to sentences in the light of the canons of rationality. For an atomist, no such test would be necessary since the theory would be confirmed or disconfirmed simply on the basis of whether words (or utterances of words) and objects stand in the (causally explicated) reference relations which the axioms say they do.

What does a holist have to say about reference? How does Davidson meet his own challenge of giving 'the semantic features of the parts of sentences'? He invokes a distinction between explanation which occurs within a theory and explanation of a theory. Within the theory of truth, the explanation of the truth conditions of sentences is indeed explained, at least in part, in terms of the reference of the parts. It is this which enables us to account for what the sentences 'snow is white' and 'snow is cold' have in common. The T-sentences of each will be derived using a common axiom, giving the reference of the word 'snow'.

However, when we come to the theory as a whole, and ask of it, in virtue of what does the theory apply to some group of speakers, the answer will not depend on ascertaining whether certain specified causal relations obtain between individual words and the objects to which they are supposed to refer. It will depend, in the ways we have been looking at, on whether the theory conforms to the Principle of Charity. It is the way in which the interpretations of sentences integrate with our general interpretation of the speakers as rational agents, with beliefs and desires, which provides the test of the theory. If a theory meets the requirements imposed by the Principle of Charity, then it can be used as a theory of interpretation. In such a case, we can see the reference relations between words and objects which are described by the axioms of the theory as theoretical constructs. Once we accept the theory, the axioms explain how the truth conditions of sentences come out as they do; they are part of the machinery of the theory. But no separate account need be given of what the relation of reference is.

It might be thought that whether or not a causal theory of reference, and hence an atomistic approach to questions of meaning, could work is an empirical question. One should simply look and see whether there is some kind of uniform causal relation between words and what they refer to. Yet if Davidson's holism rested simply on the assumption that no such relation had yet been shown to exist, this would be a very weak support. And Davidson does, indeed, have a more principled reason for rejecting the atomistic approach.

Because interpretation, truth and meaning concern whole sentences and beliefs, they are subject to the principles of rationality which Davidson thinks are so important. Reference, by contrast, concerns individual words and is therefore not directly under the aegis of the Principle of Charity. If explanatory priority is given to reference over truth, the possibility exists that the empirical semantic facts, in the shape of reference relations between words and objects, will lead to the contravention of rationality constraints which govern the relations between sentences and beliefs.

Recall Davidson's theory of anomalous monism (section 4.1). According to this theory, individual mental states are identical to physical states, but there is no correlation between types of mental and physical states. McDowell, in a defence of Davidson against an atomistic approach, emphasizes the analogy between anomalous monism and semantic holism. Holism, says McDowell:

> is quite compatible with the thesis that whenever a name, say, occurs in an utterance-event, the event is suitably related, in physically describable ways, with events or circumstances involving the name's denotation [i.e. referent]. What need not be true is a corresponding thesis with a quantifier shift: that there is some one physically describable relation which obtains between any occurrence of any name and its denotation . . . It seems right to conlude that denotation, on this view, is a non-physical relation. (McDowell 1978, p. 127)

The reasons for this are precisely the reasons for the irreducibility of the mental. Meaning, as applied to sentences, is part of the normative framework of the interpretation of people as rational agents. The normative constraints subsumed by the Principle of Charity are what govern the attributions of interpretations to sentences, as they do the attributions of beliefs, desires and actions. If types of mental states were identical to types of physical states, then the non-normative physical facts would potentially pre-empt the authority of the rational normativity of the mental. Similarly, if reference were primitive with respect to truth and meaning, if it could be explained in causal or other physical terms, then again, we would risk finding that as we assembled facts about the meanings of sentences on the basis of facts about reference, the meanings we should be forced to attribute to sentences would contravene what was required by the Principle of Charity. If reference were analysed in physical terms, there would be no way of ruling out the possibility that the correct interpretations of people's utterances made them utterers of completely false, irrational or inconsistent propositions. Since the axioms of the theory would be where its truth was tested, we would have to accept the consequences of a true set of axioms for what the truth conditions of sentences were, regardless of how rational those consequences were.

Needless to say, this is an outcome the atomist would be likely to accept. What is important is that Davidson rejects the atomist approach over this issue, the dominance of rationality, rather than the fact that, to date, no one has come up with a satisfactory theory of reference.

7.5   DUMMETT AND HOLISM

One of the most persistent and influential critics of holism, in the forms in which it is espoused by both Davidson and Quine, has been Michael Dummett, and in this section we will examine his main objection to holism. Dummett's objection springs from his insistence on the connection between meaning and understanding; in giving a theory of meaning for a language, we must be giving an account of 'what it is that someone knows when he knows the language, that is, when he knows the meanings of the expressions and sentences of the language' (Dummett 1975, p. 99).

Dummett uses this idea to motivate a distinction between what he calls 'modest' and 'full-blooded' theories of meaning. A modest theory of meaning is one the knowledge of which would only enable someone to understand the object language if he already possessed the concepts which the object language could express. In this respect, he thinks a modest theory of meaning is like a translational theory. If a theorem of a translational theory tells you '"la neige est blanche" in French is translated in English as "snow is white,"' this will only enable you to understand the French sentence if you already understand the English sentence. If the theory itself were given not in English, but in a third language, there would be a genuine possibility that someone could understand the theory without understanding the object language. Similary, Dummett argues, an axiom like '"is square" is satisfied by all and only square things,' which might feature in a Davidsonian theory of meaning, will only help you know what it is that speakers of the language know when they use the expression 'is square' if you already have the concept of squareness. The theory itself does nothing to explain the kind of (probably implicit) knowledge someone must have to use 'is square' correctly.

It might seem that if you know the axiom '"is square" is satisfied by all and only square things,' then you must genuinely understand the object language expression 'square'. But Dummett makes a distinction between knowing that a proposition is true, and knowing what that proposition says. As he correctly points out, one can know that a proposition is true without thereby knowing what truth it expresses. (Donnellan 1977 contains an interesting discussion of this distinction.) In the case of a Davidsonian theory for a language which is included in the metalanguage, we could know that the propositions which were expressed by the axioms and theorems were true merely by knowing the meanings of the connectives - 'is satisfied by', 'denotes', 'is true if and only if' - and observing that the expressions mentioned on the left of the connectives were the same as those used on their right. Dummett is worried that we could, in this sense, know a Davidsonian theory of meaning for some language without possessing whatever knowledge it is that constitutes a speaker's understanding of that language.

A full-blooded theory, by contrast, is one which says what it is to have the concepts expressible in the language for which it is a theory. Dummett's insistence on the connection between a theory of meaning and a theory of understanding means that he thinks a theory of meaning should be full-blooded. The theory of meaning must not only associate squareness with the expression 'square' but must also say what it is for someone to have the concept of squareness; and it must do this for all the primitive terms of the language. In other words, the axioms must not only connect words of the object language with words in the metalanguage, but must use the metalanguage to say what it is to have the concepts expressed by the terms of the object language.

Davidson explicitly denies that a theory of meaning should do this. He thinks it a virtue of his Tarski-inspired approach to the question that it allows one to distinguish between 'questions of logical form or grammar, and the analysis of individual concepts' (1967c, p. 31). He gives the example of evaluative terms like 'good'. These present philosophers with special problems: does 'good' express some objective property, as 'square' does, or does it express our subjective approval of those things we say are good? In a truth theory like Davidson's, however, 'what is special to evaluative words is simply not touched: the mystery is transferred from the word "good" in the object language to its translation in the metalanguage' (1967c, p. 31). Consequently, even without an analysis of what it is to possess the concept of goodness, we can accept T-sentences of the form '"A is good" is true if and only if A is good.'

Dummett thinks that holism in the theory of meaning entails modesty and this is one of his chief reasons for rejecting holism. For a theory to be full-blooded, it would have to associate with each word and sentence of the object language something that would count as a statement of what someone who understood those words and sentences knew. According to Davidson's position, we do associate with each sentence a truth condition; that is, we assert that some sentence of the metalanguage is true if and only if the corresponding sentence of the object language is. But, as we have seen, in order to make the jump from plain truth to the richer concept of meaning, in order to use the T-sentences to interpret the object language sentences, we must consider the theory as a whole. We can only use the T-sentences to interpret the sentences of the object language if we know that the theory as a whole conforms to the Principle of Charity, and meets the appropriate formal constraints.

Thus, the knowledge that enables us to use some individual T-sentence to interpret a sentence of the object language will be substantially the same in all cases. Although, at the level of truth conditions, what we say about each sentence of the object language will be different, at the level of meaning or interpretation, there will be no account of the different capacities that make up the understanding of the language as a whole. Instead of seeing knowledge of a language as the sum of all the pieces of knowledge, or capacities, which embody the understandings of the various words and sentences that make up that language, Davidson associates one block of knowledge with the language as a whole, without being able to say, for each individual word or sentence, what counts as knowing the meaning of *that*.

It was supposed to be a virtue of Davidson's account that it met the requirement that a theory of meaning should show how the meanings of sentences depend on the meanings of the words of which they are composed. Dummett is suggesting that it does not, after all, discharge this duty:

> The articulation of the theory of truth is not taken as corresponding to any articulation of the practical ability the possession of which is the manifestation of that knowledge of which the theory is presented as a theoretical model . . . To effect any such segmentation, it would be necessary to give a detailed account of the practical ability in which the understanding of a particular word or sentence consisted, whereas, on the holistic view, not only cannot a speaker's command of his language be so segmented, but no detailed description of what it consists in can be given at all. (Dummett 1975, p. 116)

In fact, this problem of not seeing knowledge of a language as composed out of knowledge of various parts of the language besets Davidson's position whether or not one invokes the distinction between modesty and full-bloodedness. In section 8.4 we shall examine some of the difficulties this raises for Davidson.

What is it that motivates Dummett's commitment to full-bloodedness in a theory of meaning? The requirement that for each word of a language, the theory of meaning must say what it is to know the meaning of that word in terms which not only enable someone who knows the theory to make the connection between the word and what it means, but also enables someone to grasp the concept expressed by the word is, essentially, a kind of semantic reductionism. It is not the kind of reductionism advocated by the causal theory of reference; it is a form of behaviouristic reductionism, seeking to equate knowledge of semantic facts with the possession of particular practical capacities. This is supported by an example given by Dummett:

> What is it to grasp the concept *square*, say? At the very least, it is to be able to discriminate between things that are square and those that are not. Such an ability can be ascribed only to one who will, on occasion, treat square things differently from things that are not square; one way, among many other possible ways, of doing this is to apply the word 'square' to square things and not to others. (Quoted in McDowell 1987, p. 62)

Davidson is not a behaviourist. The full-blown attribution of interpretations to sentences, along with the attribution of beliefs and desires, stems from the already semantic, or propositional, facts about which sentences speakers believe to be true. The attempt to use a theory of truth as a theory of meaning must therefore be seen against the presupposition that we already have some grasp of the notion of propositional content, which cannot be behaviouristically explained. (In the remainder of this section I draw heavily on McDowell 1987.) The theory is not supposed to show us how sentences have meanings from a perspective entirely outside content. It is only meant to be 'an important step in the direction of reducing complex and relatively theoretical intensional concepts [the full range of beliefs, desires and meanings] to intensional concepts that in application are closer to publicly observable behaviour' (Davidson 1980b, p. 4). Closer, but still not reducible, to publicly observable behaviour.

Dummett is right, therefore, that Davidson's theory is modest rather than full-blooded, but that is because Davidson refuses to see his theory as something which relates meaning to purely non-semantic facts (whether behavioural or of the causal physicalist kind). Davidson has thus eschewed any commitment to discharging a reduction of meaning to the non-semantic. Dummett, on the other hand, still sees it as part of the task of a theory of meaning to do this. This is, indeed, a fundamental disagreement over the nature of a theory of meaning, and what it should accomplish.

The nature of the disagreement has, however, been obscured by the fact that Davidson has inherited so much of his vocabulary from Quine. Quine, like Dummett, is essentially a behaviourist. Although his theory of radical translation is meant to have the same evidential basis as Davidson's (assent or holding sentences true), it is clear that Quine really likes to think of assent and dissent as purely behavioural, whereas for Davidson, the evidence is admitted to be irreducibly intentional. Assent is treated by Davidson as a species of belief and not behaviour. If Davidson were as close to Quine as he sometimes likes to suggest, his theory of meaning would indeed be deficient in the way Dummett thinks it is. But, in fact, Davidson is prepared, indeed, thinks it necessary, to talk in semantic, propositional or mentalistic terms right from the start. He therefore must think that Dummett's requirement that a theory of meaning be full-blooded is not just too strong, but misguided.

8

Truth, Knowledge and Relativism

In the last three chapters we have been looking at what has amounted to a general theory of propositional content. We started with the question of what determines the meanings of sentences, but it became apparent that, on Davidson's approach, the answer to this question involved simultaneously answering the question of what determines the contents of beliefs and desires, since belief, desire and linguistic meaning are interdependent. They function as theoretical constructs in a theory that explains action, including linguistic action. The explanation works by using sentences of a metalanguage, the interpretation of which is assumed, to give the truth conditions (and hence, in the sense in which we have seen, the meanings) of inscriptions and utterances, the contents of mental states such as beliefs and desires, and the intentional descriptions of actions. Since all these things interlock, the theory employs a strong normative element, the Principle of Charity, to constrain the possible assignments, and in the case of linguistic meaning, there is the further requirement that the interpretations given to utterances and inscriptions are taken from a Tarski-style truth theory which gives them on the basis of their composition out of semantically simpler parts (i.e. words). Even with all these constraints, however, it is admitted that a degree of indeterminacy remains in how we make our overall interpretations of agents.

In the next chapter, we will look at this theory of content in itself, and ask how it comports with other parts of Davidson's philosophy. First, however, we shall look at some of the consequences this theory of content has for certain metaphysical and epistemological issues. In section 8.1 we look at Davidson's views on truth. Section 8.2 turns to scepticism. In section 8.3 Davidson's rejection of empiricism, closely connected with his views on truth and content, is examined and his views on conceptual relativism are discussed. In the final section, we look at some difficulties for the views examined in this chapter.

8.1   TRUTH

Considering the importance that Tarski's semantic theory of truth has for Davidson's theory of content, it should be no surprise that his own theory, in turn, has consequences for a theory of truth. Traditionally, theories of truth have tended to be divided into two sorts, correspondence theories and coherence theories. It has been a matter of some philosophical debate how Tarski's semantic theory relates to this traditional taxonomy. Tarski himself thought of his theory as a kind of vindication of a correspondence theory. Originally, Davidson shared Tarski's conviction in this respect, but his position has become far more complicated over the years, effecting a kind of union between elements from both the correspondence and coherence theories.

The correspondence theory attempts to explain what it is for a sentence, or belief, to be true in terms of its correspondence to something else. It therefore requires something for whole sentences, rather than singular terms, to correspond, or refer, to. Facts are clearly the kind of thing one needs for a correspondence theory of truth. After all, it seems almost a truism that a sentence is true if and only if it corresponds to the facts.

Two of the most celebrated exponents of the correspondence theory of truth were Russell and the early Wittgenstein. Wittgenstein's *Tractatus Logico-Philosophicus* begins, famously: 'The world is all that is the case. The world is the totality of facts, not of things . . . The world divides into facts' (1961, 1.1 and 1.2). In elucidation of what facts are, Russell says: 'Things in the world have various properties, and stand in various relations to each other. That they have these properties and relations are *facts*, and the things and their qualities or relations are quite clearly in some sense or other components of the facts that have those qualities or relations' (1956, p. 192). These facts stand in certain relations to sentences and beliefs. 'The world contains *facts*, which are what they are whatever we may choose to think about them, and . . . there are also *beliefs*, which have reference to facts, and by reference to facts are either true or false' (1956, p. 182).

The sentence 'the cat is on the mat' is true if and only if it is a fact that the cat is on the mat. The fact that the cat is on the mat makes the sentence true (as it makes the sentence 'the cat is not on the mat' false). The fact comprises the cat, the mat and the relation of superiority in which the former stands to the latter. It therefore appears to have three elements. The relation of correspondence between the sentence and the fact can be partially illuminated by the observation that the sentence too can be fairly naturally divided into three elements, one designating the cat, one the mat and one the relation between them.

In section 2.1 I said that one of the main reasons why some philosophers have wanted to treat events as universals was because of the consequent connection between events, thus conceived, and language. Events as universals are spoken of as facts (Wilson 1974) or states of affairs (Chisholm 1970, 1971) and, in either case, are taken to be expressed by whole sentences, rather than referred to by singular terms, as Davidsonian particular events are. Thus, Davidson's advocacy of events as particulars, and his rejection of events as facts, underlies his objection to a correspondence theory of truth as understood by Russell and Wittgenstein.

Davidson deploys the Frege argument (see the Appendix for an explanation of the argument) to establish that sentences cannot correspond to facts. The Frege argument is designed to show that contexts which allow substitution of co-extensive terms must be truth-functional. Consider the sentence ' "the cat is on the mat" corresponds to the fact that the cat is on the mat.' If the cat is my favourite pet, then the fact that the cat is on the mat is the same fact as that my favourite pet is on the mat. So the sentence 'the cat is on the mat' corresponds to the fact that my favourite pet is on the mat. This shows that the context 'corresponds to the fact that . . . ' allows substitution of co-extensive terms ('the cat' and 'my favourite pet'). But once we allow this, the Frege argument shows that the context is also truth-functional; i.e. we could substitute any sentence which has the same truth value as 'the cat is on the mat' after ' "the cat is on the mat" corresponds to the fact that . . . ', and hence we would be forced to say that any sentence that corresponds to one fact corresponds to every fact that obtains. 'No point remains in distinguishing among various names of The Great Fact when written after "corresponds to"; we may as well settle for the single phrase "corresponds to The Great Fact". This unalterable predicate carries with it a redundant whiff of ontology, but beyond this there is apparently no telling it apart from "is true" ' (1969d, p. 42). If 'corresponds to The Great Fact' is indistinguishable from 'is true', we clearly have no explanation of truth in terms of correspondence to the facts.

None the less, Davidson claims that 'the semantic concept of truth as developed by Tarski deserves to be called a correspondence theory' (1969d, p. 48), and in this he follows Tarski's own evaluation of his theory. The respect in which Davidson thinks a Tarski-style truth theory deserves to be called a correspondence theory is this. Tarski's theory defines truth in terms of satisfaction, and satisfaction is a relation which holds between bits of language and bits of the world. The bits of the world, however, are not facts or states of affairs, i.e. what Wittgenstein and Russell thought were bits of the world, but particulars (objects and events). Davidson says it has been 'the nemesis of theories of truth based on facts' (1969d, p. 48) that they have always tried to include the relations or predicates that apply to the object(s) concerned in whatever is supposed to correspond to the sentence. By contrast, on his approach, the only things that correspond to sentences are the objects which satisfy them.

If, however, the only relations between sentences and things in the world are of this sort, such relations cease to explain the truth of sentences. Dolores and Dagmar both correspond to (i.e. satisfy) the sentences 'Dolores loves Dagmar' and 'Dolores is next to Dagmar,' yet the two sentences, if true, are clearly true for different reasons. The first is true because Dolores loves Dagmar; the second because she is next to him. The very fact that what is supposed to 'correspond' to the sentence does not include the relations that apply to the objects makes this sense of correspondence too tenuous to justify the idea that we have an explanation of truth in terms of correspondence.

In a recent retrospection of his work on truth, Davidson has recognized this:

> I thought . . . that the fact that in characterizing truth for a language it is necessary to put words into relation with objects was enough to give some grip for the idea of correspondence; but this now seems to me a mistake. The mistake is in a way only a misnomer, but terminological infelicities have a way of breeding conceptual confusion, and so it is here. Correspondence theories have always been conceived as providing an explanation or analysis of truth, and this a Tarski-style theory of truth certainly does not do. (1990, p. 135)

In fact, Davidson treats truth as undefinable. It is conceptually basic. We saw something of this in his reversal of Tarski's attempt to illuminate truth by using translation. Davidson used truth to throw light on what, according to him, was the far more problematic concept of meaning. Something general, however, can be said about truth: 'the truth of an utterance depends on just two things: what the words as spoken mean, and how the world is arranged.' This is a consequence of 'the disquotational feature enshrined in Tarski's Convention T', namely, that if s is the name of a sentence in the object language, and p that same sentence, or its translation, in the metalanguage, then:

(T) s is true if and only if p.

This, says Davidson, 'is enough to fix [truth's] domain of application' (1983, pp. 308–9). It is what enables us to see that it is truth that Tarski is giving a theory of.

8.2 SCEPTICISM: FOUNDATIONALISM AND COHERENCE

A correspondence theory of truth not only has nothing useful to say about the relation between truth and knowledge, it even appears to create a special problem for it. If the truth of some sentence depends on correspondence with something in the world, whether a fact or simply an object or event, it seems that the only way we could ever know that a belief was true would be by comparing the belief with the relevant bit of the world. The problem is that in making such a comparison, we can only rely on further beliefs. Our assessment of the relation between the world and one belief consists in acquiring further beliefs. The question then arises whether these further beliefs are themselves true. This is one way of putting the traditional problem of scepticism.

One approach to answering the sceptical challenge is to try to find some special beliefs which we can tell are true without having to confront them with external reality whose relations to beliefs we could only ascertain through further beliefs. If these privileged beliefs could then be shown to provide the foundations for the rest of our beliefs, we would have the makings of an answer to the sceptic since the special, foundational, beliefs could be known to be true without our having to resort merely to further beliefs.

This answer to scepticism has been common since Descartes. Descartes himself used it in attempting to show how all our knowledge could be derived, by means of deductive arguments, from the belief each person has that he exists. This belief, in turn, Descartes supposed one could know to be true merely by having it. There could be no possibility of having it unless it were true. This is the famous argument *'cogito ergo sum,'* 'I think, therefore I am.'

In more recent times, foundationalism has invoked not the belief that one exists but sensory experience. Since there is something odd about supposing that people can be mistaken over which sensations they are experiencing, it is felt that if the foundational beliefs were either identical to or based on sensations, then they might be able to provide the secure base for the rest of our knowledge. Davidson makes an incisive attack on this kind of foundationalism (see 1982c, 1983).

The first thing to notice is that the claim being made is still vague, and can be sharpened in different ways. It might be held that no distinction should be made between having, say, a sensation of a green spot, and having the belief that some spot is green. Certain beliefs would simply be identified with sensations. On this construal, foundationalism seems false. There is, surely, a great difference between having a sensation and having a belief. A sensation is a state without propositional content. It is not subject to the considerations of rationality which apply to beliefs. It cannot imply, entail or contradict anything.

Alternatively, the foundationalist might mean that certain sensations justify certain beliefs conclusively. My sensation of a green spot justifies conclusively some belief, such as that I am seeing a green spot, or that there is a green spot in my perceptual field. Against this, Davidson argues that a sensation of a green spot only justifies some belief if the person having the sensation believes that he is having that sensation. For there is nothing incompatible in his having the sensation and yet believing that he is not having it. The sensation alone, therefore, cannot justify his belief. On the other hand, if he does believe that he is having the sensation, then his belief that there is a green spot is being justified not by a sensation but by another belief. And now, of course, we have to contend with the possibility that this other belief is false, since someone could believe that he was having a certain sensation and yet be mistaken (1983, p. 311). In the face of this line of argument, it is tempting for the foundationalist to fall back on the identification of the sensation with a belief, but as we have seen, Davidson thinks this identification is false.

Davidson does not deny that there is some relation between, say, a sensation of a green spot and believing that there is a green spot. What he is denying is that this relation is a logical, justificatory or evidential relation, as it would have to be if sensations were to provide an answer to scepticism. It may be that our sensations cannot lie to us, but if so, that is because they do not say anything at all; they are not propositional and therefore cannot justify, or serve as evidence for, beliefs or other propositional attitudes. Only things with content, such as beliefs or interpreted sentences, can be evidence for beliefs.

This is compatible, however, with the view that sensations cause certain beliefs and this view Davidson embraces. In chapter 3, we saw Davidson invoking the distinction between causes and reasons, in order to argue that intentional actions are events that have descriptions such that they are caused (in the right way) by things which are reasons for them under those descriptions. The present distinction, between cause and justification or evidence, is essentially the same. As with action, Davidson must say that when we come to hold one belief because of another belief which is a reason for it, the reason must cause the belief for which it is a reason. The trouble with sensations is that they are *merely* causes; they can cause beliefs but cannot be reasons for them because they do not have propositional content.

Foundationalism, however, is only one way of attempting to answer the sceptic. A second approach is provided by a coherence theory of truth. Acknowledging that one cannot get outside one's beliefs, and that only a belief can be a reason for another belief, the coherentist suggests that a belief is true not if it corresponds to something which is not a belief, but rather if it coheres with other beliefs. In the pursuit of knowledge, our goal should not be the unobtainable one of comparing our beliefs with reality, but that of maximizing the coherence and consistency of our set of beliefs.

This involves a radical shift away from the intuitions about truth which motivate the correspondence theory. The correspondence theory, whatever its faults, at least acknowledged that truth was something to do with the relation between language and the world. As Davidson put it: 'the truth of an utterance depends on just two things: what the words as spoken mean, and how the world is arranged.' In a coherence theory, this link with the world is lost. Truth becomes something that sentences have merely in virtue of their relations to other sentences. This free-floating view of truth leads to the greatest problem that faces the coherence theory. It is clearly possible that we can frame two different sets of consistent sentences which are none the less inconsistent with each other. If truth is merely consistency, then we will have to say that two sets of sentences which are inconsistent with each other are both true. This violates one of our most basic intuitions about truth, that a sentence and its negation cannot both be true.

This problem for the coherence theory has a counterpart in Davidson's theory of interpretation. Coherence and consistency bulk large in Davidson's theory of content. While it may be true that 'the truth of an utterance depends on just two things: what the words as spoken mean, and how the world is arranged,' what any sentence means, for Davidson, is itself determined by the holistic and normative theory of radical interpretation. On that theory, the meaning of a sentence depends on its relations to other sentences, and these relations must, by and large, be those of consistency, coherence and rationality. Davidson puts this by saying that an interpreter must find the object of his interpretation largely true by the interpreter's own standards. That is, he must interpret so as to maximize the consistency and coherence of his beliefs and the beliefs of the interpretee.

So far, this qualification, that the truth which the Principle of Charity requires us to maximize is truth by the interpreter's own lights, has always been assumed. But the question now forces itself on us, what ensures that the interpreter's own beliefs are true? If he is mistaken in the first place, won't the method of radical interpretation lead him to interpret others so that they are indeed consistent, in agreement with him, and therefore in his opinion believers of truths, but are in fact mistaken? Ultimately, the Principle of Charity and radical interpretation depend on, and are only entitled to demand, consistency and truth according to the interpreter. Unless the interpreter has some way of guaranteeing the truth of his own beliefs, he can come with nothing more. Yet the consistency and coherence of his own beliefs do not seem to be incompatible with their falsity.

Davidson's theory of interpretation thus appears to face the same dilemma as the coherence theory of truth. It can either guarantee that the mere agreement generated by the Principle of Charity suffices for objective truth (and not just truth according to the interpreter) by identifying truth with (some qualified form of) agreement. In this case, it pays the price of divorcing truth from the world and sacrificing our intuitions about truth. Or else, it allows that truth exceeds mere agreement, in which case interpretation, and the coherence and consistency it brings, do not ensure that what is agreed upon is objectively true. In order, therefore, to answer the sceptical challenge, Davidson has to show 'that coherence yields correspondence' (1983, p. 307), where correspondence is understood in the weak, Aristotelian sense which Tarski liked to quote: 'to say of what is that it is not, or of what is not that it is, is false, while to say of what is that it is, or of what is not that it is not, is true.' This he attempts to do in two different ways. The first is a clearly articulated argument, the second an extension of his theory of content. Let us look first at the argument.

The method of radical interpretation takes us as far as ensuring that between interpreter and interpretee there must be a large amount of agreement, and that therefore the interpreter must take the interpretee to be largely a believer of truths. But it does not appear to guarantee the truth of the beliefs of either. To do this, Davidson introduces the fiction of an omniscient being, someone who believes all and only truths. If such a being were to adopt the stance of an interpreter, it too would have to find its interpretee largely in agreement with itself; but the special feature of this case is that the interpreter has been stipulated to be omniscient. To be largely in agreement with such a being is, *ipso facto*, to be largely a believer of truths (Davidson 1983, p. 317).

This argument is interesting from several points of view. For one thing, it emphasizes a feature of Davidson's theory of content that we have already seen to some extent, that content is a theoretical notion which only exists in the context of interpretation. This is emphasized by the argument because it is assumed that the omniscient being's knowledge does not already include knowledge of what the content is of the beliefs and utterances of the interpretee (see Rasmussen 1987). If content were determined independently of the context of interpretation, then an omniscient being would not be required to adopt the position of a radical interpreter, and hence could possibly find itself in extensive disagreement with fallible, non-omniscient beings.

Another interesting point raised by this argument concerns the question of knowledge of one's own mind, and the meanings of one's own sentences. Davidson, of course, must mean his theory of content to apply to oneself. But the idea that the contents of one's own beliefs and utterances are an artefact of interpretation, or of those facts which interpretation makes explicit, is much more difficult to accept than is the corresponding position about the contents of other people's mental states. The way in which the present argument raises this question is this. The argument is essentially the claim that the following three theses are incompatible: (1) we could be largely wrong about how things are; (2) radical interpretation must put interpreter and interpretee largely in agreement; and (3) we must be interpretable by an omniscient being. Accepting (2) and (3) entails rejecting (1), the sceptic's position. The argument against scepticism is not, therefore, mounted only on the basis of Davidson's theory of interpretation (as Davidson sometimes suggests), but also requires premise (3). And our conviction that premise (3) is true depends, in turn, on our conviction that we do indeed have beliefs and utter meaningful sentences, since it is only on this supposition that we can assert that we *must* be interpretable. But if content is a theoretical notion, what convinces us that the theory applies to us? Does not the thought that we must be interpretable imply that, in our own cases, we think of content not as a theoretical construct, but as a real presence? We will return to the issues raised by this argument in sections 9.1 and 9.3.

Let us turn now to the more general considerations which Davidson advances against scepticism. His claim is that truth is generally ensured, and scepticism refuted, not by foundational beliefs which guarantee their own truth, nor by a vacuous identification of truth with coherence, but rather by what he calls the 'veridical nature of belief'. In determining what the content is of a belief, Davidson has tended more and more to stress that we should, in radical interpretation, identify the object that a belief is about (in those cases where we are considering singular beliefs) with the cause of that belief. 'What stands in the way of global skepticism of the senses is, in my view, the fact that we must, in the plainest and methodologically most basic cases, take the objects of a belief to be the causes of that belief' (1983, pp. 317–18).

Take, for example, the sceptic's case of the brain in a vat. The sceptic argues that there could be a brain kept alive in a vat in a laboratory somewhere, being stimulated in such a way that it seemed to the brain as if it were a person climbing the Himalayas or whatever. Its experience of looking down from the summit of K2 would be indistinguishable from the experiences of someone really in that position. If the brain were linked to a voice producer, it would utter sentences such as 'the air here in Nepal is so wonderful and clear.' But we would know that all such sentences were false, since 'here' for the brain is really floor – 19 in the Pentagon, and the air there may in fact be tired and stale.

If there could be such a brain it could surely be fed experiences which were indistinguishable from the ones you're having right now. In fact, the sceptic concludes, for all we know, we could be just brains in vats. All the beliefs which we have about our environment could be false. Since it is at least possible that we are brains in vats, it must at least be possible that we are massively in error. If Davidson claims that his theory of content makes it impossible for us to be generally mistaken about such matters, then he has to address the brain-in-a-vat problem. His assertion that we should take the objects of beliefs to be the causes of those beliefs is designed to do just that.

The plausibility of the sceptic's attack lies in our seeing the contents of the brain's beliefs as determined independently of their causes. The brain believes it has blue eyes, but this is a mistake because in fact the belief was caused by the stimulation of the scientist; the brain itself has no eyes. 'But,' says Davidson, 'if I am right, we can't in general first identify beliefs and meanings and then ask what caused them. The causality plays an indispensable role in determining the content of what we say and believe' (1983, p. 317). So whatever words the brain uses in expressing its beliefs, we, as interpreters, cannot accept that it consistently talks demonstratively about mountains and glaciers when it is lodged in a Washington basement. As interpreters, the Principle of Charity, now explicitly taken to include the injunction to take the objects of certain beliefs as their causes, means that we must interpret the brain's demonstrative sentences as being about its actual environment, the environment that causes the assertions of those sentences and the presence of the corresponding beliefs. Although the brain's words appear to be English words referring to exotic mountain locations, we must conclude that they are not English at all, but really Vatese and that they express the brain's beliefs about what it actually encounters, such as probes and electrical stimulations in a Pentagon basement.

8.3   THE DISAPPEARANCE OF MIND

The claim that the brain in a vat's beliefs must be about its environment may seem like a difficult doctrine. The sceptic's challenge, it might be felt, is being side-stepped, or answered by some form of trickery. All those more traditional attempts to rebut scepticism, attempts which have relied on trying to show that, in some sense or other, we have good evidence for the beliefs we seem to have, will have been shown to be useless since Davidson turns the trick by finding 'a *reason* for supposing most of our beliefs are true that is not a form of *evidence*' for those beliefs (1983, p. 314). This reason is that we cannot, in many basic cases, identify what a belief is about independently of saying what caused it. Some philosophers have felt that any theory of content or interpretation which does away with scepticism in such a summary fashion should be rejected for that very reason. For instance, McGinn writes: 'I had the idea of using the anti-sceptical consequences of the principle of charity as a *reductio* before I learned that Davidson regarded this as a *virtue* of his account of interpretation' (McGinn 1986, p. 359).

For this reason, it is important to see Davidson's views against a wider background. Davidson identifies, and ultimately rejects, a common, two-tier picture of the mind which is particularly a feature of the empiricist tradition in philosophy. According to this picture, there is a level of 'sensory experience', 'the given', 'sense-data' or whatever which the mind receives passively, through the senses. Secondly, there is something which applies to this raw experience, a mechanism of the mind, concepts, a conceptual scheme or perhaps a language, to produce beliefs and other cognitive mental states. Davidson call this view the dualism of scheme and content.

The dualism of scheme and content has been advocated since the beginning of modern empiricism (Locke and Hume). Kant, although not obviously an empiricist according to the traditional history of philosophy, shared with that tradition this dualism and he has probably proved its most influential exponent. Kant held that the senses provide us with experience, or intuition, and the mind, necessarily using certain categories or concepts, such as cause and effect, necessity and probability, and others, organizes this raw experience to form knowledge.

> Our knowledge springs from two fundamental sources of the mind; the first is the capacity of receiving representations . . . the second is the power of knowing an object through these representations . . . Intuition and concepts constitute, therefore, the elements of all our knowledge, so that neither concepts without an intuition in some way corresponding to them, nor intuition without concepts, can yield knowledge . . . Thoughts without content are empty, intuitions without concepts are blind. (Kant 1933, A50–1, B74–5)

Quine too is part of this tradition. When we looked at the differences between Quine's radical translation and Davidson's radical interpretation (section 6.2) I said that the most important difference was over what it was that should characterize the conditions under which sentences are assented to or dissented from. For Quine, translation depended on the notion of stimulus meaning, the set of sensory stimulations which prompt assent to and dissent from a given sentence. Davidson, however, insisted that the conditions should be specified directly in world-involving terms. Instead of trying to insulate the content of sentences from the world, by introducing a sensory mediation, a level of how it seems to the subject, we should determine content directly in terms of the things in the world which prompt assent and dissent.

We can now appreciate the full significance of this. Quine is subscribing to the dualism of scheme and content by invoking a level of sensory stimulations that act as epistemological intermediaries between the world and the meanings of sentences or the contents of beliefs. Sensory stimulations are treated by Quine not merely as what prompt assent and dissent to various sentences, but as evidence for those sentences. Davidson, as we saw in the previous section, repudiates any epistemological intermediary between belief and the world. Experience can remain in a purely causal role, but Davidson denies it any epistemological, evidential role. Davidson goes straight to the world itself to help fix what mental states and sentences are about.

To return to the brain-in-a-vat case, the reason why we might feel that Davidson's anti-sceptical move is somehow a trick is that we are still thinking of the case in the light of the dualism of scheme and content. We assume that the brain has a certain characteristic experience which is given to it by the scientist. This experience, through its own nature, constrains what beliefs the brain can have on its basis. If the scientist so determines it, that experience could be such as to constrain the beliefs to be somehow about mountains and glaciers; and whatever experience could constrain beliefs in that way certainly could not also permit judgements made directly on the basis of it to be about scientists in a laboratory as well.

By rejecting the dualism of scheme and content, Davidson is rejecting the possibility of this defence of scepticism. There is no such thing as the 'given', or experience, which constrains the contents of the beliefs. The contents of the brain's mental states are determined directly by radical interpretation, guided by the Principle of Charity which includes the principle that the objects of beliefs are, in certain common cases, their causes. Our attribution of beliefs and interpretations to the brain in a vat is not constrained by any sensory intermediary.

If the 'given' drops out of the theory of content in this way, then it is clear that the other part of the traditional empiricist theory, the scheme which organizes the experience, the categories that are applied to it, must also drop out. One of the most prominent ways in which the dualism of scheme and content manifests itself, and where Davidson's rejection of an organizing scheme is most forceful, is in the doctrine of relativism.

Empiricist epistemology as I have characterized it raises the possibility of relativism for this reason: once one allows a distinction between scheme and content, one can envisage different people, or groups of people, who share the same content (whose common physiology ensures that they have the same sensory experience of the world), and yet have different schemes, or sets of concepts, for organizing or interpreting their experience. Furthermore, if the concepts used by one person or group are different from those used by another, then the thoughts which each is capable of thinking may be unthinkable by the other.

Given the idea the different people may be capable of having different beliefs, it is tempting to become relativist about truth as well. What, it can be asked, is the point of insisting that the beliefs of some tribe about its pantheon are false? They are, surely, just its way of conceptualizing experience which we conceptualize through science. Neither way produces beliefs which are absolutely 'true' or 'false'. For us, their beliefs are false and ours are true; for them, the opposite is the case. But since each of us makes this claim from within some conceptual scheme, neither can lay claim to any absolute authority.

We have seen how Tarski's theory of truth is really truth relative to a language (section 5.3), but this sort of relativism is harmless since it concerns uninterpreted sentences. What may be true in one language and false in another is an uninterpreted syntactic string. By contrast, conceptual relativism allows one to say, of a sentence with a single interpretation, that it may be true in one conceptual scheme but not in another. This position is extremely prevalent in many circles ('the young in California *do* say "true for me" ': Putnam 1979, p. 168). Standards of truth and rationality, which for Davidson are central to interpretation, are viewed by relativists as distinctively Western, and inapplicable to members of other cultures. They argue that we should not assess the beliefs of one culture by standards applicable only to another.

Relativism, requiring different intermediaries between experience and belief, can locate these intermediaries in different places. The most obvious intermediary is the mind. And indeed, after Kant's influential work in epistemology, it became commonplace in the nineteenth century to discuss 'the pre-logical mind of savages', to compare the Hebrew and Greek minds, and so on. Such views, of course, were frequently made to serve racist and imperialist ends. Today, the same views are still current, though now they are usually taken as grounds for respecting other forms of life rather than subjugating them.

A very prevalent form of relativism finds the intermediary not directly in the mind and its mechanisms, but in language.[1] A language is taken to express, or embody, a conceptual scheme. Where two languages express different conceptual schemes, it may be impossible to translate from one language to the other satisfactorily. Speakers of one language may be uninterpretable to speakers of another.

This idea has been influentially developed by the American anthropologists and linguists Edward Sapir and Benjamin Lee Whorf. The Sapir–Whorf hypothesis, as their view is called, is that languages conceal metaphysics, and that speakers of a language are implicitly committed to its metaphysics. Whorf writes:

The Hopi language and culture conceals a METAPHYSICS, such as our so-called naive view of space and time does, or as the relativity theory does; yet it is a different metaphysics from either. In order to describe the structure of the universe according to the Hopi, it is necessary to attempt – insofar as it is possible – to make explicit this metaphysics, properly describable only in the Hopi language. (Whorf 1956, p. 58)

This passage includes all the elements of relativism: the idea that different cultures have different views of the world; that what we take to be the truth about space and time is merely *our* metaphysics; that how one culture sees the world is only partially, if at all, accessible to members of other cultures, or speakers of other languages.

How does Davidson address the question of conceptual schemes? Putting the question in terms of interpretability of language, he writes that 'nothing . . . could count as evidence that some form of activity could not be interpreted in our language that was not at the same time evidence that that form of activity was not speech behaviour' (1974a, p. 185). What justifies this is the theory of content that has emerged through the last three chapters. The Principle of Charity, which assures agreement between interpreter and interpretee, implicitly defines the very notions of meaning, belief and action. Thus, if someone is uninterpretable, there is no basis for the application to him of the concepts of meaning, belief and action (see section 6.6).

Of course, as we have seen, the Principle of Charity is not intended to rule out any possibility of error according to the interpreter, and hence disagreement with him. Davidson's point is that too much disagreement simply undermines the possibility of communication. Some failure to be interpretable may be tolerated, but the more we allow, the more we compromise what makes interpretation possible at all. 'We improve the clarity and bite of declarations of difference, whether of scheme or opinion, by enlarging the basis of shared (translatable) language or of shared opinion' (1974a, p. 197).

8.4   RATIONALIST IDEALISM AND SOME OF ITS PROBLEMS

Davidson regards the dualism of scheme and content as the 'third dogma of empiricism' (the first two being the analytic/synthetic distinction and the dogma of reductionism, rejected by Quine in 'Two Dogmas of Empiricism' of 1951). In rejecting this dogma, along with the first two, Davidson rightly sees that there is nothing distinctively empiricist about his position anymore.

Empiricism, in the sense in which Davidson is rejecting it, is largely a study of the nature of the intermediaries between world and belief, the most common intermediary being 'the mind'. Philosophers like Hume attempted to account for the possession of concepts in terms of sensory experience. This meant identifying the principles which the mind uses to deal with the experience it receives, passively, from the senses. Putative laws, about such things as the association of ideas, laws intended to stand to ideas in the same relation as the Newtonian laws of physics stand to physical phenomena, underpin traditional empiricist epistemology. This tradition led directly to the emergence of psychology, as the study of the laws of the mind, in the hands of the late eighteenth-century disciples of Hume such as David Hartley, Thomas Brown and James Mill.

For all those who continued to subscribe to the dualism of scheme and content, a central task of philosophy has been the study of the intermediary between belief and knowledge on the one hand, and the world on the other. Whether this intermediary was taken as the mind, as language, as scientific theory or as something else, the problems of the philosophy of mind and epistemology have been dictated by this picture.

Against this background, we can see just how radically Davidson has changed philosophy. Epistemology ceases to be the study of some sort of intermediary; in a sense one could say that for Davidson, epistemology is no longer a real issue. We saw, in section 6.4, how in the philosophy of language, Davidson now writes: 'there is no such thing as a language, not if a language is anything like what many philosophers and linguists have supposed' (1986, p. 446). Thus, for the study of linguistic communication, too, the presence of 'a language', as something that mediates between the world and communication about the world, falls away. But the most decisive and explicit revision of the traditional philosophical agenda comes in the philosophy of mind, which ceases to be the study of the nature of mind. The mind, conceived of as a passive receiver of sensory information together with a way of processing that information in terms of concepts or theory, no longer has any place. Davidson replaces the study of the mind with the study of the mental; as he says, 'in my view the mental is not an ontological but a conceptual category' (1987b, p. 46). There is no object or entity, whether material or immaterial, whose nature it is the philosopher's task to study. What Davidson's philosophy of mind recognizes are a purely ideal, normative system: what it is rational to believe, say and do; a physical world, including the biological species of human beings; and, emerging out of these, at the point of contact between the material and the rational ideal, people, beings who have beliefs and desires, utter meaningful sentences and perform intentional actions.

To this view I give the name 'rationalist idealism'. Idealism as a theory about the nature of the world is often associated with just that form of empiricism at which we have been looking. Once it is admitted that between people and the world, there stand sensations or ideas as real mental items, inhabiting the mind, the world itself is in danger of being lost to knowledge. This is why scepticism is such a problem for traditional epistemologists, and why Davidson's dismissal of it seems too easy. If our knowledge of the world is mediated by the mind then how can we justify the claim that what we know is more than what is in our minds? To salvage our claims to knowledge, empiricists such as Berkeley identified the world itself with ideas. The logical positivist programme of reducing empirical sentences to sentences about sensory experience is a similar move.

This kind of idealism is utterly alien to Davidson. He stresses that 'given a correct epistemology, we can be realists in all departments. We can accept objective truth conditions as the key to meaning, a realist view of truth, and we can insist that knowledge is of an objective world independent of our thought or language' (1983, p. 307). But Davidson's realism, in this sense, is secured by his rejection of an empiricist philosophy of mind according to which 'the mind' stands between the world and our knowledge of it. The approach to the mental which replaces it is one in which mental states are constituted directly by the ideal of rationality (the Principle of Charity) and the way the world is (the veridical nature of belief). About *propositional content*, therefore, Davidson is an idealist, since what people actually believe, desire and mean is, at least partly, constituted by what it is ideally rational for them to believe, desire and mean.

In chapter 9 we shall look at this idealist theory of content and compare it with what I shall characterize as a realist theory of content. But for the remainder of this chapter, I want to look at some problems which are internal to Davidson's rationalist idealism.

The first problem is this. Content is partially constituted by considerations of rationality, consistency and coherence. Yet it is also partially constituted by the causal relations between mental states and the world they are about. This is not an internal, normative and holistic consideration. These two features in the theory of content are echoes of the two approaches to truth at which we looked in sections 8.1 and 8.2. In so far as Davidson stresses considerations of rationality, he is following the lead of the coherence theory of truth. This theory's greatest problem was that, if it identified truth with coherence, it severed all links with our intuitions about truth as a connection between beliefs or sentences and the world. This intuition is served better by some form of correspondence theory (though not of the sort advocated by Russell and Wittgenstein), and is catered for in Davidson's theory of content by the claim that an object of a belief is its cause. But the correspondence and coherence theories are traditionally seen as incompatible. How viable, therefore, is Davidson's theory of content?

Consider the following passage by Davidson:

How clear are we that the ancients – some ancients – believed that the earth was flat? *This* earth? Well, this earth of ours is part of the solar system, a system partly identified by the fact that it is a gaggle of large, cool, solid bodies circling around a very large, hot star. If someone believes *none* of this about the earth, is it certain that it is the earth that he is thinking about? (1975, p. 168)

This predates Davidson's growing reliance on the idea that the object of a belief is its cause. What determines the object of a belief here is what other beliefs someone has. The possibility of identifying the object of a belief as this earth is undermined if we cannot also attribute many beliefs about large, hot stars and cool, solid bodies circling them. This recalls David Lewis's ideas about theoretical identification which we looked at in section 6.6. Various sentences or beliefs are taken as defining what it is for something to be the referent of a particular term, 'this earth' for instance. Any object of which (enough of) these other beliefs were not true could not be the referent of the expression 'this earth'.

But, of course, now Davidson thinks that what would make some object the object of a belief is whether that object was the cause of the belief. There is, therefore, a way of saying whether the ancients believed, of this earth, that it was flat, independently of determining what else they believed about the solar system. (McGinn 1977 discusses the quoted passage, criticizing it on just these grounds.)

The difficulty in combining the two positions is this. It is part of the point of holism and normativity that one cannot have too many beliefs that an interpreter considers to be false. 'False beliefs tend to undermine the identification of the subject matter; to undermine, therefore, the validity of a description of the belief as being about that subject' (1975, p. 168). By making the identification of the subject matter of some belief depend on what else is believed, Davidson ensures that interpreter and interpreted cannot have radically different beliefs about the same objects.

Causation, however, is a non-holistic relation between a belief and an object or event. If we hold that what a belief is about is determined by what causes it, we allow the possibility of a gap between what a belief is about, and what else is believed about that thing. It might turn out that a belief is about a certain object, on the grounds that that object is the cause of the belief, and yet what is believed about the object may be false, peculiar and even inconsistent.

The problem is partially mitigated by the realization that for Davidson, what is at issue is not, as it is for the causal theory of reference (section 7.4), a relation which holds between words and objects independently of the knowledge of speakers and interpreters. Davidson's conception is that, in interpretation, the interpreter should interpret beliefs and utterances as being about what he, the interpreter, identifies as their causes in the world. (Perhaps it is misleading to think in terms of causation, a relation which has a scientific, theoretical air to it. Davidson seems to be after a much more primitive relation of contact: we should interpret people as talking and thinking about the objects with which they come into contact.)

But now, of course, the old problem of scepticism is raised again. For, as an interpreter, I can judge someone to be in contact with, or causally related to, various objects; he can judge himself to be in contact with them; and yet we can both be mistaken. As long as we talk only in terms of constraints which can actually be applied by interpreters and speakers, we risk the possibility of massive error. All we can ensure is coherence and consistency, not real correspondence. But if we invoke relations which hold independently of the knowledge of interpreters and speakers, we open up the possibility of a gap between reference and truth, on the one hand, and consistency, agreement and rationality on the other. We also risk making content inscrutable, to ourselves and others, since we may ourselves not have knowledge of the causes of beliefs, and hence not have knowledge of the contents of those beliefs.

This is a very serious problem, and it is one which Davidson has, I believe, insufficiently appreciated. Until quite recently, the emphasis in his work was on coherence and rationality, and the truth that the Principle of Charity spoke of was always taken to be 'truth according to the interpreter'. On the other hand, the rejection of empiricism is largely based on the claim that content is determined directly by the way the world is, thus removing the need for actual intervening states with a distinctively mental nature that affects what content they can have. It is difficult to see, therefore, how this problem can be resolved.

Another problem with rationalist idealism is one which we have already anticipated in section 7.5. Anti-relativism is also anti-historicism. Some forms of historicism are merely temporalized versions of conceptual relativism, and these will present no special difficulties of their own. Thomas Kuhn (1962), for instance, has argued that, in science, theoretical advances are made within a paradigm. At certain junctures, a crisis will be precipitated, and a new paradigm will replace the old one. When this has taken place, it will not necessarily be the case that every sentence which was accepted as true in the first paradigm will have a counterpart in the new paradigm. It is not just that a revision takes place of which sentences are held true, but rather that one paradigm can express propositions which simply have no place in another. Different paradigms are incommensurable.

Paradigms, here, are just another form of conceptual schemes, and Davidson's position with regard to them will be the same. Of course, as science develops and theories change, theoretical terms which are defined by what a theory says about them, terms such as 'mass', 'force' and 'vacuum', will change their meanings. If we ask whether Aristotle believed in the existence of vacuums, we must be careful to distinguish whether we are asking if he believed in vacuums as characterized in our paradigm, or in vacuums as defined by himself. The answers to these questions may well be different. But our very ability to distinguish these two questions shows that we need have no trouble in principle in understanding Aristotle's scientific views. It may be more cumbersome to express them but this is not a case of genuine incommensurability.

But we are forced to recognize that there is another kind of historicism which is not so easily dealt with as this. People acquire a first language, or the ability to deploy a range of concepts, from nothing. Holism means that 'if one or another important part of the system of concepts with which we operate is lopped off, what remains cannot be made intelligible simply as the remainder; we may be quite unable to make sense of the truncated structure. The same point holds for language' (1976c, p. 18). Yet unless we want to maintain, implausibly, that we acquire our language or concepts all in one go, we will surely have to allow that there is some time at which individuals can operate with inferior linguistic or conceptual capabilities. Psychologists such as Piaget have done much work on precisely the question of how and when children acquire the ability to reason logically, and how and when they acquire the concepts of causality, space and time. The existence of 'genetic epistemology' seems to pose a serious threat to Davidson's position.

The problem of language or concept acquisition has its counterpart at the supra-individual level. Although Davidson's anti-relativism precludes our contrasting the conceptual schemes of different historical eras, or of stigmatizing the mentality of savages as somehow 'pre-logical', there is still the question to be asked of how humanity as a whole came to be rational and use language. If one accepts the idea of the evolution of *Homo sapiens* one cannot avoid wondering how a species which evolved from the single-cell amoeba should have acquired rationality. It surely could not have done it in one fell swoop. How could any single evolutionary change mean the difference between non-rationality and rationality? Again, we seem forced to admit that at some stage, the species must have had some, but not all, of its present linguistic and conceptual capabilities.

The ideal of rationality which constitutes mental content is integral, but individuals and the species are, at some points in their histories, imperfect. Both individuals and the species have a childhood. Similarly, the same problem arises for other creatures that we wish to describe as mentally impoverished, idiots and animals, for instance. Members of both these categories may well appear to us to have some beliefs and some desires, and to be able to use a certain amount of language, yet we would hesitate about ascribing to them the full panoply of mental states and meanings, and a complete grasp of reason. (Davidson discusses the question of animal rationality in 1975 and 1982a, and strongly suggests that it is wrong, as a matter of fact, though not principle, to attribute mental states to non-human animals.)

These problems, of the acquisition of language, concepts and rationality, either by the individual or by the species as a whole, are real problems for any theory which, like Davidson's, insists that the identities of concepts are determined by their places in an entire network, since until that network is in place, the parts of it have not assumed their final identities. There is no room for learning piece by piece. This is connected with one of Dummett's criticisms of Davidson's holism (section 7.5). Dummett argued that a theory of meaning must associate with each concept something which would count as knowing that concept. If it did that, then we could account for learning a language; it would simply be the, possibly serial, acquisition of a number of different capacities. But Davidson could only associate one piece of knowledge with a language as a whole.

Davidson goes some way towards answering these problems, but he does not say nearly enough. Concerning the problem of the acquisition of language by the individual, he has written: 'in so far as we take the "organic" [i.e. holistic] character of language seriously, we cannot accurately describe the first steps towards its conquest as learning part of the language; rather it is a matter of partly learning' (1965, p. 7). But it is not altogether clear what this distinction between learning a part of a language and partly learning a language amounts to. For it to do the work Davidson wants it to, it seems that he would have to give the distinction a clear empirical realization, and it is difficult to imagine what this might look like.

More recently, Davidson has suggested a new approach to the question of the mental states of animals and small children. We have seen how Davidson thinks that radical interpretation is necessarily subject to some indeterminacy (section 7.3). He now hints that we might be able to attribute some thought to small children and animals, if we recognize that in doing so, our attributions are subject to much greater indeterminacy than they are for rational adult humans. For instance, for a rational creature, we can sensibly and determinately distinguish between his believing that Jones is home, and his believing that his boss is home, when Jones is his boss. But for Jones's dog we cannot make similar distinctions. There is thus greater indeterminacy in how we characterize the beliefs of Jones's dog. 'The fewer acceptable transformations,' Davidson says, 'the more thought' (1985a, p. 252). This rather tantalizing suggestion has not, to my knowledge, been followed up in detail by Davidson.

Whether or not Davidson can come up with satisfactory solutions for these problems, they force us to realize how *metaphysical* his philosophy is. It is easy to see the problems raised here as providing a straightforward *reductio* of Davidson's views, given that these views developed out of an empiricist, and generally anti-metaphysical tradition, and are often framed in the vocabulary of this tradition. Any theory which has consequences as unacceptable as these, it might be argued, must be false. But in fact, as I have tried to show, Davidson has now stepped entirely outside this empiricist tradition. It is far more useful to see him in the company of Plato (on whom, incidentally, he wrote his doctoral dissertation in 1949), and Hegel, with all their metaphysical baggage, than in the company of the Vienna Circle and Quine, with their austere, anti-metaphysical scientism.

This, of course, does not mean that we should ignore the difficulties that afflict Davidson's holistic approach, nor that we should accept it just because it is metaphysical. But it does help to see the implausible consequences as part of a theory, or worldview, which is, possibly, quite distant from that which we initially expected. Davidson's problems are of a piece with the problems that have always afflicted rationalist idealists such as Plato and Hegel: how can people, as finite, limited and material creatures, participate in the ideal?

9

Realism and Idealism

In the previous chapter, we saw something of the problems facing what I called Davidson's rationalist idealism. This idealism concerned only propositional content, and did not in any way imply the non-existence of an independent material world. In section 9.1, I propose to compare this idealist theory of content with two other theories of content, one realist, and the other more explicitly idealist than Davidson's. I believe that Davidson does not fully accept the consequences of his idealist theory of content because some of his most important philosophical intuitions rely, in fact, on a realist theory of content. There is thus a tension running through his whole work generated by these two conflicting approaches to content. I will then go on, in sections 9.2 to 9.4, to examine three areas in which this tension is most manifest.

9.1   TWO THEORIES OF CONTENT

One of the most fully worked-out versions of 'intentional realism', i.e. realism about propositional content, is the language of thought hypothesis advocated by Jerry Fodor (1975, 1987). Fodor regards propositional attitudes as relations between a person and an internal representation of a proposition. The nature of the relation determines whether the state is one of belief, fear, hope, etc.; the internal representation determines the content of the state. Internal representations, which in human beings are states of the brain, are syntactically and semantically structured. A representation *that Will is happy* will be composed of components which represent Will and being happy. These components can enter into other representations, such as *that Will is tall*, and *that Mary is happy*.

Our thoughts are thus constituted like a language; internal representations are like sentences of a language, we can call it Mentalese, that has its own syntax and semantics. Sentences of the natural languages that people speak gain their contents by their associations with the sentences of Mentalese which they are used to express. If sentences of English have their contents determined by sentences of Mentalese, the question obviously arises, how do sentences of Mentalese have their contents determined? If a brain state is a representation *that Will is happy*, what makes it have just that content, rather than some other content?

Davidson's idealism is a consequence of his semantic holism. Intentional realism, therefore, must reject holism and treat the semantics of Mentalese as atomistic (see section 7.4). If a representation has the content *that Will is happy*, then the components out of which it is composed, representing Will and being happy, must have their contents determined by some real and independent semantic property. Our question therefore becomes, how do Mentalese words get their meanings? Fodor offers a causal theory to answer this. A type of brain state is a representation with the content *is happy* if and only if instances of it are regularly caused to occur by things that are happy, and are not regularly caused to occur by things that are not happy. (This requires considerable elaboration to avoid various counter-examples. See Fodor 1987, pp. 97–127.)

Given the importance that we have seen causation has for Davidson's theory of content, we should stress the differences between the way it works for Davidson and for Fodor. There are two main differences. First, for Davidson, causation relates external circumstances to entire beliefs or sentences, and not to the words or concepts that comprise them. But secondly, and more importantly, Davidson takes causation to determine the contents of individual mental states, mental state-tokens, and not mental state-types. For Fodor, on the other hand, there is meant to be a correlation between a type of brain state and its typical cause which makes any token of that state-type a token with a content that represents that cause.

This second feature, the ascription of content to state-types, explains why Fodor sees his view on content as the foundation of a science of the mental. As he says:

Mental representations do two jobs in theories that employ them. First, they provide a canonical notation for specifying the intentional contents of mental states. But second, mental symbols constitute domains over which *mental processes* are defined. If you think of a mental process – extensionally, as it were – as a sequence of mental states each specified with reference to its intentional content, then mental representations provide a mechanism for the construction of these sequences; they allow you to get, in a mechanical way, from one such state to the next *by performing operations on the representations.* (Fodor 1987, p. 145)

In other words, Fodor envisages psychological laws, laws which relate mental state-types, described in terms of their contents, to each other. (It was Fodor's criticism of Davidson's arguments against the possibility of psychological laws that we looked at in section 1.4.)

Since principles of rationality relate mental states to each other, Fodor's view implies that these principles will themselves be naturalized, or taken as empirical, psychological laws. Fodor thus hopes for a naturalized theory of rationality. For instance, he holds that what makes it true that mental states cause actions for which they are *reasons* is that 'there are true, contingent generalizations which relate mental state *types* in virtue of their contents' (Fodor 1978, p. 183). If these generalizations are contingent, then there is no logical reason why they might not hold. Were they not to hold, people's actions might regularly be caused by mental states which were not reasons for them, and mental states might be related to each other in non-rational ways. This complete failure to be related rationally would not, for Fodor, impugn the fact that these states still had propositional content.

It is just this kind of bizarre possibility that Davidson's approach rules out. He stresses that to have propositional attitudes at all is to be more or less rational. There is no possibility that, as a general rule, people's actions or mental states should be related to other mental states to which they were not rationally related. Rationality is not naturalized (that is, there are no psychological laws in the way in which there are laws of physics) and, by continuing to act normatively in the very constitution of propositional content, rationality constraints prevent the possiblity that mental states could ever, by and large, be related in non-rational ways.

The price that Davidson pays for sustaining this strong position for rationality is that he cannot see psychology as a science, in the way Fodor does. Correlatively, the price Fodor pays for being able to see psychology as a science is that he is unable to account for the strong normative force considerations of rationality have with us (see Evnine 1989b, pp. 11–18).

Daniel Dennett (1978, 1987) has developed an approach to content which is the antithesis of Fodor's. Dennett is concerned with our attempts to explain and, especially, predict the behaviour of things. He identifies three stances we can adopt in doing this and uses the example of a chess-playing computer to illustrate them. Suppose we want to anticipate the computer's next move. One way we could do this is to trace the progress of input, in the form of electrical charges, through the cicuitry of the computer's insides, until it ends up as the activation of certain lights on the screen, or characters of a printer. We will have made no use of the concept of representation or content, but will have treated the computer purely as a physical mechanism. This method would, in principle, yield entirely correct predictions (assuming the determinacy of physical processes). The disadvantage with it is that it would be unbelievably complicated to use, even in the very simplest cases. When one thinks about employing this method in the case of the prediction of human action, it is clear that, at our present state of knowledge, it is at the very best only a theoretical possibility.

But there are other ways of attempting to predict the computer's behaviour besides this mechanistic stance. We can adopt what Dennett calls the design stance. Here, we use our knowledge of how the computer has been programmed to make chess moves. A programme, for instance, might work by assigning values to the different pieces, which are then weighted by their positions relative to other pieces, and so on. A total value can then be computed for each of the different possible states of the board that can be reached after permissible moves. The computer selects the move which would yield the highest value.

If we knew the programme the computer was designed to perform, we could predict its moves on the same basis. We could go through just the processes described and thus anticipate what the computer will do. This is clearly much less cumbersome than the mechanistic stance but the increased elegance is bought at the price of greater fallibility. In order to use the design stance, we have to *assume* that the computer will actually do what it is designed, or programmed, to do. This assumption may be unwarranted if, for instance, someone has just spilled some coffee in the machine, or if one of the electrical components has short-circuited. Various possibilities, having nothing to do with questions of programme, can prevent something from doing what it is designed to do. They would not present a problem for the mechanistic stance since there, we are using a level which employs no normative assumptions about what ought to happen. We explain or predict on the basis of what is there, coffee and all.

By making even stronger assumptions about something's functioning, we can gain even simpler and more compact methods of dealing with it. Dennett describes the final position we can adopt as the intentional stance. Here, we assume that the computer will make the move that it is rational to make, the best move it can given its information. We can then predict its behaviour by deciding what is the rational move for it to make. This, of course, is how we work in a game with an expert chess player. We look at the board and think what our opponent ought to do and predict that he will do that. We need not make any assumptions about how a computer is programmed to find the rational move, much less about the mechanical or electronic apparatus that implements the programme. The attendant dangers of the intentional stance are equally great, however, since now there is not only the possibility that the mechanism will fail to implement the programme, through spilled coffee or whatever, but also the possibility that the programme will be inadequate to find the best move for the computer. That is, although the computer may do what it is supposed to, what it is supposed to do may not be what it is best for it to do, if it is to win the game; whether it is will depend on the success of the programme. But as long as we are willing to assume that the mechanism is in order, and the programme is adequate, assuming that the computer is rational will prove the easiest way of predicting its moves.

Dennett thinks that, in attributing beliefs and desires to people, we are adopting the intentional stance with respect to them. We assume that people will do, believe and desire what they ought, given their natures and their perceptual capabilities, to do, believe and desire. Generally, these assumptions are warranted, since the intentional stance is usually successful. Attributing beliefs and desires, states which have rational, normative connections to each other and to action, is a good strategy for explaining and predicting human behaviour. But sometimes, for various reasons, people's behaviour cannot be explained or predicted well on the basis of attributions of rational mental states, and in these cases explanation and prediction will be more successful if we can drop to the design or mechanical stance. For instance, when we explain an aphasic's speech on the basis of lesions in the brain rather than on the basis of the subject's beliefs, we are adopting the mechanistic stance.

Dennett's views have much in common with Davidson's. For both, intentional states like beliefs and desires are only applicable given the assumption of rationality; and the contents of these states are constituted by the ideal of what contents would be rational. Although beliefs and the rest are seen as semantically complex, in that their contents depend on the contents of their parts, which in turn can combine in infinitely many ways to form new beliefs, neither Dennett nor Davidson agrees with Fodor that this complexity is accounted for by brain states which are themselves composed out of semantically representational parts. Semantic complexity is a feature of our semantic descriptions and not of the actual states we are describing.

There are, however, differences between Davidson and Dennett. Although Dennett shares with Davidson a general commitment to physicalism as an ontological thesis, he does not think that this requires that we identify mental, intentional states, with physical states. 'If we are to have identity,' he writes, 'it will have to be something like Davidson's "anomalous monism". But what ontic house-cleaning would be accomplished by identifying each and every intentionally characterized "state" or "event" in a system with some particular physical state or event of its parts?' (Dennett 1978, p. 28). One reason Dennett gives for being reluctant to identify each intentional state with a physical state is that there is no saying 'how many *different* intentional states to ascribe to [a] system . . . Is the state of believing that 100<101 distinct from the state of believing that 100<102, and if so, should we then expect to find distinct physical states of the system to ally with each?' (Dennett 1978, p. 28).

Dennett does not think that the refusal to identify each and every intentionally characterized event with a physical event will lead to ontological dualism. But the only way it can not lead to dualism is if the intentional events are somehow not real events. In explanation of this position, he writes:

> Folk psychology is *abstract* in that the beliefs and desires it attributes are not – or need not be – presumed to be intervening distinguishable states of an internal behavior-causing system . . . The role of the concept of belief is like the role of the concept of a center of gravity, and the calculations that yield the predictions are more like the calculations one performs with a parallelogram of forces than like the calculations one performs with a blueprint of internal levers and cogs . . . Reichenbach distinguished between two sorts of referents for theoretical terms: *illata* – posited theoretical entities – and *abstracta* – calculation-bound entities or logical constructs. Beliefs and desires of folk psychology . . . are *abstracta*. (1981a, pp. 52–3)

Dennett's views on these matters spring from premises which are similar to Davidson's, premises about the relations between mental states and rationality. But Davidson resists the idea that mental states are calculation-bound entities, or logical constructs. Indeed, his causal theory of action and anomalous monism require that he treats beliefs and so on as 'intervening distinguishable states in an internal behavior-causing system'. The question therefore arises, are these two parts of Davidson's theory consistent with the idealist theory of content that stems from his views on holism and the Principle of Charity? Or do they rely implicitly on a realist theory of content? In the following three sections we shall look at problems in Davidson's philosophy which arise from the conflict of these two approaches to content.

9.2   CAUSATION AND CONTENT

The reasons why Davidson insists on identifying mental events with physical events are two. First, failure to do so makes it difficult to explain what it is to act for a reason. Secondly, and relatedly, it makes it difficult to show how the mental is dependent on the physical.

In section 3.2 we saw that Davidson wanted to explain what it is to act for a reason, rather than merely act and have a reason for that act. He identified (non-deviant) causation as the salient factor. When one acts for some reason, that reason must cause the action for which it is a reason. This clearly requires that reasons, i.e. intentional mental states, are 'intervening distinguishable states of an internal behavior-causing system'.

If a reason causes an action then there is some law that these events instantiate, but the anomalism of the mental means that there are no laws which are instantiated by events under mental descriptions. The law which a reason and action instantiate will therefore be a physical law and the reason and action will instantiate it under physical descriptions.

An event instantiates a law by virtue of various of its properties. If a law says that any *A*-type event is followed by a *B*-type event, then an event will instantiate it because it is *A*. We can call the properties by virtue of which an event instantiates a causal law its causally relevant properties. The anomalism of the mental entails that no mental properties can be causally relevant. Since for an event to have what propositional content it does is a mental property, this means that when beliefs and desires cause actions, their being just the beliefs and desires they are, rather than states with some other content, is causally irrelevant. They cannot cause what actions they cause *because* they have the content they do, since all their causally relevant properties are physical. This in itself does not mean mental events cannot be causes of actions. But it does mean that there is no connection between their having what causal powers they do and their having what propositional content they do. (Arguments similar to this can be found in Honderich 1982; Stoutland 1985; Antony 1989.)

In this light, we can also understand the problems that beset Davidson in trying to defend the supervenience of the mental on the physical (section 4.3). The rather aimless position that one gets by combining the thesis that reasons cause actions with the admission that the mental properties of states are not causally relevant, is just what one gets if one advocates anomalous monism without supervenience. Anomalous monism ensures that each mental state is identical to some physical state. Hence, each mental state is capable of standing in causal relations. But the mental properties a state possesses are unconstrained by anomalous monism itself, since anomalous monism is consistent with the possibility that two creatures could be exact physical replicas but differ with respect to which mental states they had. This means that if some mental state causes some other state, it cannot be because of its mental content.

In section 4.3, I asked why Davidson held the supervenience thesis. The answer, I believe, is because without it, the mental is obviously causally irrelevant. Causal relevance of the mental is not ensured by the ontological materialism of anomalous monism alone. But we saw that supervenience was not as straightforward as it seemed. It is impossible satisfactorily to reinstate the causal relevance of the mental while at the same time holding onto the anomalism of the mental. For supervenience to be plausible, one has to limit the properties upon which a mental property supervenes to properties which are themselves causally relevant, since otherwise, mere difference in the length of eye-lashes could be the *only* physical difference between two creatures with different mental states. However, in order to say which physical properties are causally relevant to some mental property, we have to have some way of saying which other physical and psychological properties the given mental state is connected with. This can only be done by supposing that there are, after all, some sorts of psychophysical and psychological laws, systematic ways of determining what other kinds of events a given kind of mental event will cause.

These laws or generalizations would also provide an answer to the problem that faces the causal theory of action. If there were laws or generalizations which related types of mental events, then the properties by virtue of which an event instantiated them would be mental, and, in some sense to be determined, causally relevant.

Thus, the causal theory of action and anomalous monism would both be better served by a theory in which mental properties were causally relevant, or nomologically connected to causally relevant properties. This was the position of Fodor's 'intentional realism'. Fodor held, it will be remembered, that 'there are true, contingent generalizations which relate mental state *types* in virtue of their contents' (Fodor 1978, p. 183). He held, in other words, that there are psychological laws and, hence, that mental properties can be causally relevant.

It is therefore interesting to note that Davidson himself takes some steps in this direction, as a response to the difficulties which I have been urging. When we looked at his views on the dispositional nature of mental events described in terms of content (section 3.4), we saw that he was prepared to allow that dispositional statements were psychological laws, only different in kind from physical laws in that they inevitably could never be made precise, or formulated without *ceteris paribus* clauses. The criticism that on Davidson's view, mental properties must be causally irrelevant, fails, he says, to note:

> the difference between events described in terms that allow the application of laws without *ceteris paribus* clauses, laws that make no use of causal tendencies, potentialities or dispositions, and laws that, by using such devices, allow us to choose what we call the cause according to our special explanatory interests . . . Explanation in terms of the ultimate physics, though it answers to various interests,

is not interest relative: it treats everything without exception as a cause of an event if it lies within physical reach . . . Special sciences, or explanatory schemes, take note of more or less precise correlations between effects of certain kinds and far more limited causes of certain kinds. These correlations, of the sort we find in economics, geology, biology, aerodynamics and the explanation of action, depend on assumptions about other things being more or less equal – assumptions that cannot be made precise . . . [D]epending on the sort of explanation we are interested in, different properties of events are treated as causally efficacious. But, interest aside, every property of every event is causally efficacious. (1987b, pp. 45–6)

There are several things one might be unhappy about in Davidson's answer. First, why should the ultimate physics treat every event as a cause of another if it lies within physical reach? Secondly, even if it did, this would not support the claim that every property of every event is causally efficacious, and this latter claim seems palpably false. If the motion of one atom causes the motion of another, the property of the first motion of being thought of by me is certainly not causally efficacious. Davidson may mean to include only every intrinsic property; this would exclude the property of being thought of by me. But it is not clear that the distinction between extrinsic and intrinsic properties can be made wholly independently of the distinction between causally efficacious and inefficacious properties.

The passage also gives the impression that Davidson now takes psychology to be one of the special sciences, along with geology and the rest. Although he goes on, after the quoted extract, to differentiate psychology from the other special sciences on the grounds of the role of normative principles in psychology, he does not indicate that this undermines the way in which he uses psychological generalizations to rebut the objection of the causal irrelevance of the mental. The generalizations of the special sciences are not, in principle, unconnected to the laws of physics. The properties with which they deal are not separated from the properties of which physics treats by a qualitative leap, in the way in which normative, psychological properties are.

As we saw in section 1.4, the generalizations of the special sciences are vague for epistemological reasons; there is often no way, within the language of one special science, of subsuming all the ways in which its generalizations can be violated. But there is, none the less, some underlying geological, or biological, reality to which the generalizations strive to be adequate. By contrast, psychological generalizations are vague because the mental is inherently holistic and normative. There is no underlying, mental reality of which the vague generalizations are shadows and whose laws we could formulate precisely if only the mental were not acted upon by the non-mental. The mental is constitutionally anomalous. Accordingly, it is difficult to see how psychological generalizations can make mental properties causally relevant. There will always be precise physical laws which mental events instantiate under physical descriptions, and whatever mental generalizations they instantiate through their mental properties will be totally unconnectable, as the generalizations of the other special sciences are *not*, with the underlying laws of physics.

The idealist theory of content, with the anomalism of the mental and the Principle of Charity at its centre, thus works against the causal theory of action. It does not entail the falsity of the claim that reasons cause actions, but it does mean that we cannot say that a reason causes an action for which it is a reason because the mental states which constitute the reason have the propositional contents they do. And given this lacuna, it becomes doubtful how attractive the thesis is that reasons cause actions at all. This latter thesis, in turn, was supposed to provide the motivation for identifying mental states with physical states, rather than seeing them as calculation-bound entities, or logical constructs, in the way that Dennett described and that Davidson's work on radical interpretation encourages.

Conversely, as we have seen in this section and in section 3.4, to the extent that Davidson wants to hold onto the claims that reason explanation is a form of causal explanation, and that the mental is supervenient on the physical, he begins to talk, first of psychophysical and psychological generalizations, and ultimately of laws. Even though these are still distinguished from physical laws by their vague and qualified nature, it is clear that pressure is being placed on the anomalism of the mental by both supervenience and the thesis that reason explanation is a form of causal explanation.

9.3   KNOWING ONE'S OWN MIND

Let us now turn to another area in which the tension between realism and idealism about content comes to the fore in Davidson's work. Realism not only sees beliefs and desires as real, causally efficacious states, but also treats their contents as causally relevant. This encourages the view that there exist propositional objects, the objects of belief and desire. For Fodor, the propositional object of a belief such as the belief that snow is white is a brain state of the person which, in the language of thought, means that snow is white. The person will stand in one relation to this propositional object if he believes that snow is white, and in a different relation to the same object, if he hopes that snow is white. For Fodor, propositional objects exist in a very real sense.

With this intentional realism goes a particular epistemology. The mind is seen as a kind of theatre, or container, in which propositional objects, the objects of beliefs, desires and so on, parade and perform before some internal spectator (the mind's eye). We thus know what mental states we are in by coming into contact with the relevant propositional objects. We deploy our 'inner sense' to survey our mental landscapes, just as we use our outer senses to view the external world.

Davidson's idealism, on the other hand, treats beliefs and desires as theoretical constructs. This does not mean that people do not genuinely have beliefs. 'Of course people have beliefs, wishes, doubts, and so forth; but to allow this is not to suggest that beliefs, wishes and doubts are *entities* in or before the mind, or that being in such states requires there to be corresponding mental objects' (1987a, p. 454). What is having a belief if it is not standing in some relation to a propositional object? It is behaving, and being situated in your environment, in such a way that the Principle of Charity requires that you be interpreted as having such a belief.

Each of these two views, the realist and idealist, appears to pose its own epistemological problem. For the realist, the apparent problem is this. If beliefs are objects which exist in people's minds, then there should be no special difficulty in seeing how people know what beliefs they have themselves. But it will require some explanation how they know what beliefs other people have. What access can one person have to the propositional objects that inhabit another's mind? Thus, with regard to content, the traditional sceptical problem, predicated on the assumption of intentional realism, has always been the so-called problem of other minds.

For idealism, the apparent problem is the converse of this. The notion of contentful mental states has been developed as part of a theory which we apply to people to make sense of them. This seems most plausible when one considers somebody else, and asks in virtue of what he believes what he does. But when one thinks of one's own case, the idea that beliefs and the rest are part of a theory applied to make sense of one seems wrong. Our own beliefs seem to have an immediacy for us which makes us think they must have some real presence.

It is implausible to deny that each person knows better what he believes than what others believe. But this fact is not easily accommodated by an idealist theory of content. Forerunners of Davidson in rejecting the 'objects of thought' view of the mind, such as Ryle, were prepared to bite the bullet and maintain that we only know about our own beliefs with such authority because we know in much greater detail the behaviour which, on Ryle's view, constitutes those beliefs. For Ryle, we find out about ourselves in the same way as we find out about others, but we happen to be particularly well-placed to observe ourselves. (This is also the view of some contemporary psychologists.) But this amounts simply to denying that we do have special authority about our own mental states, and

Davidson does not want to deny this. If the epistemological problem for the intentional realist was the knowledge of other minds, the stumbling block for idealism is the knowledge of our own minds.

Davidson suggests that both the realist's ability and the idealist's inability to deal with knowledge of one's own mind are spurious. With respect to the realist claim that knowledge of our own mental states is transparent, he claims that 'if to have a thought is to have an object "before the mind", and the identity of the object determines what the thought is, then it must always be possible to be mistaken about what one is thinking. For unless one knows *everything* about the object, there will always be senses in which one does not know what object it is' (1987a, p. 455). This fails to take into account the fact that, for those who consider that thoughts are objects before the mind, such objects are considered to be precisely such that one could know everything about them. This is just what is special about propositional as opposed to ordinary objects. However, recognition of this only makes the realist view more implausible, since the nature of such transparent objects is a mystery.

With regard to the apparent problem for idealism, Davidson thinks he can explain why we know our own thoughts with an authority that is lacking in the case of others. Indeed, he goes so far as to say that his idealism is the best way to explain this fact. The explanation is as follows. Suppose Rebecca utters the sentence 'your camels are thirsty.' She and we all know that, if she is making an assertion, then her belief is whatever the sentence 'your camels are thirsty' means. If we can interpret the sentence, we can know what her belief is. The difference between her and us is that she, unlike us, does not have to interpret what her sentence means. Davidson writes:

> There can be no general guarantee that a hearer is correctly interpreting a speaker; however easily, automatically, unreflectively and successfully a hearer understands a speaker, he is liable to general and serious error. In this special sense, he may always be regarded as interpreting a speaker. The speaker cannot, in the same way, interpret his own words ... Neither speaker nor hearer knows in a special or mysterious way what the speaker's words mean; and both can be wrong. But there is a difference. The speaker, after bending whatever knowledge and craft he can to the task of saying what his words mean, cannot improve on the following sort of statement: 'My utterance of "Wagner died happy" is true if and only if Wagner died happy.' An interpreter has no reason to assume this will be *his* best way of stating the truth conditions of the speaker's utterance. (1984c, pp. 110–11)

It must be said that it is highly doubtful whether this approach represents a viable way of meeting the requirements that Davidson has imposed on himself, of accounting for the special authority we have about our own mental states within the context of his idealist theory of content. First we should notice that Davidson has indeed argued that there is a guarantee that an interpreter, in general, can correctly understand a speaker – that an interpreter can do this was the main argument against the possibility of scepticism (section 8.2).

But a more serious flaw in Davidson's account of first-person authority is this. The theory of content which does away with beliefs as objects of thought, and which Davidson, for the sake of consistency, must apply to the first-person case, is a theory not only of the meanings of utterances but of the contents of mental states as well. The content of what a speaker knows when he knows what his words mean is therefore also something which is determined by that theory of content. Davidson is seeking to explain a speaker's authority about what he believes by invoking another fact of the same kind, what the speaker knows (about what his words mean). But the question then arises, what determines the content of the speaker's knowledge, and is he authoritative with respect to that? If so, how?

It is of no use for Davidson to say that a speaker always knows that the truth conditions of his sentences can be given by using those sentences themselves, whereas an interpreter cannot. The reason why, in general, a homophonic theorem of a truth theory, such as ' "is bald" is satisfied by something if and only if it is bald' is not trivial is that it 'states an eminently learnable and forgettable relation between an English word and a set of men' (Evans and McDowell 1976, p. xi). But in so far as one can always give a homophonic T-sentence for any sentence of one's own, one is not stating a learnable and forgettable relation between a piece of language and something in the world. Thus, suppose I have forgotten the meaning of the word 'freebooter'. I can still say ' "Morgan was a freebooter" ' is true if and only if Morgan was a freebooter,' but I do not thereby remind myself of what 'freebooter' means. If I uttered the sentence 'Morgan was a freebooter' I would, consequently, be unable to interpret what I had said, even though I could give a T-sentence for it. (See Donnellan 1977, pp. 23–5 for an interesting discussion of some related issues.)

What all this amounts to is that if we are to apply the idealist theory of content to the first-person case, then even in our own cases thoughts and beliefs are theoretical constructs, or calculation-bound abstract entities, and we must give up the idea that people have some special knowledge about their own mental states. Like Ryle, we would have to say that whatever authority we have about our own mental states derives merely from the fact that we are so much better placed to observe ourselves than we are to observe other people.

In this context, we should remember the argument about the omniscient interpreter in section 8.2. One of the premises of this argument, designed to show the impossibility of massive error in our beliefs, was that we must be interpretable by an omniscient interpreter. Our conviction that we must rests on the immediacy which our mental states have to us. But if Davidson's idealist theory of content applies to the contents of one's own mental states, then this conviction must be abandoned. Whether we are interpretable will depend on whether our behaviour can be described in the rational ways demanded by the Principle of Charity. How things seem with us will be no assurance that we do indeed have beliefs and desires. Some philosophers treat this as a *reductio* of the view of content which leads to it (for instance, Searle 1987). But whether or not we take this attitude, we should note that Davidson's own theory of content, if applied to the first person case, threatens to undermine his argument against the possibility of scepticism.

To the degree that we want to hang on to the idea that we do have a special authority about our own mental states, we must give up the application of the idealist theory of content to the first person case and offer some other theory about how one's own mental states have their contents constituted. We would have to become realists about our own mental content, while being idealists about the contents of other people's mental states. Such asymmetry would be a serious weakness for any theory.[1]

9.4   IRRATIONALITY

We come now to the last example of a tension between realist and idealist approaches to content within Davidson's philosophy. Davidson has devoted much attention to the problem of irrationality. That he should have to do so is, perhaps, obvious on reflection. The idealist approach to content seeks to show how what people really believe, desire, mean and do is constituted by what it is rational for them to believe, desire, mean and do. This penetration of the real by the ideal is what gives the theory its greatest asset, an explanation of the importance of rationality to rational creatures. But it also raises a big question, since people are clearly not optimally rational. How are we to account for all those cases where people fail to conform to the standards required by the Principle of Charity, cases where they act against their better judgement, or hold inconsistent beliefs? Indeed, how can we even allow that such cases exist?

Davidson takes it as a datum that such cases of irrationality do exist. The problem he faces is how to account for this within the context of his idealist theory of content and, just as with the question of first person authority, I shall suggest that his account is at odds with this theory of content. I shall concentrate on the case of irrational action, though what I say could be applied to irrationally held beliefs as well.

An example of the kind of irrational action which we are considering is as follows. I have been told to lose weight by my doctor. After an already splendid dinner, a friend offers me some baked alaska. An assessment of all the relevant pros and cons leads me to conclude that I should not have any dessert. Yet having reached this all-things considered judgement, I deliberately eat the baked alaska.

There are two ways one could redescribe this case to avoid the imputation of irrationality. First, one could say that since my better judgement was against eating the dessert, it must have been the case that when I ate it, I was temporarily overcome by passion or desire. Reason was set aside. This would, of course, cast doubt on the description of what I did as an action since an action is intentional under some description, and to be an intentional action, according to Davidson, an event must be caused by something which is a reason for it. Davidson insists, however, that many cases of irrational action are not like this. I need not be overcome by passion to eat the baked alaska, and my action of eating it is done for a reason, namely, that I desire to eat the baked alaska.

The other way of avoiding the imputation of irrationality is the converse of this. Since I perform the intentional action of eating the dessert, it cannot be that I really judged it best all things considered not to eat it. My very action shows that what we took to be the all-things considered judgement did not, in fact, take everything into account. Here, the performance of an intentional action is taken as a sufficient condition for the presence of an all-things considered judgement in favour of that action. Davidson calls this the Plato Principle because it holds, as Plato's Socrates did, that we never intentionally act against our better judgement. This diagnosis is encouraged by the Principle of Charity which includes the Principle of Continence, a principle which tells the rational man always to do what, all things considered, he thinks it best to do. Davidson's refusal to diagnose the case in this way, the way which is suggested by his own theory of content, is what makes apparent irrationality a problem for him.

Given Davidson's insistence that the case of the baked alaska should not be redescribed in either of these ways, it might seem as if the agent of the irrational action must be credited with contradictory judgements about what he ought to do. On the one hand, I judge it best to refrain from eating; on the other, I perform the intentional action of eating, and therefore must judge in favour of eating. The first stage in Davidson's account of irrationality, therefore, is to use the structure of practical reason which we developed in section 3.5 to show how the agent of an irrational act is not implicitly holding contradictory judgements about what he should do (see 1969b). The judgement that I ought not to eat the dessert is my best, all-things considered judgement, the outcome of my practical reasoning. As such, it has the form of a prima facie judgement: eating the baked alaska is not desirable, *in so far* as R, where R represents all those things which are considered. As a relative judgement (albeit relative to all relevant considerations) it does not logically contradict the all-out, or un-conditional, judgement which I must have in favour of eating the dessert if I eat it intentionally. This judgement has the form: eating the baked alaska is desirable. The two judgements, the all-things considered, relative judgement, and the all-out, unconditional judgement, have different log-ical forms. But this rather technical solution still leaves the problem of why, given that one has reached an all-things considered judgement against some course of action, one should none the less intentionally take that course of action?

There are three elements in the story of the baked alaska. First, there is a piece of practical reasoning which takes into account my desire for the dessert, my health, my doctor's advice, my present weight and so on. This results in the prima facie, all-things considered judgement against eating the baked alaska. Secondly, there is another piece of reasoning which goes from my wanting the dessert to my intention to eat it, and ultimately my action of eating it. Davidson's account of practical reasoning shows how the judgements involved in these two elements are not logically contradic-tory. We can therefore describe someone as acting irrationally without having to represent him as a mere logical blunderer. But how is the agent in this case irrational, if he does not, after all, hold contradictory judge-ments here?

What makes the case one of irrationality is the presence of the third element. This is the Principle of Continence, a principle which, as a ratio-nal man, I accept. It tells me that I should always perform that action which I consider it best to perform, all-things considered. It thus links prima facie, all-things considered judgements on the one hand, with all-out judgements, intentions and actions on the other hand. Once we take this principle into account, the question, why I eat the dessert, can be seen as the question, why is the Principle of Continence not operative on this occasion? Why do I fail to make the transition between prima facie judge-ment and all-out judgement that it requires? Davidson's answer is that my desire to eat the dessert acts as a cause which suppresses the operation of the Principle of Continence but without being a reason against the Principle.

Davidson illuminates this idea with the case of irrationally held beliefs. If I desire that I appear glamorous, then, in a sense, that is a reason for believing that I appear glamorous – the belief will satisfy my desire. But although the desire may thus be a reason to hold the belief, it is not a reason for the belief. It does not support the truth of the belief. Hence, if it causes me to hold the belief, I will hold it irrationally. In the same way, my desire to eat the baked alaska is, in some sense, a reason for ignoring the Principle of Continence, since if I ignore it, I will satisfy the desire. But my desire does not make my setting aside the Principle a rational thing to do, and hence, if it causes me to ignore the Principle, and eat the dessert, my action is irrational.

What is irrational is not that I have no good reason for my action, for I do have a good reason, namely, that I want to eat the alaska; what is irrational is that I suppress the operation of the Principle which connects prima facie, all-things considered judgements with intentions and actions, and that this suppression is caused by a desire which does not make the suppression rational. This account allows us to see how the action is both irrational and, at the same time, done for a reason (indeed, the reason is even a good reason).

Davidson, however, sees that his account raises problems when taken in conjunction with his idealist theory of content. In the following passage, the cause referred to would be the desire to eat the dessert, and the effect, the ignoring of the Principle of Continence.

> If we think of the cause in a neutral mode, disregarding its status as a belief or other attitude – if we think of it merely as a force that works on the mind without being identified as part of it – then we fail to explain, or even describe, irrationality. Blind forces are in the category of the non-rational, not the irrational. So, we introduce a mental description of the cause, which thus makes it a candidate for being a reason. But we still remain outside the only clear pattern of explanation that applies to the mental, for that pattern demands that the cause be more than a candidate for being a reason; it must *be* a reason, which in the present case it cannot be. (1982b, p. 299)

This is a difficult passage but it is important to understand it. If the events or states which stand in the causal relation are given descriptions, like neurophysiological descriptions, that do not attribute propositional content to them, then the case will appear as neither rational nor irrational, since only events under mental descriptions can be rational or irrational. If we want to reveal the irrationality of the case, we must supply mental descriptions for the events involved. However, when we give mental descriptions, the Principle of Charity, which governs 'the only clear pattern of explanation that applies to the mental', requires that the descriptions of the events are related in rational, coherent and consistent ways. The idealist theory of content requires that intentional descriptions of events are related rationally, while the account of irrationality requires that we be able to see mental events, described as such, related in ways which contravene the Principle of Charity.

Davidson's account of irrationality thus requires that we can describe events as mental, but in ways which do not conform to the Principle of

Charity. The contents of the mental events, the mental descriptions which are true of them, must be determined in ways other than their places in a normatively governed holistic network. Content must be able to be divorced from considerations of rationality. In other words, the account of irrationality conflicts with an idealist theory of content.

Davidson attempts to mitigate the problem that the Principle of Charity militates against ascribing to someone the necessary mental states to see him as irrational by invoking the idea of partitions within the mind. Each part would be defined as an area in which the Principle of Charity does apply, and mental states are related in the rational ways they should be. But a mental state from one part can causally interact with a mental state from another part without being rationally connected to it. But Davidson recognizes that 'there is no question but that the precept of unavoidable charity in interpretation is opposed to the partitioning of the mind. For the point of partitioning was to allow inconsistent or conflicting beliefs and desires and feelings to exist in the same mind, while the basic methodology of all interpretation tells us that inconsistency breeds unintelligibility' (1982b, p. 303).

In any case, it is doubtful whether partitioning improves the acceptability of non-rational mental causation. Davidson admits that the picture he has of partitions is one of 'overlapping territories'. Particular beliefs or desires can exist in more than one partition without appearing twice over (without 'double registration' to use Freud's term). Given this, the only thing in virtue of which two mental states are in different parts of one mind is their standing in the relation of non-rational causation. Nothing is added to or subtracted from the original, unpalatable conflict between non-rational mental causation and the Principle of Charity by the idea of partitioning.

It may be suggested that with partitions, we can at least rescue the Principle of Charity to some extent by holding that it continues to reign supreme within each partition, although not across partitions. But in fact, this is simply equivalent to saying that, without partitions, the Principle holds partially, in that it governs large chunks of a person's mental states, but does not govern them all. Whether we introduce partitioning or not, Davidson's account of irrationality encroaches on the hegemony of the Principle of Charity.

What ought to be the attitude to irrationality of someone who unequivocally held an idealist theory of content? Dennett writes, of a case in which someone makes a mistake in a simple calculation, that 'we must descend from the level of beliefs and desires to some other level of theory to describe his mistake, since no account in terms of his beliefs and desires will make sense completely. At some point our account will have to cope with the sheer senselessness of the transition in any error' (1981b, p. 87). This applies to irrationality as well. If beliefs and desires are constituted by normative standards of correctness and rationality, as Davidson holds, then failure to be rationally explainable at the level of beliefs and desires must mean failure to be explainable at that level at all. We must, as Dennett says, descend to a non-rational level (i.e. a level which does not involve intentional mental states) to explain, or even describe, what happens. (See Evnine 1989a, pp. 93–9 and 1989b, pp. 11–18 for a more positive account of Davidson's troubles in this area.)

Conclusion:

Davidson's Two Projects

We have now concluded our examination of the various parts of Davidson's philosophy. I have tried to emphasize the systematic interconnections between these parts, and to show something of the many ways the parts fit together. In pursuing a philosophical system, Davidson is in a minority among philosophers. David Lewis has written: 'I should have liked to be a piecemeal, unsystematic philosopher, offering independent proposals on a variety of topics' (1983, p. ix). Although Lewis admits the failure of this wish, its expression is indicative of the current disfavour in which systematic philosophy stands in many quarters. It is often felt that systems are to philosophical intuitions as steam-rollers may be to eggs.

Davidson's system does, as we have seen, sometimes have counterintuitive consequences. That the sentence 'Ferdinand married Christine' is really a quantification over events; that psychology cannot be made a precise science; that no one can be considered as having any beliefs at all, if they cannot be considered as having largely rational, and even true, beliefs; that to know the meaning of a sentence one must know the whole language to which it belongs; these, and other theses of Davidson's system, may seem quite unacceptable to some people (though, almost certainly, different things would be unacceptable to different people).

But the virtues of Davidson's work are not the enshrinement and preservation of isolated philosophical intuitions (though this does not by any means imply that his system does not answer to some very powerful intuitions). By offering a philosophical vision, he has provided a direction for philosophy, not just in the sense that many people now work on problems set by his agenda, though this is so, but in placing before us a certain substantive goal: to account for the importance of rationality and the role it has in logic, science, thought and life.

None the less, at various points during this book, and especially in chapter 9, we have seen that Davidson's philosophical system is subject to the irruption of internally generated tensions. This is, I believe, because he has simultaneously been engaged in pursuing two quite different projects. On the one hand, there is a causal, explanatory project which rests on his work on events and causation and seeks to explore topics in the philosophy of mind, such as the explanation and production of action, and the relation between mind and body, in terms of these fundamental concepts. On the other hand, there is an interpretative, hermeneutic project, which rests on his insights about the importance of rationality for the mental, and attempts to describe our confrontation with rational agents as a single, though complex and articulated, application of the normative Principle of Charity to the entire mental and linguistic lives of people. Each of these projects carries with it, or at least comports well with, a characteristic theory of propositional content (the two theories described in section 9.1). The causal explanatory project allies itself to a realist theory of content while the interpretative hermeneutic project goes with an idealist theory of content.

Since these two projects have many of their topics in common, and since the projects are not clearly and explicitly distinguished by Davidson, we find, not surprisingly, that at a number of places conflicts, problems, tensions and sometimes downright inconsistencies arise in what Davidson writes on particular questions.

Davidson placed great emphasis, we saw, on the thesis that events are particulars, very like individual material objects. As particulars, they are subject to indefinite redescription. Furthermore, they can stand in causal relations to each other, and when they do so, this will be quite independent of any linguistic devices used to pick them out and state that they are causally related. Thus, the assertion 'event a caused event b' will not necessarily enable us to infer that causal relations exist between other pairs of events just because they can be described in the same way as events a and b are described in our assertion.

Similar consequences apply to identity. If particular events a and b are identical this does not allow us to infer that other events which can be given a-type descriptions can also be given b-type descriptions. As Davidson puts it: 'causality and identity are relations between individual events no matter how described' (1970b, p. 215). Accordingly, statements that assert that either of these relations hold between individual events carry no implications at all for when and where these relations hold between other events, even if those other events are of the same *general types* as those which feature in the original singular assertion.

This fundamental idea is used by Davidson to approach two important issues in the philosophy of mind. Actions, the deeds of people, are events; they too, therefore, can stand in causal relations to other events or states, and Davidson suggested, very much against the then prevalent ortho-doxy, that this could explicate what it is to act *for* a reason. What is distinctive about acting for a reason, rather than merely acting and having a reason for that action, is that one's action is caused by the mental states or events which constitute one's reason. But this fact does not imply that there are laws which connect reasons with actions, since laws are framed in terms of properties, or types of events, or descriptions of events and, as we have just seen, the existence of causal relations between individual events does not entitle one to assume anything about the types of events to which the individual events belong, or the descriptions which apply to them.

Similarly, with respect to the question of the relation between mind and body, Davidson argued that individual events or states could have both mental and physical descriptions. Thus, it could be the case that every event which has a mental description also has some physical description, and in this sense one could hold that mind was identical to matter. In-deed, Davidson had a specific argument to show that at least all proposi-tional mental states and events (as opposed to sensations) that interact causally with physical states or events must have physical descriptions (see section 4.1).

This token-identity theory, however, does not entail that there are any connections between *types* of mental and physical states and events. From the fact that one state is describable as 'a belief that snow is white' and 'a firing of neurons x, y, and z' we cannot infer anything at all about beliefs that snow is white in general. Other instances of this belief may be iden-tical to quite different physical states. Thus, one can be a materialist about individual states and events, and thus avoid the necessity of positing non-material entities in the world, and yet not have to subscribe to unlikely psychophysical laws which, as we saw in section 1.3, Davidson rejects.

Davidson, however, was not content with either the causal theory of action or anomalous monism in the way I have so far described them. In each case he wanted to supplement the original thesis with claims that concern not just the relations between events, no matter how described, but the relations between events under descriptions, or between types of events, or between properties.

In the case of the causal theory of action, the supplementary claim was that reasons not only cause actions, but causally explain them. Unlike causation, which relates events no matter how described, causal explana-tion requires the existence of some general links between types of events or states. Thus, if a reason causally explains an action, there must be some kind of general connection between states or events which are of the same kind as the given reason and events which are of the same kind as the given action. Statements expressing these general connections would either be, or approximate to, psychophysical or psychological laws.

Although Davidson took steps to try to distinguish the generalizations involved from genuine laws (see sections 3.4 and 9.2), we saw that there was undoubtedly a certain tension in his views here.

With anomalous monism, the supplementary claim was that mental states are supervenient on physical states (section 4.3). Supervenience is a form of constraint imposed on the attribution or existence of mental states by the presence of certain physical states. Thus, once again, Davidson is led towards the existence of some kinds of general connections between the mental and the physical which do not comport well with his strictures on the anomalism of the mental.

Although in both cases the supplementary claims are quite independent, logically, from the main theses, these main theses would be much less attractive without their supplements. However, it is the supplements, and not the main theses, that conflict with the idealist theory of content, derived from the anomalism of the mental and the Principle of Charity, and that call for a realist theory of content. Both supervenience, and the thesis of the causal explanatoriness of reasons for actions, imply a view of content according to which mental states have their propositional content independently of considerations of overall rationality, and in such a way that mental states can cause other mental states in virtue of their propositional content. In other words, mental properties must be causally relevant. It is precisely this requirement that makes the two supplementary claims imply the existence of some sort of psychological or psychophysical laws, since causally relevant properties are the properties the possession of which makes individuals fall under causal generalizations.

Thus, Davidson's project of placing causation in the mental, and its attendant claims about the causal explanation of actions by reasons, and the supervenience of the mental on the physical, relies, implicitly, on a realist theory of propositional content, and thus falls into some conflict with those parts of Davidson's philosophy, such as the anomalism of the mental and the Principle of Charity, which underlie the idealist theory of propositional content.

Davidson's other project is interpretative and hermeneutic. It is not about explanation, in the sense of explanation derived from the sciences and associated with causation, but rather about understanding. It concentrates on the interdependencies of mental states, actions and linguistic behaviour, and accounts for the fact that all of these intentional phenomena are thoroughly permeated by rationality. The leading ideas of this second project are the anomalism of the mental and the Principle of Charity. The anomalism of the mental stresses the freedom of the mental from constraint by the non-rational. The Principle of Charity articulates a positive conception of the mental by delineating the various rational constraints that operate in the domain of intentional phenomena.

The main work that the Principle of Charity does is in providing a theory of propositional content, a theory which I have suggested deserves to be called an idealist theory of content, since it holds that what people actually believe and mean is constituted by what, according to the 'epistemological' considerations included in the Principle of Charity, it is ideally rational for them to believe and mean.

Davidson introduced the Principle of Charity in answering the question, how can we tell whether some formal theory which assigns truth conditions to sentences applies to a given language? The answer he gave was that a truth theory would apply to a given language if interpreting the speakers on the basis of that theory would make them conform to the constraints that comprise the Principle of Charity better than (or, given the possibility of indeterminacy, at least as well as) any other truth theory.

Although, therefore, the main part of Davidson's work in the philosophy of language appears to be, and is often taken to be, the elaboration of a theory of formal semantics, it becomes clear once one considers the question of how to apply a truth theory, that his real concern is with the interpretation of speakers of a language. The formal part of his work underpins the larger, hermeneutic aim which places language within the sphere of the intentional, and unifies this area by the general application of the principles of rationality.

The interpretative project essentially is the provision of a theory of propositional content. But at a number of places, the implications of such a theory become unpalatable for Davidson, and in these places we see the conflict between his two projects from the other side. The greatest conflict comes about because the idealist theory of content suggests that beliefs and other mental states are not, to use Dennett's phrase, 'intervening distinguishable states of an internal behavior-causing system' (Dennett 1981a, p. 52). They are not concrete enough to be the kinds of things to stand in causal relations. Thus, at one stroke, Davidson's work on events and causation threatens to lose its relevance for the philosophy of mind. Mental states, according to the idealist theory of content, would not be concrete events with causal properties, but some sort of abstract, or calculation-bound entities (to use Dennett's phrases again). And although actions and the utterances of sentences would appear to be unassailably real events, their descriptions as actions, or as meaningful utterances, would be largely, if not completely, unconstrained by what those events were *really* like.

The idealist theory of content makes irrationality hard to explain, or even describe. If what people actually believe is constituted by what it is ideally rational for them to believe, then how can they have irrational beliefs, and perform irrational actions? To answer these questions, Davidson offers an account which, as we saw, did not comport well with his hermeneutic project, since it required us to see mental states as non-rational causes of other mental states. Furthermore, although they would have to be non-rational causes, they would still have to be causes in virtue of their propositional content. Hence, the theory of irrationality was based on the view that mental states are not only causes but that their mental properties are causally relevant. It needed a realist theory of content.

A similar problem occurred with the question, how do we know the contents of our own minds better than we know the contents of other people's minds? For an idealist position, according to which content is a kind of theoretical construct, there ought to be no asymmetry; or if there is asymmetry, it ought only to be because each of us is in a better position to see whether the theory applies to himself than to others. But Davidson did not want to relinquish the intuition that we do have special insight into our own mental lives. This, we saw, was problematic for him and his attempted solution was beset by difficulties.

It may be that Davidson can yet convince us that his two projects are not inconsistent. The idealist theory of content does not, at least, put pressure on the claim of mere identity between the mental and the physical, and the thesis that reasons cause actions. What it does put pressure on are Davidson's views about the relations between mental and physical properties. Where he attempts to forge links between mental and physical properties, as in supervenience, or the causal explanatoriness of reasons for actions, the two projects seem inevitably to come into conflict and the aims of one must yield to the aims of the other.

Of the two projects, it is the interpretative hermeneutic project, with its work on the link between propositional content and rationality, that, I believe, is the most important. No other philosophical approach comes as close to accounting for the importance that rationality has for rational creatures such as we are. Davidson has placed in centre stage the crucial insight that rationality, consistency, coherence and logic are not 'optional extras' for creatures that have content-bearing mental states and use language. They lie right at the heart of these capacities. David Lewis has said that 'what we accomplish in philosophical argument' is to 'measure the price' of a philosophical theory (1983, p. x). Whatever difficulties Davidson's work on rationality faces, the insight that without reason there is no thought is so valuable that I believe it should be bought at almost any price.

Appendix: The Frege Argument

The Frege argument is designed to show that any sentential operator which permits the substitution of co-extensive terms within the sentences being operated on must be truth-functional. In section 2.3, the operator under consideration was 'the fact that . . . caused it to be the case that . . .'. In section 8.1, the operator was '*s* corresponds to the fact that . . .'. I give the argument here in terms of the former connective but it should be clear how it applies to the latter. If, from

> (1)   The fact that Aquinas was fat caused it to be the case that Aquinas was heavy

we can infer

> (2)   The fact that the Angelic Doctor was fat caused it to be the case that Aquinas was heavy

on the grounds that 'Aquinas' and 'the Angelic Doctor' have the same extension, the Frege argument would show that we could also infer from (1)

> (3)   The fact that Frege was a logician caused it to be the case that Aquinas was heavy

since the sentence 'Frege was a logician' has the same truth value as 'Aquinas was fat.' Assuming that this is unacceptable, the Frege argument means we would either have to prohibit substitution of co-extensive terms within sentences, and hence rule out the apparently acceptable inference from (1) to (2), or, as Davidson urges, give up the sentential connective 'the fact that . . . caused it to be the case that . . .'.

The argument works as follows. Two sentences are logically equivalent if it is impossible for them to differ in truth value. It is assumed that we can always substitute logically equivalent sentences for each other. The following sentence is logically equivalent to 'Aquinas was fat':

(4) $\hat{x}(x = x$ and Aquinas was fat$)$ $=$ $\hat{x}(x = x)$.

This rather complicated looking sentence requires some explanation. The symbol '$\hat{x}$' is the set abstraction operator and is read 'the set of things x such that . . .'. Thus (4) contains descriptions of two sets and asserts their identity. What is in these sets? On the right-hand side, we have '$\hat{x}(x = x)$'. This is the set of things x such that $x = x$, that is, the set of things which are self-identical. It includes everything. The name of the set on the left-hand side is more complicated. It is the set of things which meet two conditions, that they are self-identical, and that they are such that Aquinas was fat. The locution 'x is such that Aquinas was fat' is not like anything in ordinary speech and this is one of the things that makes the Frege argument hard to grasp. If the sentence 'Aquinas was fat' is true, then the predicate 'x is such that Aquinas was fat' will apply to everything, since any possible value of x will be such that Aquinas was fat. If it is false, the predicate will apply to nothing. Since everything meets the condition of being identical to itself, the contents of the left-hand set depend entirely on whether Aquinas was fat. If he was, then this set includes everything, and the identity of sets asserted by (4) obtains; if it is false that Aquinas was fat, then the set contains nothing, and the identity asserted by (4) does not obtain. This is what makes (4) logically equivalent to 'Aquinas was fat.' Under any circumstances in which the sentence 'Aquinas was fat' is true, (4) is true, and under any circumstances in which it is false, (4) is false. The two sentences could never come apart in truth value. Since (4) and 'Aquinas was fat' are logically equivalent, we can substitute one for the other in (1) to obtain:

(5)   The fact that $\hat{x}(x = x$ and Aquinas was fat$)$ $=$ $\hat{x}(x = x)$ caused it to be the case that Aquinas was heavy.

By the principle that we can substitute co-extensive singular terms within sentences, if there were another name for the set which at present is referred to by the singular term '$\hat{x}(x = x$ and Aquinas was fat$)$', then we could substitute it for that name. Since, in fact, Aquinas was fat, this name is the name of the set which includes everything. We can, therefore, take any true sentence, such as 'Frege was a logician,' and make a name for the set which contains everything on the same pattern: '$\hat{x}(x = x$ and

Frege was a logician)'. Again, since everything meets the first condition, that it be self-identical, this will name the set which contains everything if Frege was a logician, and if Frege was not a logician, it will name the empty set.

By substituting co-extensive terms, we now obtain:

(6)   The fact that $\hat{x}(x = x$ and Frege was a logician) $= \hat{x}(x = x)$ caused it to be the case that Aquinas was heavy.

The first of the connected sentences is logically equivalent to the sentence 'Frege was a logician' in just the same way in which '$\hat{x}(x = x$ and Aquinas was fat) $= \hat{x}(x = x)$' is logically equivalent to 'Aquinas was fat.' So by substituting logically equivalent sentences we finally reach:

(7)   The fact that Frege was a logician caused it to be the case that Aquinas was heavy.

Since the only thing that the sentences 'Aquinas was fat' and 'Frege was a logician' were required to have in common was that they have the same truth value, it turns out that the 'the fact that . . . caused it to be the case that . . .' connective is truth functional. All that matters is the truth values of the sentences it connects. We should therefore reject the causal connective. This is what the Frege argument set out to prove.

An evaluation of this argument, and of the criticisms that have been made of it, would introduce too much logic to make it appropriate in a book like this. Interested readers can follow up this issue in the following literature. Mackie (1974, pp. 248–57) discusses a number of different criticisms, some of which are developed in greater detail in Horgan (1978, 1982) and Lycan (1974). McGinn (1976) answers Lycan's objection.

Notes

Chapter 1 The Anomalism of the Mental

1 This restriction to propositional attitudes has led some writers to identify a 'serious lacuna' in Davidson's argument, since 'it is . . . occurrent experiences [such as pains, sensations etc.] that have often been supposed to provide the greatest difficulty for the materialist' (Smart 1985, p. 175). In response to such criticism, Davidson has made a few remarks to encourage the view that such 'occurrent experiences' do fall within the scope of his arguments. See Davidson 1985a, p. 246.

2 Strictly speaking, bridging laws need not claim identity of properties, but only that whenever an object instantiates one, it instantiates the other.

Chapter 2 Events, Causation and Causal Explanation

1 This solution was suggested to me by the reader for Stanford University Press.

2 We cannot say that if the singular term does not refer, the sentence must be false, or that if the sentence is true, the singular term must refer, since a singular term would fail of reference if there were more than one thing which fit the description. In that case, the sentence would be true but the singular term would not refer. Consider the sentence 'Richard Burton and Elizabeth Taylor were married,' which is true even though the singular term 'the marriage of Burton and Taylor' does not refer because there is more than one event which fits the descriptive phrase.

Chapter 3 Action

1 Davidson's fullest discussion of deviant causal chains is in the last four or

five pages of 1973b. However, this discussion is somewhat confusing since what seems to be under discussion is not the question of sufficient conditions for the application of the concept of intentional action, but rather sufficient conditions for the production of an intentional action. The problem with deviancy is then that if the condition is supplemented with mentalistic vocabulary, it will become a piece of conceptual analysis, whereas if it is supplemented with physicalist vocabulary, it would constitute a psychophysical law.

2 Whether this is actually what Aristotle thought or not is a complicated exegetical question. See Charles 1984, pp. 84–96.

3 This approach goes back to Ross 1930, some of whose ideas are very Davidsonian *avant la lettre*.

Chapter 4 Mind and Matter

1 This passage makes it quite clear that Davidson wishes 'anomalous' to be understood as a privative form of 'nomological', despite the fact that the two words are etymologically unconnected. 'Anomalous' is not from ' a-nomos' but from 'an-omalos', the privative form of the word for 'regular' or 'even'.

2 I say this despite the fact that Davidson has been reported as saying, in conversation, that supervenience should be understood as 'no more than the holding of certain universal material conditionals' (Honderich 1982, p. 64). This cannot really be what Davidson thinks since supervenience is obviously meant as an interesting philosophical claim, whereas whether such material conditionals or psychophysical generalizations hold is an empirical matter, of no philosophical interest.

Chapter 5 Meaning and Truth

1 An ordered pair (or n-tuple) is a pair in a specific order. It is represented by pointed brackets. Unordered pairs (or n-tuples, i.e. sets) are represented by curly brackets. Thus, {a,b} and {b,a} are the same pair, but <a,b> and <b,a> are different ordered pairs.

2 In his Letter to Dr Dunning, originally published in 1778, John Horne Tooke, desirous of establishing that the demonstrative and conjunctive 'that's are etymologically related, offered, in effect, Davidson's analysis of indirect discourse as evidence. He also recognized the importance of the independence thus accorded to the embedded content sentence. At his trial (the Letter was written while he was in prison) it was allowed that 'she knowing that Crooke had been indicted for forgery, did so and so,' yet it was denied that an averment that Crooke had been indicted had been made. The analysis of the sentence, however, into 'Crooke had been indicted. She, knowing that, did so and so' means that 'the Averment said to be omitted, was, not only substantially, but literally made' (1829, p. 685). Davidson would resist this further conclusion since, although he claims that the

analysis of 'Galileo said that the earth moves' entails that one has said one-self 'the earth moves', it does not entail that one has said it assertorically, or, to use Tooke's terms, that one has averred it.

Curiously, Tooke claims that his analysis shows the 'unsuspected construction, not only in our own but in every language in the world, where the conjunction THAT (or some equivalent word) is employed.'

Chapter 6   Radical Interpretation

1   Davidson has actually denied that he holds that decision theory, or by extension, the Principle of Charity, is analytic (1976b, pp. 272–3), in the way that Lewis held that the theory which defines belief, desire and meaning is analytic, though his recent remarks about how the question of whether people are rational is not an empirical question suggest that he would no longer make this denial.

Chapter 7   Holism and Meaning

1   Causation is often treated as the best candidate for a naturalist, or physicalist, account of reference (see Field 1972). In what follows, therefore, I shall sometimes speak indifferently of causal or physicalist theories of reference, though strictly speaking they should not be confused in this way.

Chapter 8   Truth, Knowledge and Relativism

1   The idea goes back at least to Condillac, but is particularly associated with German romantic thinkers such as Herder and Humboldt. See Aarsleff 1988, pp. xxxii-lxv for a historical picture of the progress of the idea from French eighteenth-century to German nineteenth-century thought.

Chapter 9   Realism and Idealism

1   It has been reported of Quine that, despite his many brave assertions that radical translation begins at home, he holds 'that our situation is "asymmetrical": he is a "realist" with respect to his own language but not with respect to other languages' (Putnam 1983, p. 242n.). This, if true, is a remarkable admission of Quine's and testifies to the difficulties that first-person authority poses for an idealist theory of content.

Bibliography

Note: Wherever works are listed as having been reprinted, page references in the text are to the reprinted version.

WORKS BY DONALD DAVIDSON

1963 'Actions, Reasons, and Causes', reprinted in Davidson 1980a, pp. 3–19.
1965 'Theories of Meaning and Learnable Languages', reprinted in Davidson 1984a, pp. 3–15.
1967a 'The Logical Form of Action Sentences', reprinted in Davidson 1980a, pp. 105–48.
1967b 'Causal Relations', reprinted in Davidson 1980a, pp. 149–62.
1967c 'Truth and Meaning', reprinted in Davidson 1984a, pp. 17–36.
1968 'On Saying That', reprinted in Davidson 1984a, pp. 93–108.
1969a 'Facts and Events', reprinted, as part of 1967a, in Davidson 1980a, pp. 129–37.
1969b 'How is Weakness of Will Possible?', reprinted in Davidson 1980a, pp. 21–42.
1969c 'The Individuation of Events', reprinted in Davidson 1980a, pp. 163–80.
1969d 'True to the Facts', reprinted in Davidson 1984a, pp. 37–54.
1970a 'Semantics for Natural Languages', reprinted in Davidson 1984a, pp. 55–64.
1970b 'Mental Events', reprinted in Davidson 1980a, pp. 207–27.
1970c 'Events as Particulars', reprinted in Davidson 1980a, pp. 181–7.
1971 'Agency', reprinted in Davidson 1980a, pp. 43–61.
1973a 'In Defense of Convention T', reprinted in Davidson 1984a, pp. 65–75.
1973b 'Freedom to Act', reprinted in Davidson 1980a, pp. 63–81.
1973c 'Radical Interpretation', reprinted in Davidson 1984a, pp. 125–39.

1973d 'The Material Mind', reprinted in Davidson 1980a, pp. 245–59.

1973e 'Psychology as Philosophy', reprinted in Davidson 1980a, pp. 229–44.

1974a 'On the Very Idea of a Conceptual Scheme', reprinted in Davidson 1984a, pp. 183–98.

1974b 'Belief and the Basis of Meaning', reprinted in Davidson 1984a, pp. 141–54.

1975 'Thought and Talk', reprinted in Davidson 1984a, pp. 155–70.

1976a 'Reply to Foster', reprinted in Davidson 1984a, pp. 171–9.

1976b 'Hempel on Explaining Action', reprinted in Davidson 1980a, pp. 261–75.

1976c 'Introduction and Discussion', in S. Harnad, H. Steklis and J. Lancaster (eds), *Origins and Evolution of Language and Speech*, pp. 18–19; 42–5. New York: New York Academy of Sciences. Published as vol. 280 of the Annals of the New York Academy of Sciences.

1977 'Reality without Reference', reprinted in Davidson 1984a, pp. 215–25.

1978a 'What Metaphors Mean', reprinted in Davidson 1984a, pp. 245–64.

1978b 'Intending', reprinted in Davidson 1980a, pp. 83–102.

1979 'The Inscrutability of Reference', reprinted in Davidson 1984a, pp. 227–41.

1980a *Essays on Actions and Events*. Oxford: Clarendon Press.

1980b 'Towards a Unified Theory of Meaning and Action', in *Grazer Philosophische Studien*, 2, pp. 1–12.

1982a 'Rational Animals', reprinted in E. Lepore and B. McLaughlin (eds) *Actions and Events. Perspectives on the Philosophy of Donald Davidson*, pp. 473–80. Oxford: Basil Blackwell, 1985.

1982b 'Paradoxes of Irrationality', in Richard Wollheim and James Hopkins (eds) *Philosophical Essays on Freud*, pp. 289–305. Cambridge: Cambridge University Press.

1982c 'Empirical Content', reprinted in E. Lepore (ed.) *Truth and Interpretation. Perspectives on the Philosophy of Donald Davidson*, pp. 320–32. Oxford: Basil Blackwell, 1986.

1983 'A Coherence Theory of Truth and Knowledge', reprinted in E. Lepore (ed.) *Truth and Interpretation. Perspectives on the Philosophy of Donald Davidson*, pp. 307–19. Oxford: Basil Blackwell, 1986.

1984a *Inquiries into Truth and Interpretation*. Oxford: Clarendon Press.

1984b 'Communication and Convention', reprinted in Davidson 1984a, pp. 265–80.

1984c 'First Person Authority', in *Dialectica*, 38, pp. 101–11.

1984d *Expressing Evaluations*. The Lindley Lecture (monograph). Lawrence: University of Kansas.

1985a Replies to Essays, in B. Vermazen and M. Hintikka (eds) *Essays on Davidson: Actions and Events*, pp. 195–229; 242–52. Oxford: Clarendon Press, 1985.

1985b 'Adverbs of Action', in B. Vermazen and M. Hintikka (eds) *Essays on Davidson: Actions and Events*, pp. 230–41. Oxford: Clarendon Press, 1985.

1985c 'A New Basis for Decision Theory', in *Theory and Decision*, 18, pp. 87–98.

1985d 'Reply to Quine on Events', in E. Lepore and B. McLaughlin (eds) *Actions and Events. Perspectives on the Philosophy of Donald Davidson*, pp. 172–6. Oxford: Basil Blackwell, 1985.

1986 'A Nice Derangement of Epitaphs', reprinted in E. Lepore (ed.) *Truth and Interpretation. Perspectives on the Philosophy of Donald Davidson*, pp. 433–46. Oxford: Basil Blackwell, 1986.

1987a 'Knowing One's Own Mind', in *Proceedings and Addresses of the American Philosophical Association*, 1987, pp. 441–58.

1987b 'Problems in the Explanation of Action', in P. Petit, R. Sylvan and J. Norman (eds) *Metaphysics and Morality: Essays in Honour of J.J.C. Smart*, pp. 35–49. Oxford: Basil Blackwell.

1990 'Afterthoughts, 1987 (to "A Coherence Theory of Truth and Knowledge")', in Alan Malachowski (ed.) *Reading Rorty*, pp. 134–7. Oxford: Basil Blackwell.

OTHER WORKS CITED

Aarsleff, Hans (1988) 'Introduction', in Wilhelm von Humboldt, *On Language*, translated by Peter Heath. Cambridge: Cambridge University Press.

Antony, Louise (1989) 'Anomalous Monism and the Problem of Explanatory Force', in *Philosophical Review*, 98, pp. 153–87.

Bennett, Jonathan (1985) 'Adverb-dropping Inferences and the Lemmon Criterion', in Lepore and McLaughlin (eds) 1985, pp. 193–206.

Blackburn, Simon (1985) 'Supervenience Revisited', in Ian Hacking (ed.) *Exercises in Analysis*, pp. 47–67. Cambridge: Cambridge University Press.

Burge, Tyler (1986) 'On Davidson's "Saying That" ', in Lepore (ed.) 1986, pp. 190–208.

Carnap, Rudolf (1932) 'Psychology in Physical Language', reprinted in A. J. Ayer (ed.) *Logical Positivism*, pp. 165–98. Glencoe, Illinois: The Free Press, 1959.

Carnap, Rudolf (1956) *Meaning and Necessity*, enlarged edition. Chicago: Chicago University Press.

Charles, David (1984) *Aristotle's Philosophy of Action*. Ithaca: Cornell University Press.

Chisholm, Roderick (1970) 'Events and Propositions', in *Nous*, 4, pp. 15–24.

Chisholm, Roderick (1971) 'States of Affairs Again', in *Nous*, 5, pp. 179–89.

Church, Alonzo (1951) 'A Formulation of the Logic of Sense and Denotation', in P. Henle, H. M. Kallen and S. K. Langer (eds) *Structure, Method and Meaning: Essays in Honour of H. M. Scheffer*, pp. 3–24. New York: Liberal Arts Press.

Danto, Arthur (1963) 'What We Can Do', in *Journal of Philosophy*, 60, pp. 435–45.

Danto, Arthur (1965) 'Basic Actions', in *American Philosophical Quarterly*, 2, pp. 141–8.

Dennett, Daniel (1978) *Brainstorms. Philosophical Essays on Mind and Psychology*. Montgomery: Bradford Books.

Dennett, Daniel (1981a) 'Three Kinds of Intentional Psychology', reprinted in Dennett 1987, pp. 43–68.

Dennett, Daniel (1981b) 'Making Sense of Ourselves', reprinted in Dennett 1987, pp. 83–101.

Dennett, Daniel (1987) *The Intentional Stance*. Cambridge, Mass.: MIT Press.

Donnellan, Keith (1977) 'The Contingent *a Priori* and Rigid Designators', in P. A. French, T. E. Uehling Jr and H. K. Wettstein (eds) *Midwest Studies in Philosophy, 2: Studies in the Philosophy of Language*, pp. 12–27. Morris: University of Minnesota Press.

Ducasse, Charles (1926) 'The Nature and Observability of the Causal Relation', reprinted in Ernest Sosa (ed.) *Causation and Conditionals*, pp. 114–25. Oxford: Oxford University Press, 1975.

Dummett, Michael (1975) 'What is a Theory of Meaning?', in Samuel Guttenplan (ed.) *Mind and Language*, pp. 97–138. Oxford: Oxford University Press.

Edwards, Ward and Tversky, Amos (eds) (1967) *Decision Making*. Harmondsworth: Penguin Books.

Elgin, C. Z. (1980) 'Indeterminacy, Underdetermination, and the Anomalism of the Mental', in *Synthese*, 45, pp. 233–55.

Evans, Gareth and McDowell, John (eds) (1976) *Truth and Meaning*. Oxford: Oxford University Press.

Evnine, Simon (1989a) 'Freud's Ambiguous Concepts', in *Journal of Speculative Philosophy*, new series, III, pp. 86–99.

Evnine, Simon (1989b) 'Understanding Madness?', in *Ratio*, new series, II, pp. 1–18.

Feigl, Herbert and Sellars, Wilfrid (eds) (1949) *Readings in Philosophical Analysis*. New York: Appleton-Century-Crofts, Inc.

Field, Hartry (1972) 'Tarski's Theory of Truth', in *Journal of Philosophy*, 69, pp. 347–75.

Fodor, Jerry (1975) *The Language of Thought*. New York: Thomas Y. Crowell.

Fodor, Jerry (1978) 'Propositional Attitudes', reprinted in J. Fodor, *Representations*, pp. 177–203. Brighton: Harvester Press, 1981.

Fodor, Jerry (1987) *Psychosemantics*. Cambridge, Mass.: MIT Press.

Foster, John (1976) 'Meaning and Truth Theory', in Evans and McDowell (eds) 1976, pp. 1–32.

Frege, Gottlob (1952) 'On Sense and Reference', in Peter Geach and Max Black (eds) *Translations from the Philosophical Writings of Gottlob Frege*, pp. 56–78. Oxford: Basil Blackwell.

Frege, Gottlob (1953) *The Foundations of Arithmetic*, second, revised edition. Oxford: Basil Blackwell.

Goldman, Alvin (1970) *A Theory of Human Action*. New York: Prentice Hall.

Grandy, Richard (1973) 'Reference, Meaning and Belief', in *Journal of Philosophy*, 70, pp. 439–52.

Grice, H. P. (1957) 'Meaning', reprinted in P. F. Strawson (ed.) *Philosophical Logic*, pp. 39–48. Oxford: Oxford University Press, 1967.

Grice, H. P. (1971) *Intention and Uncertainty*. London: Oxford University Press.

Haack, Susan (1978) *Philosophy of Logics*. Cambridge: Cambridge University Press.

Hempel, Carl (1966) *Philosophy of Natural Science*. Englewood Cliffs, NJ: Prentice-Hall Inc.

Honderich, Ted (1982) 'The Argument for Anomalous Monism', in *Analysis*, 42, pp. 59–64.

Horgan, Terence (1978) 'The Case against Events', in *Philosophical Review*, 87, pp. 28–47.

Horgan, Terence (1982) 'Substitutivity and the Causal Connective', in *Philosophical Studies*, 42, pp. 47–52.

Hornsby, Jennifer (1980–81) 'Which Physical Events are Mental?', in *Proceedings of the Aristotelian Society*, 81, pp. 73–92.

Hornsby, Jennifer (1985) 'Physicalism, Events and Part-Whole Relations', in Lepore and McLaughlin (eds) 1985, pp. 444–58.

Hume, David (1975) *Enquiries Concerning Human Understanding and Concerning the Principles of Morals*, edited by Peter Nidditch. Oxford: Clarendon Press.

Kant, Immanuel (1933) *Critique of Pure Reason*, translated by Norman Kemp Smith, second impression with corrections. London: Macmillan.

Kim, Jaegwon (1976) 'Events as Property Exemplifications', in M. Brand and D. Walton (eds) *Action Theory*, pp. 159–77. Dordrecht: Reidel.

Kim, Jaegwon (1978) 'Supervenience and Nomological Incommensurables', in *American Philosophical Quarterly*, 15, pp. 149–56.

Kim, Jaegwon (1985) 'Psychophysical Laws', in Lepore and McLaughlin (eds) 1985, pp. 369–86.

Kuhn, Thomas (1962) *The Structure of Scientific Revolution*. Chicago: University of Chicago Press.

Lepore, Ernest (ed.) (1986) *Truth and Interpretation. Perspectives on the Philosophy of Donald Davidson*. Oxford: Basil Blackwell.

Lepore, Ernest and McLaughlin, Brian (eds) (1985) *Actions and Events. Perspectives on the Philosophy of Donald Davidson*. Oxford: Basil Blackwell.

Lewis, Clarence Irving (1923) 'A Pragmatic Conception of the *a Priori*', reprinted in Feigl and Sellars (eds) 1949, pp. 286–94.

Lewis, David (1966) 'An Argument for the Identity Theory', reprinted in Lewis 1983, pp. 99–107.

Lewis, David (1969) *Convention*. Oxford: Basil Blackwell.

Lewis, David (1970) 'General Semantics', reprinted in Lewis 1983, pp. 189–232.

Lewis, David (1972) 'Psychophysical and Theoretical Identifications', in *Australasian Journal of Philosophy*, 50, pp. 249–58.

Lewis, David (1974a) 'Radical Interpretation', reprinted in Lewis 1983, pp. 108–21.

Lewis, David (1974b) ' 'Tensions', reprinted in Lewis 1983, pp. 250–60.

Lewis, David (1975) 'Languages and Language', reprinted in Lewis 1983, pp. 163–88.

Lewis, David (1983) *Philosophical Papers. Volume I*. New York: Oxford University Press.

Lewis, David (1986) 'Causal Explanation', in David Lewis, *Philosophical Papers. Volume II*, pp. 214–40. New York: Oxford University Press.

Lewis, Harry (1985) 'Is the Mental Supervenient on the Physical?', in Vermazen and Hintikka (eds) 1985, pp. 159–72.

Loar, Brian (1976) 'Two Theories of Meaning', in Evans and McDowell (eds) 1976, pp. 138–61.

Lycan, William (1974) 'The Extensionality of Cause, Space and Time', in *Mind*, 83, pp. 498–511.

Mackie, John (1974) *The Cement of the Universe*. Oxford: Clarendon Press.

McDowell, John (1978) 'Physicalism and Primitive Denotation: Field on Tarski', reprinted in Mark Platts (ed.) *Reference, Truth and Reality*, pp. 111–30. London: Routledge and Kegan Paul, 1980.

McDowell, John (1980) 'Quotation and Saying That', in Mark Platts (ed.) *Reference, Truth and Reality*, pp. 206–37. London: Routledge and Kegan Paul.

McDowell, John (1985) 'Functionalism and Anomalous Monism', in Lepore and McLaughlin (eds) 1985, pp. 387–98.

McDowell, John (1987) 'In Defence of Modesty', in Barry Taylor (ed.) *Michael Dummett: Contributions to Philosophy*, pp. 59–80. Dordrecht: Nijhoff.

McGinn, Colin (1976) 'A Note on the Frege Argument', in *Mind*, 85, pp. 422–3.

McGinn, Colin (1977) 'Charity, Interpretation and Belief', in *Journal of Philosophy*, 74, pp. 521–35.

McGinn, Colin (1978) 'Mental States, Natural Kinds and Psychophysical Laws', in *Proceedings of the Aristotelian Society*, suppl vol., pp. 195–220.

McGinn, Colin (1986) 'Radical Interpretation and Epistemology', in Lepore (ed.) 1986, pp. 356–68.

Melden, A. I. (1961) *Free Action*. London: Routledge and Kegan Paul.

Montague, Richard (1974) *Formal Philosophy*, edited by Richmond H. Thomason. New Haven: Yale University Press.

Nagel, Thomas (1986) *The View from Nowhere*. New York: Oxford University Press.

Peacocke, Christopher (1979) *Holistic Explanation: Action, Space, Interpretation*. Oxford: Clarendon Press.

Putnam, Hilary (1975) 'The Meaning of "Meaning"', in H. Putnam, *Mind, Language, and Reality*, pp. 215–71. Cambridge: Cambridge University Press, 1975.

Putnam, Hilary (1979) 'Reflections on Goodman's *Ways of Worldmaking*', reprinted in H. Putnam, *Realism and Reason*, pp. 155–69. Cambridge: Cambridge University Press, 1983.

Putnam, Hilary (1983) 'Why Reason Can't Be Naturalized', in H. Putnam, *Realism and Reason*, pp. 229–47. Cambridge: Cambridge University Press.

Quine, Willard Van Orman (1951) 'Two Dogmas of Empiricism', reprinted in W. V. Quine, *From a Logical Point of View*, pp. 20–46. Cambridge, Mass.: Harvard University Press, 1953.

Quine, Willard Van Orman (1960) *Word and Object*. Cambridge, Mass.: MIT Press.

Quine, Willard Van Orman (1969) 'Propositional Objects', in W. V. Quine, *Ontological Relativity and Other Essays*, pp. 139–60. New York: Columbia University Press.

Quine, Willard Van Orman (1970) *Philosophy of Logic*. Englewood Cliffs, NJ: Prentice-Hall, Inc.

Quine, Willard Van Orman (1981) 'On the Very Idea of a Third Dogma', in W. V. Quine, *Theories and Things*, pp. 38–42. Cambridge, Mass.: Belknap Press of Harvard University Press.

Quine, Willard Van Orman (1985) 'Events and Reification', in Lepore and McLaughlin (eds) 1985, pp. 162–71.

Rasmussen, Stig Alstrup (1987) 'The Intelligibility of Abortive Omniscience', in *Philosophical Quarterly*, 37, pp. 315–19.

Ross, William David (1930) *The Right and the Good*. Oxford: Clarendon Press.

Russell, Bertrand (1956) *Logic and Knowledge*. London: Unwin Hyman Ltd.

Ryle, Gilbert (1949) *The Concept of Mind*. London: Hutchinson.

Searle, J. R. (1987) 'Indeterminacy, Empiricism, and the First Person', in *Journal of Philosophy*, 84, pp. 123–46.

Smart, J. J. C. (1985) 'Davidson's Minimal Materialism', in Vermazen and Hintikka (eds) 1985, pp. 173–82.

Stoutland, Frederick (1970) 'The Logical Connection Argument', in *American Philosophical Quarterly Monograph*, IV, pp. 117–29.

Stoutland, Frederick (1985) 'Davidson on Intentional Behavior', in Lepore and McLaughlin (eds) 1985, pp. 44–59.

Strawson, P. F. (1970) 'Meaning and Truth', reprinted in Ted Honderich and Miles Burnyeat (eds) *Philosophy as It Is*, pp. 519–39. Harmondsworth: Penguin, 1979.

Strawson, P. F. (1976) 'On Understanding the Structure of One's Language', in Evans and McDowell (eds) 1976, pp. 189–98.

Tarski, Alfred (1944) 'The Semantic Conception of Truth', reprinted in Feigl and Sellars (eds) 1949, pp. 52–84.

Tarski, Alfred (1956) 'The Concept of Truth in Formalized Languages', in A. Tarski, *Logic, Semantics, Metamathematics*, pp. 152–278. Oxford: Clarendon Press.

Thalberg, Irving (1985) 'A World without Events?', in Vermazen and Hintikka (eds) 1985, pp. 137–55.

Thomson, Judith Jarvis (1971) 'The Time of a Killing', in *Journal of Philosophy*, 68, pp. 115–32.

Tooke, John Horne (1829) *Epea Pteroenta or, The Diversions of Purley*. London: William Tegg.

Valberg, Jerry (1970) 'Some Remarks on Action and Desire', in *Journal of Philosophy*, 67, pp. 503–20.

Vermazen, Bruce and Hintikka, Merrill (eds) (1985) *Essays on Davidson: Actions and Events*. Oxford: Clarendon Press.

Wallace, John (1977) 'Only in the Context of a Sentence do Words have any Meaning', in P. A. French, T. E. Uehling Jr and H. K. Wettstein (eds) *Midwest Studies in Philosophy, 2: Studies in the Philosophy of Language*, pp. 144–64. Morris: University of Minnesota Press.

Weinstein, Scott (1974) 'Truth and Demonstratives', in *Nous*, 8, pp. 179–84.

Whorf, Benjamin Lee (1956) *Language, Thought, and Reality*. Cambridge, Mass.: MIT Press.

Wilson, Neil (1959) 'Substance without Substrata', in *Review of Metaphysics*, 12, pp. 521–39.

Wilson, Neil (1974) 'Facts, Events, and their Identity Conditions', in *Philosophical Studies*, 25, pp. 303–21.

Wittgenstein, Ludwig (1961) *Tractatus Logico-Philosophicus*, translated by D.F. Pears and B.F. McGuiness. London: Routledge and Kegan Paul.

Wittgenstein, Ludwig (1983) *Remarks on the Philosophy of Psychology*, vol. I. Oxford: Basil Blackwell.

Index